Bare-Bones Logic

John H Bolen

INFINITY
PUBLISHING

ISBN 978-1-4958-1222-4
eISBN 978-1-4958-1223-1

Published December 2016

INFINITY PUBLISHING
1094 New DeHaven Street, Suite 100
West Conshohocken, PA 19428-2713
Toll-free (877) BUY BOOK
Local Phone (610) 941-9999
Fax (610) 941-9959
Info@buybooksontheweb.com
www.buybooksontheweb.com

TABLE OF CONTENTS

INTRODUCTION TO BARE-BONES LOGIC

This textbook is intended to introduce the reader to, "Simplicity beyond complexity". What does that mean? We can go back to Oliver Wendell Holmes, a 19th century writer, philosopher and Supreme Court Justice who is attributed with having said *"I would not give a fig for the simplicity this side of complexity, but I would give my life for the simplicity on the other side of complexity."* What did he mean when he made that statement? Read the excerpt borrowed from Matthew May below:

The Simplicity on the Far Side of Complexity

This enigmatic expression, when better understood, describes the essence of what Systems Thinking and Strategic Thinking are all about, and in practical terms, how they work. Let's see if we can break this opaque aphorism down into ideas that are more easily visualized and applied to the real world problems we need to solve.

The answer to most dilemmas often turns out to be ridiculously simple. But in order to see and understand the simple answers, we must first wade through what seems like overwhelming complexities in order to organize, prioritize, and unify them so that simple solutions can emerge.

Matthew E. May, in his recent book, *The Elegant Solution:Toyota's Formula for Mastering Innovation*, made this seemingly complex concept abundantly clear:

"Customers don't want products and services, they want solutions to problems."
"Simple is better when talking about solutions, and Elegant is better still."
"An elegant solution is one in which the optimal or desired effect is achieved with the least amount of effort."
"In a mathematical proof, elegance is the minimum number of steps to achieve the solution with greatest clarity. In dance or the martial arts, elegance is minimum motion with maximum effect. In filmmaking, elegance is a simple message with complex meaning. The most challenging games have the fewest rules, as do the most dynamic societies and organizations. An elegant solution is quite often a single tiny idea that changes everything."
"Elegance is the simplicity found on the far side of complexity."

– The Elegant Solution:Toyota's Formula for Mastering Innovation,
Matthew E. May, Free Press, 2007

This is exactly what we want to accomplish through the study of logic. We want to achieve that level of elegance in being able to understand and determine whether an argument is valid and true and therefore sound. We also want to be able to write elegantly sound arguments.

That is why you must work through what will seem very complex, but once mastered will open up what at first seemed like a complex argument to reveal the simplicity of its conclusion. Through the application of the rules of logic the elegance of analyzing and crafting arguments will amaze you. However, first we must get through the apparent complexity of logic and its rules. You will be tested, and there will be times you will wonder if you will ever understand and remember all of the rules. I assure you, you will understand, and when you do, how wonderful that will be.

Chapter One

ORIENTATION TO LOGIC

How often we have heard the word "logic" tossed around as if everyone truly understood what it meant. Many associate logic with Mr. Spock of Star Trek fame or with the great sleuth, Sherlock Holmes. Logic is often viewed, therefore, as being devoid of emotion and cold to reality. While it is true that logic must operate without emotional influence it is not true that logic is devoid of passion and indifferent to reality. Logic assists those passionate about discovering truth. Logic, properly used, can separate what is true from what is false in a reality that can be both complex and confusing. Logic can assist one in making sense of statements made in complex arguments, or promises made by politicians, or accusations appearing in the local newspapers. In the world around us, it seems nothing is simple or straightforward, logic helps us maneuver through that complex maze we call reality.

Logic is often neglected and not understood so what is false often passes for what is true with no one being the wiser. The discipline of logic has been neglected so much that today the average person really has no idea what "logic" is. Students are often confused from the beginning in any study of logic due to the apparent absence of any clear understanding of "logical processes of thought." While we will break down the study of logic in this course into its various forms and categories, the main focus of this course will be to apply logical thought processes to actual arguments. Logic is a very powerful tool, but one will not appreciate the power of logic if one does not understand how it is applied and how it can assist anyone who masters it in evaluating complex arguments and in crafting complex arguments. Perhaps most importantly, knowing logic well will empower the student to recognize a fallacy when they see one. Understand that what counts as a fallacy is something that otherwise looks right, but in fact is fallacious. (For example, the recent commercial where a physicist says, "One would think that you have to be a "Rocket Scientist" in order to understand which LCD TV to purchase, well, as a matter of fact, I am a Rocket Scientist, and…;" who cares if he is a rocket scientist, has he designed LCD TV's? And even if he had designed LCD TV's, is he a disinterested third party? Who is paying him to do the commercial? Yet, it seems somehow valid when in fact it is fallacious! A fallacy referred to as an Appeal to Inappropriate Authority).

We will break down Logic into two categories, "Formal Logic and Informal Logic".[1] The kind of logic that is used most often in analyzing and making arguments is "Informal Logic".[2] Informal logic is made up of statements or propositions that are used as premises and conclusions, whereas formal logic replaces propositions with symbols and forms.[3] Informal logic is the type of logic that we will focus on first. It is the more practical of the two types of logic. Whereas formal logic helps us to see in a graphic and symbolic way the connection that exist within arguments and helps us find ways of creating formal proofs of validity.

Even in informal logic we will break down arguments by using symbols to represent the main elements of the argument. The method being suggested by this text on logic is to help the student first understand the underpinnings of logic, first get the "hang" of arranging symbols in an orderly fashion that best demonstrates the inner relationship between the various "components" of a statement before trying to interpret complex arguments using language. While we have to use language in informal logic, we will only use language to help us identify what each symbol stands for in the symbolic breakdown of a syllogism (argument form).[4] If the student can begin to organize her/his thoughts to conform to the discipline of logic without dealing with the ambiguities of language, then it will be easier for the student to approach the difficulties of language.

Language is indeed ambiguous. While most of us seem to have no difficulty communicating with each other, we often overlook the fact that we purposefully make constant compromises in order to communicate with each other. For example, when a wife says to her husband, "The screen door needs fixing" is she requesting that he fix it now, or is she using the term "fixing" to imply that the door is broken and beyond repair and therefore needs to be replaced? In a case like this it helps if they have been married for several years because he will more easily interpret what she means, but more than likely, he will still wonder what she truly means. You see the point! Or if you have a roommate who says to you, "I'll be just a minute" does that mean:five minutes; twenty minutes; 30 minutes? Again, if you know this person fairly well, you may have a pretty good idea what he/she means. Later in the text we will discuss several different fallacies that are fallacies of language in all of its ambiguous glory. While the examples I just gave seem to be trivial, if you have a presidential candidate who promises that he/she will reduce the deficit in four years, what does he/she mean? Does it mean cutting all military spending, all Medicare spending, all social security spending? If we did all of that anyone could balance the budget and get rid of all of our debt, but what would it truly cost us and our society? It is important to cut through all the rhetoric and figure out whether or not the candidate is giving a good and true argument. Precision is the logician's most important goal, precision of meaning and argument structure expressing a truth. To reach that precision we must first be able to identify all that is ambiguous about language and then begin to look at the structures of arguments.

Once the student has mastered an understanding of the ambiguities of language, then he/she will begin to study the structures of arguments. Once that has been mastered, the student then may begin breaking down simple arguments into symbols, the text will move the student to considering more complex arguments within the discipline of symbolic logic.

To use the metaphor of the architect and the builder, before we can rearrange a pile of bricks into a building, it helps to have first developed a clear design on how to arrange the building material. Language is the building material and logic is the architectural design.

INFORMAL LOGIC AND THE AMBIGUITY OF LANGUAGE

Is language truly ambiguous? Think for just a moment, how many ways can you tell someone that you do not like something? First, you will choose a way to express that depending upon the situation. If it is a very close friend and they have just baked a cake for you and it tastes terrible, and you know your friend is a bit sensitive about his/her baking skills, how will you communicate to the friend that you really don't like the cake? How about, "No, no more, I am really full, but thanks anyway. The cake was not bad." Now, did you see anywhere the actual words, "The cake is terrible!" no, you didn't. Yet, in a gentle way you conveyed to your friend that it was not all that good.

Ok, so what if the situation involves a perfect stranger who asks you for your opinion on whether to purchase a particular car, there is probably a better chance that you will actually say, "I've heard that this car is no good, and besides, I don't like the way it looks." Or, how about a friend says to another friend, "Where were you last night?", again, we know that depending upon the situation and whether the two friends are romantically involved, this question could be interpreted any number of ways. For example, if the couple were romantically involved it might express just a bit of jealousy. It would, of course, help if we could actually hear the question being asked, because again, the tone of the voice in asking such a question could make all the difference in the world! If the tone were playful then it just may be that one was teasing the other. If the tone were harsh, then definitely one is accusing the other of cheating.

Just the fact that you can convey so many different attitudes in so many different ways while using the same words begins to demonstrate how flexible our language is, but being flexible is also what makes it ambiguous. **EXERCISE:Can you come up with three of your own examples demonstrating the ambiguity of language?**

Ambiguous Example #1

Ambiguous Example #2

Ambiguous Example #3

Now, how about more serious issues, issues that we do not want to be confused about, for example, issues surrounding your health. If you go to a doctor and she says to you that your cholesterol is a bit high, what does that mean? Am I about to have a stroke? Is it above 300? Is it above 200? So, you ask, "What is my cholesterol count?" At this point it would be helpful if you understood what count would be considered high or "bad" and what count would be considered OK. What this means is that after the doctor tells you, "Well, your cholesterol is about 215..." what does that mean? So, you ask a further question, "Is 215 considered dangerous?" The doctor then says, "Well, we would prefer it be below 200, but you are not at risk with this kind of count, just watch your diet." You see what is going on here; one way to overcome ambiguity is to LEARN about something that is confusing to you.

To be a good logician also means you have to have a lot of knowledge, and what you don't know you have to have the hunger to learn for yourself. The less knowledge you have the easier for you to believe just about anything! The more you actually know about something, the more difficult it will be for someone to fool you with bogus information. You may have heard the saying, "If you stand for nothing you will fall for everything." Ok, I get what is being said here, but just to stand for something is not enough. You need to do your homework. You could stand for something that is totally false without realizing it because you haven't done your research.

For example, there are many who stand for the belief that President Obama was not born in the United States, and yet none of his detractors has ever been able to prove it. Does it make sense to continue to stand for something when there is no evidence to support it? Or how about those who stand against Mitt Romney because he is known as a "flip-flopper", that is, someone who changes his mind just to suit the political agenda at the time. Is this actually true? What about a person who constantly wants to learn the truth about anything and everything and as a result may change his/her mind? Is that flip-flopping? Again, just standing for something is not enough, you need to do your research.

Now, going back to a political campaign, it helps if you know something about what a politician is promising. For example, if a politician says to you that our healthcare system is a mess and the government should not be involved in it, what do you know about the healthcare system and what role the government is playing in the system? If you know nothing but what politicians are telling you, do you honestly believe a politician will give you an unbiased, fair assessment of the healthcare system, especially if doing so would shed a negative light on their position? The problem is, even if the politician wanted to do that, because of the complexity of the healthcare system, it would be no easy task. So, what do you do? One way to overcome ambiguity in language is to study the issue yourself and find out what people on both sides of the issue believe. Only by investigating both sides are you more likely to overcome the ambiguity that often leads to suffering for many people and more fiscal messes for the government.

I know, this is not easy, but Plato once said if there is going to be a democracy, those who vote must be well informed. The less you know about something the more likely you will suffer from the ambiguity of language and as a result not know the difference between good arguments and bad arguments. So, there are at least two different points when it comes to the ambiguity of language, **one**, words themselves are ambiguous because they can mean so many different things, and **second**, how much one knows or does not know about a subject will impact the level of ambiguity one faces in trying to understand an argument.

Before we get to the structure of arguments, how do we overcome the ambiguity of language? I am not sure we will ever completely do away with the ambiguity of language, but it helps if we are at least aware that there is quite a lot of ambiguity in the language we use. What are some steps we might employ to assist us in overcoming ambiguity and attain clarity in what we or anyone else might mean? I have listed some suggestions below:

1. Do **not** assume you understand the definition of a word being used, in other words, have a dictionary handy!

2. Discover the origin of the word, and how many different ways it can be used. It would help to have a Thesaurus to look up possible synonyms and antonyms. How many

different ways can the word "load" be used? It can be used to refer to how many courses a student is taking, or how much material is in the back of a truck, or whether or not something someone is saying is a "load of ____!"

3. What is the context in which the word or words are being used? When I say context I mean who said it, to whom was it said, what were the circumstances of the statement, what was it referring to, what are other opposing views on the subject, was the person saying it with ulterior motives? Or, another way of saying it, what will the person gain by making such a statement? Etc…

4. Restate the argument using different and simpler words, in other words, restate it as clearly as possible.

5. Determine if any fallacies were used in the use of language. (See Chapter Eight)

6. Understand the structures of arguments and their internal valid forms.

What is so important about understanding how ambiguous language can be? Simple, we bring something to every exchange of communication involving humans. When you hear an argument, you might not think it is ambiguous at all because you have brought your own beliefs about the subject to the conversation, or to the speech, and therefore you fill in the blanks for the person making the speech, even if it is not what that person meant.

For example, a person states that abortion is a tragic event in the death of the unborn child. If you are pro-choice, you will probably agree, but will not be happy because you will think the speaker stands against legalized abortions, however, you will not think there is any ambiguity involved. If you are pro-life, you will agree and rise to your feet in support, and of course will not think there is any ambiguity. However, what do you do when you discover that the one making the statement is the chairman of the board of a local Planned Parenthood clinic? Now, what do you think? Someone could easily see that abortion is tragic, and yet still believe women should have the right to make the choice.

Context makes all the difference, and if we are not willing to exercise our higher level of critical thought, we will simply bring our own beliefs to the speech and think we heard what we heard, when in fact we completely misunderstood the speaker. Sometimes politicians are accused of "double-speak" which means they will say something that is ambiguous enough without really saying anything. For example, if you are courting the conservative vote you might speak about abortion by saying, "Abortion is tragic, and we must find ways to make it unnecessary…" Such a statement leaves the pro-life crowd pleased, and those who are pro-choice can convince themselves that the politician left open the possibility that until abortions are unnecessary, they will remain legal. It all depends on what you bring to the conversation!

We have not exhausted the subject of the ambiguity of language, but suffice it to say that such ambiguity exists, and we must do all we can to overcome ambiguity and achieve clarity. In addition to the five "tips" listed above in helping to clarify ambiguous language, we added a sixth point, understanding the structures of arguments. We borrow from the great philosopher and "founder" of logic, Aristotle.[5] He developed the concepts of the syllogism, propositions, premises, conclusion, and distribution, deductive and inductive arguments. We owe our understanding of informal logic to Aristotle. According to Aristotle, arguments all have an internal structure, and that structure will either be valid or invalid, regardless of the meaning of the language being used. We will also come to discover that a truly good argument is a "sound" argument, which means the structure is valid and the content of the statements in the argument are true. But before we look at the structures of arguments, what is an argument?

DEFINITION OF AN ARGUMENT

One of the difficulties in understanding logic emerges from how we understand terms we think we already know. For example, the word "argument", conjures up for most people an image of two people yelling at each other over a disagreement. However, in logic, the definition of "argument" is a bit less exciting than the image of two people fighting it out! ***An argument is any group of statements that together make a point (conclusion).*** Not nearly as exciting, is it? An argument is made up of statements, also known as propositions that together form a conclusion. A statement or proposition is any phrase that is either true or false. Therefore, an argument does not necessarily mean two people disagreeing with each other, or fighting over something, it means in its simplest form, something is being claimed through premises leading to a conclusion which is either true or false.

While it would avoid the ambiguity of language to start with just symbols in near algebraic fashion, in order for the student to properly understand the purpose as well as the discipline of logic it will be important for us to start with a simple argument and demonstrate how we can break it down into symbols. At that point we will then be able to move solely into symbolic logic. Before we reach that point, however, we will need to understand the basic rules governing what makes an argument valid.

CATEGORICAL SYLLOGISMS

There are two general types of arguments, *inductive* and *deductive*. The difference is simple, **inductive arguments** are those in which the conclusion **probably** follows from the premises.[6] **Deductive arguments** are those in which the conclusion **necessarily** follows from the premises.[7]

What is a premise, you might ask? A premise is a proposition that leads to or implies another proposition.[8] The conclusion is a proposition that follows from a premise or premises.[9]

For example:

	1.	All mammals are warm-blooded	(premise)
	2.	All horses are mammals	(premise)
Therefore:	3.	All horses are warm-blooded	(conclusion)

What is a proposition? It is a statement that is either true or false.[10] For example, "All horses are mammals". On the other hand, a statement such as, "I like the color red" or "I don't want to go to the play" are not proper propositions because they are neither true nor false. They are statements of preferences or exclamations. You might object and say that stating "I like the color red" is true for the person who just said it because they do like the color red, but when we say that a statement is either true or false, we mean it is true in all circumstances or false in all circumstances, so to point to a ball that is red and say, "That ball is not red" either means we make a false statement on purpose or we are color blind, whatever the circumstance, we can verify by using the conventional meaning of the word "red" that the ball IS red, and therefore the statement is false. It addressed nothing about whether we prefer a red ball or a blue ball. (True, color blindness is different for each person who is color-blind. Sometimes red can appear purple, or shades of grey. Here we simply make the point that for people who are not color-blind a red ball conforms to the understood meaning of "red".)

Using symbols to break down an argument is a tool that allows us to see more clearly the "structure" of the argument and as a result the simplification of a very complex argument into a format that makes it easy to see whether or not an argument is a good argument or a bad argument.

Before we tackle complex arguments, let us have a look at this simple argument given above. This is an example of a deductive argument.

On the one hand, it seems fairly simple to see that the conclusion, "All horses are warm-blooded" does follow from the two premises. However, if we are going to be able to break down more complex arguments, we need to see how we can simplify this argument even more and trace how we can show that the conclusion necessarily follows (definition of a deductive argument) from the premises.

Let's allow H to represent "horses" and M to represent "mammals" and W to represent "warm-blooded".

In deductive logic, we understand that arguments are either valid or invalid[11] and we can demonstrate the validity of this argument by building the argument using symbols. This argument is in the form of a syllogism.

DEFINITION OF A CATEGORICAL SYLLOGISM

A syllogism is an argument with two premises and a conclusion, such that the conclusion necessarily follows from the premises (deduction).[12]

The argument from above would look like this using the symbols H, M and W:

	All M is W	(1)	(All Mammals are Warm-blooded)
	All H is M	(2)	(All Horses are Mammals)
∴	All H is W	(3)	(∴ *this symbol means "therefore"*; All Horses are Warm-blooded)

So what is a Categorical Syllogism? You see the definition above, but why did Aristotle use the term "Categorical"? If you look at the argument, we have the category known as "Horses" and a category known as "Warm Blooded" and finally a category known as "Mammals". What Aristotle was interested in clarifying were the relationships among these categories. It was Aristotle that organized all of reality (at least all of reality that he could think of) into categories. By so organizing reality he could more easily determine what affected what and how.[13]

Now, let's take a look at this structure. First, line (1) is what Aristotle called a universal affirmative proposition[14] which is also referred to as an "A" form of proposition. It is "universal" because it is referring to all members of the category "Mammals", and it is "affirmative" because it is "affirming" something about all Mammals. It is claiming that all Mammals are Warm Blooded, a fact we cannot dispute because it is, after all, part of the definition of being a mammal.

We look at the second premise and see that it too is a universal affirmative "A" type of proposition. It is affirming something about all members of the category known as "Horses". It is claiming that all horses are mammals, again, a fact not in dispute. Now, look at the conclusion, it too is a universal affirmative proposition that affirms something about all horses. Look at the structure of the argument, if all mammals are warm-blooded and all horses are mammals, then it simply follows that therefore all horses are warm-blooded. That makes sense, and if you were to negate the conclusion to read "All horses are NOT warm-blooded" we know enough about horses and mammals and being warm-blooded that we would think this is a crazy argument. But the truth is, in this particular case it matters not whether or not we know anything about Horses or Mammals or being "Warm-blooded"! Let's just assume that we do not know what the letters H, W, M stand for in the above argument and determine whether or not we can see that the conclusion as originally stated MUST follow from the premises.

$$\text{All M is W} \quad (1)$$
$$\text{All H is M} \quad (2)$$
$$\therefore \quad \text{All H is W} \quad (3)$$

Look at the structure of this syllogism, if all M is W, and all H is M, then it seems to naturally follow that all H would be W. What does H and W have in common? They are both connected someway to M. If we remember how Aristotle used categories we would look at it this way:

CATEGORY M   CATEGORY H

W	M (W)

In Category M we see the W, and in Category H we see the M. Why no category W? Do any of the propositions above say All W is _____? No, they do not, so we do not include the category W. What the propositions above do say is that in ALL categories of M you will find W and in ALL categories of H you will find M. The argument structure simply makes the connection, that if in all cases of M we have W and in all cases of H we have M, then it would make sense that where the M is the W will be as well. Thus, we see in Category H not only the M but the W in () to indicate that the M implies the W. So, Category H included two qualities of being H, both the M and the W. Thus, we see why the conclusion: All H is W, necessarily follows from the premises.

You can see that the structure of the argument is what makes it valid. It does not matter what M, W, or H stand for, the structure is what makes it valid. However, to determine if the argument is both valid and sound, we would need to know the content of the propositions to determine if they are in fact true.

MIDDLE TERM, SUBJECT TERM, PREDICATE TERM

Now that we have the structure of a categorical syllogism, let's look at the component parts. In every categorical syllogism you will have a SUBJECT, a PREDICATE, and a MIDDLE TERM. The conclusion determines the SUBJECT and PREDICATE. In the proposition which is the conclusion of the argument...

All $^{\#1}$H is $^{\#2}$W

...the Subject term is the H and the predicate term is the W. This is based upon the POSITION of these letters in the proposition, not whether they are subjects and predicates as we would think of them in English grammar. Therefore, whatever term is in position #1 is the Subject and whatever is in position #2 is the predicate: All <u>#1</u> are <u>#2</u>. For all categorical syllogisms *THE CONCLUSION ALWAYS DETERMINES WHAT IS THE SUBJECT AND THE PREDICATE.* So, whatever term appears in position #1 in the conclusion will be the subject term and whatever term appears in position #2 in the conclusion will be the predicate term.

There is another way of referring to the Subject and Predicate. The SUBJECT term is also known as the MINOR term and the PREDICATE term is also known as the MAJOR term. Let's look at the original argument again:

All M is W (1) (major premise)
All H is M (2) (minor premise)
∴ All H is W (3)

The proposition in line (1) is known as the Major Premise and the proposition in line (2) is referred to as the Minor Premise. You may have guessed at this point that if the Subject Term in the conclusion is referred to as the Minor Term then it must appear in the Minor Premise, and the same would be true for the Predicate Term or the Major Term, that it must appear in the Major Premise. If you thought that, you are correct! <u>Basically what this means is, if all you know about the argument is the conclusion, you at least know something about the structure of the argument, because you know the Subject Term or Minor Term must appear in the second or Minor Premise, and the Predicate Term or Major Term must appear</u>

in the first or Major Premise. But in this argument, what do we call the "M" that appears in both premises but not the conclusion?

We refer to the "M" as a middle term. **What is the "middle term" in a syllogism?** It is the term that appears in both premises but is not in the conclusion. So, in the case of line #1, I would say that the middle term "M" is in the subject position.

For our purposes with this argument, in line (1) "M" is the middle term in the subject position, and in line (2) "M" is the middle term in the predicate position. Because the "M" or middle term can be in either the Subject or Predicate positions, is why we caution you against confusing these terms with how they are used in English grammar.

Let's break down the conclusion one more time, shall we?

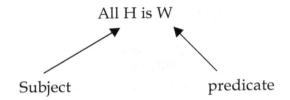

All H is W

Subject   predicate

In this proposition, the symbol in the subject position is referred to as the "minor term" and the symbol in the predicate position in the conclusion is referred to as the "major term".[15] The first premise of any syllogism is always the "major premise", that is, the premise in which the major term appears. The second premise in any syllogism is the "minor premise" or the premise that contains the minor term. This order can never change, the predicate term in the conclusion MUST always appear in the first premise and the subject term in the conclusion MUST always appear in the second premise. (Note: The major term must always appear in the major premise (1st premise) but may be in either the subject position or the predicate position. The same is true with the minor term. While the minor term must always appear in the minor premise (2nd premise) it too may be in either the subject or predicate position, depending upon the argument.)

What about the "M"? It does not appear in the conclusion, why? The "M" in this particular syllogism is, as stated above, referred to as the "middle term", that is, any term that appears in each of the two premises of a syllogism but not in the conclusion.[16] The middle term is the "glue" that holds the argument together.

Notice that the subject and predicate of the conclusion both have the same relationship with the middle term, therefore we could write a rule to determine validity of a syllogism this way:

Draft #1 "For a syllogism to be logically valid, the minor term and the major term of the conclusion must share a similar relationship with the middle term of that syllogism."

But wait, what about this argument, is it valid?

Most Democrats are liberal
Most Republicans are Conservative
John is a Republican
∴   John is not a liberal

On the surface it certainly appears to be valid, but something is not right. First, it is not in true syllogistic form, that is, there are more than two premises and no apparent middle term.

Remember, a categorical syllogism is an argument form with TWO premises and a conclusion. Therefore, if we ever see more than two premises we know we have more than one argument.

Because there are three premises instead of two, we know we have more than one argument. We can re-write this argument into two arguments with both being in proper syllogistic form with just three terms, a minor term, a major term and a middle term. The two arguments would look like this:

Argument #1

> Most Republicans are Conservative
> John is a Republican
> ∴ John is a Conservative

Argument #2

> Most Democrats are liberal
> John is Not a Democrat
> ∴ John is not a liberal

Now, these arguments are in proper syllogistic form, and they both sort of make sense, but something still seems to be wrong. What if we changed things around and did this:

Argument #1

> Most Republicans are Conservative   (major premise)
> John is Conservative   (minor premise)
> ∴ John is a Republican   (conclusion)

Do you think that is true? If you recall the Categories we used above, we were saying something about ALL "M" and something about ALL "H", but in this argument, if we use R for Republicans and C for Conservatives, are we saying something about ALL "R"? No, we are not while we are saying something about all "J" if "J" stands for John. *(When you see a proposition using a proper name, as in John is a Republican, we treat that proposition as a universal.)* So, what we cannot do is conclude something about ALL "J" based upon this argument structure. In the argument itself, in the first or major premise, it states that "Most" Republicans are conservative, not ALL Republicans. Therefore, does it make sense to say that just because John is a conservative that he is a Republican? If we are treating this as a deductive argument, we have a problem. It seems we have some ambiguity creeping into our argument. But look what happens if we treat this as an inductive argument by adding the term "probably" to the conclusion:

> Most Republicans are Conservative
> John is Conservative
> ∴ John is probably a Republican

Now that seems reasonable. The problem is, now it is no longer a deductive argument. Why? Because in a deductive argument there is no room for probability! It is now in the form of an inductive argument, which means the conclusion PROBABLY follows from the premises. Note that the inductive argument can claim nothing conclusive about John, only that he is PROBABLY a Republican, which is certainly not conclusive. You see, as a deduction, the argument was claiming too much. This is precisely the problem with how arguments are made today, we treat what are inductive arguments as if they should be deductive arguments, when in fact the argument does not claim that much. In order to allow the conclusion, "John is a Republican" to be deductively valid, we would have to change the first or major premise to read this way:

> ALL Conservatives are Republicans
> John is a Conservative
> ∴ John is a Republican

We would then be able to reduce the argument form to symbols thusly:

> All C is R
> All J is C
> ∴ All J is R

Which gives us the following Categories:

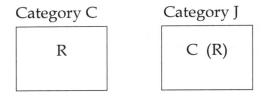

Category C

Category J

Of course, there is one problem with this argument, if someone were to come up with a Conservative that was not a Republican, this argument would be defeated. Why? Because we have claimed that ALL Conservatives are Republican and if we find one who is an actual Conservative who is not Republican, then the argument fails.

That is why we argue as if we are using deduction when in fact we are using induction because with induction I could present any number of moderate Republicans who were not conservatives and the inductive argument would remain strong, because the inductive argument would claim as its conclusion that John is "probably" a Republican based upon the claim that only "most" Republicans are Conservative. However, in order to put more force behind the argument we treat it AS IF it is deductive. Why? Because with a deduction we have a level of certainty and thus force that we simply don't have in an induction. For example, it seems more satisfying and righteous to say "All liberal/conservative politicians are crooks and cannot be trusted." Why is that more satisfying? Because we want an excuse to dislike politicians so we can blame someone for all of our troubles. Besides, it's easier than actually having to find out whether or not someone is trustworthy! Never mind that many liberal/conservative politicians are very moral and trustworthy. But a radio talk show host is not going to get much buzz by saying, "Some liberal/conservative politicians are crooks and cannot be trusted." Thus, it stands to reason that most arguments out there can be defeated by first exposing the deductive implication and then presenting one case that contradicts the claim.

Or to restate, listen carefully to arguments that try to claim a deductive conclusion and then decide whether or not the premises support such deduction.

OK, so what just happened? A thing called "distribution" just happened. What does "distribution" mean?

We will cover "distribution" in the next chapter. So, we are not yet done drafting a definition of a valid syllogism. We will continue this conversation in the next chapter.

REVIEW GLOSSARY

DEDUCTIVE ARGUMENT	The conclusion necessarily follows from the premises
INDUCTIVE ARGUMENT	The conclusion probably follows from the premises
PROPOSITION	Any statement that is either true or false, and not an exclamation, a question, or a feeling
PREMISE	A proposition that leads to or implies another proposition
CONCLUSION	A proposition that follows from other propositions
SYLLOGISM	An argument form that has two premises and a conclusion and is made up of a minor term, a major term and the middle term
MINOR TERM	The term in the subject position of the conclusion in a syllogism
MAJOR TERM	The term in the predicate position of the conclusion in a syllogism
MAJOR PREMISE	The first premise of a syllogism and the premise that contains the major term of the conclusion
MINOR PREMISE	The second premise of a syllogism and the premise that contains the minor term from the conclusion
TRUE/FALSE	Propositions are either true or false
VALID/INVALID	Deductive arguments are either valid or invalid

EXERCISES

Re-write the following from symbols into a regular argument.

1.

S   =   Socrates
M   =   Men
MO =   Mortal

All M is MO
All S is M
∴ All S is MO

_____

_____
∴ _____

2.

E   =   Electric Cars
EF =   Efficient with gas
P   =   Prius

All E is EF
All P is E
∴ All P is EF

_____

_____
∴ _____

3.

F   =   Ford (or pick any car you wish)
J   =   Junk
B   =   I don't Buy

(Is this argument valid? What would this argument look like if it was in valid form? See Chapter Four)

All F is J
All B is J
∴ All B is F

_____

_____
∴ _____

Write the following arguments into symbolic categorical syllogisms:

1.

U = Unicorns
W = White horse
B = Bessie

All Unicorns are White horses
Bessie is a White horse
Bessie is a Unicorn

_____

_____

∴ _____

2. Why does the above argument seem wrong somehow? What additional argument could you write using the following symbols to show that this argument is not quite right?

U=Unicorns
H=Horses with a horn in the middle of their forehead
B=Bessie

(hint:write an argument that shows Bessie is not a Unicorn even though she is a white horse)

_____

_____

∴ _____

3. Sam is lonesome, but of course anyone who is without a date for this dance would be lonesome, so it stands to reason to conclude that Sam is without a date.

S=Sam
L=is lonesome
D=Without a date

_____

_____

∴ _____

4. All people who exercise will live longer. Joe exercises every day, so it stands to reason that Joe will live longer.

_____

_____

∴ _____

5. Some people are people who are terrified of heights. No people who are terrified of heights are people who will climb a tall ladder. Some people will not climb a tall ladder.

_____

_____

∴ _____

6. All men who take a baby aspirin daily are men who lower the chance for heart attack. John is a man who takes a baby aspirin daily. It stands to reason, then, that John will lower his chance of a heart attack.

_____

_____

∴ _____

7. People who are a higher risk pay more for their insurance. People who have multiple speeding tickets are people who are considered a higher risk. Therefore, people with multiple speeding tickets pay more for their insurance.

_____

_____

∴ _____

ADVANCED EXERCISES

Below are some conclusions, see if you can construct a categorical syllogism from just the conclusion, give it a try (some of the answers are in the back of the book, but don't look until you have tried your hand at it!) Because the conclusion determines the minor and major terms, and because we know where they are supposed to go in the premises, we can reconstruct valid arguments from just the conclusion. However, you will need to create a middle term. For example, say the conclusion is:Therefore, All politicians are untrustworthy. Here we see the major term is "untrustworthy" and the minor term is "politicians". We also know we have a universal affirmative proposition for a conclusion, so all of the premises must also be universal affirmative propositions. So, the argument would begin to look like this:

1. All _____ are untrustworthy. (Major Premise with the major term in the predicate position.)
2. All politicians are _____. (Minor Premise with the minor term in the subject position.)
3. Therefore, All politicians are untrustworthy. (What is missing is the middle term. What is something that is always untrustworthy? How about a liar? So, what if we make the middle term "liar". Then this is what the argument would look like:
   1. All liars are untrustworthy.
   2. All politicians are liars.
   3. Therefore, all politicians are untrustworthy. (The problem we face is that all we have accomplished is to call all politicians liars. Is that true? Probably not. You see,

creating the middle term begins to shed some light on the nature of the argument we are building. Try some other possible middle terms and you will begin to see the flaw in this argument. Now try your hand at it with the following...)

1. Therefore, Kentucky won the NCAA College Basketball Championship.

_____

∴ _____

2. Therefore, all people in the Navy are people who can swim.

_____

∴ _____

3. Therefore, all Red Tractors are better than Green Tractors.

_____

∴ _____

4. Therefore, the Cow jumped over the Moon.

_____

∴ _____

5. Therefore, I am not a monkey's uncle!

_____

∴ _____

6. Therefore, Republicans only care about the wealthy.

_____

∴ _____

7. Therefore, Democrats only care about the poor.

_____

∴ _____

Chapter Two:

THE CATEGORICAL SYLLOGISM

We left our last chapter wondering what had happened in the argument. Let's re-cap:

Argument #1

Most Republicans are Conservative	(major premise)
John is a Conservative	(minor premise)
∴ John is a Republican	(conclusion)

Do you think that is true? In the argument itself, in the first or major premise, it states that "Most" Republicans are conservative, not ALL Republicans. Therefore, does it make sense to say that just because John is a conservative that he is a Republican? If we are treating this as a deductive argument, we have a problem. But look what happens if we treat this as an inductive argument by adding the term "probably" to the conclusion:

Most Republicans are Conservative	(major premise)
John is a Conservative	(minor premise)
∴ John is probably a Republican	(conclusion)

Now that seems reasonable. You see, as a deduction, the argument was claiming a certainty which is out of the reach of this argument. This is precisely the problem with how arguments are often made; we want the force of a deductive conclusion "John IS a Republican" by using an argument that could, at the most, claim only that John is PROBABLY a Republican. In order to allow the conclusion, "John is a Republican" to be deductively valid, we would have to change the first or major premise to read this way:

ALL Conservatives are Republicans	(major premise)
John is a Conservative	(minor premise)
∴ John is a Republican	(conclusion)

We would then be able to reduce the argument form to symbols thus:

All C is R
All J is C
∴   All J is R

But is it a true statement that "ALL Conservatives are Republicans"? It certainly would seem odd to many moderate Republicans to make such a claim. So, people use the statement that is true, "Most Conservatives are Republicans" but treat it as if we are actually saying "ALL Conservatives are Republicans", thus the need to be alert to what is being claimed in any given argument.

This is precisely the reason people have so much trouble with profiling, it often attempts to claim too much and is treated as a deduction, when in fact it is inductive in nature. What do we do with profiling? Look at the following argument as an example of profiling:

Many men who look like they are from the Middle East are Muslim

Many Muslims wish to kill Americans

Therefore, Men who look like they are from the Middle East are men who wish to kill Americans.

You have two premises that only claim that SOME men who look like they are from the Middle East are Muslims, and only that SOME Muslims wish to kill Americans. So how can we conclude that just because you look like a Middle Eastern male you wish to kill Americans! You MIGHT be able to conclude that PERHAPS a person who looks like a Middle Eastern Male and who MIGHT be Muslim MIGHT want to harm Americans. So, of course, this is the person who is searched at the airports. The danger of profiling is that in the hands of a smart criminal a very good disguise could be used to get right past the authorities. So, if you are a terrorist, but you happen to be blond haired and blue-eyed, who would ever suspect you of wanting to harm Americans?

Obviously there are some very good uses for profiling; the problem is when authorities treat profiling as a deduction, when it is at best an inductive process. (Remember the difference between deduction and induction. A deduction has a conclusion that necessarily follows from the premises while an induction has a conclusion that probably follows from the premises. In a deduction, more information would not change the conclusion, whereas in an induction the more information you discover the more likely you are to "tweak" the conclusion.)

DISTRIBUTION[17]

OK, so what is this all about? A thing called "distribution", and what does "distribution" mean? The definition of distribution is a quality of a proposition that makes a claim affecting all members of a particular class of things. In order for us to understand the concept of "distribution" we need to go back a few steps. Remember early in the first chapter we saw that the propositions we were using are called "universal affirmative" propositions or "A" propositions as a symbolic way of referring to a universal affirmative proposition form. There are actually four propositional forms that cover any type of proposition.[18] According to Aristotle, every proposition will be in one of these four forms. They are:

A   Universal Affirmative   (All A is B)
E   Universal Negative   (No A is B)
I   Particular Affirmative   (Some A is B)
O   Particular Negative   (Some A is not B)

QUALITY & QUANTITY

When we refer to the "quality" of a proposition, we are referring to whether or not it is Affirmative or Negative, and when we refer to the "quantity" of a proposition we are referring to whether it is Universal or Particular.[19]

So, to review:

Proposition Type	Quantity	Quality
A	Universal	Affirmative
E	Universal	Negative
I	Particular	Affirmative
O	Particular	Negative

(Ok, now I know this all seems a bit much just to be able to determine whether or not a simple argument is valid, but once we get through all of this complexity, it will make finding valid arguments so much easier! So, hang in there!)

Now we have these four propositional forms. How does that help me understand "distribution"? Well, we have to have a propositional form to work with to help us determine distribution, and it helps that now we have every possible propositional form in these four. Thus, once we determine distribution in these four forms, we have answered the distribution question for all propositions.

PROPOSITION "A" DISTRIBUTION

Let's begin with proposition "A", the Universal Affirmative proposition. In this proposition, the term in the subject position is distributed and the term in the predicate proposition is not. What does that mean?

Let's take the proposition,

All Horses are Mammals

The reason the term "Horses" is "distributed" is because this proposition tells us something about ALL horses, but does this tell us something about all mammals? No, it does not. Therefore, the term in the predicate position is NOT distributed.[20]

We can use what are called Venn Diagrams[21] to help us "see" this distribution of the subject term in the A proposition.

The "S" stands for Subject and the "P" stands for Predicate:

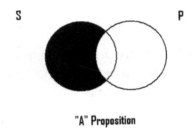

S   P

"A" Proposition

Notice that the circles overlap, and that the part of the "S" (or subject) circle that is shaded in does NOT overlap the "P" (predicate) circle, which means, that part of S is outside of P. How can that be? Well, even though ALL horses are mammals, there is more to a horse than the fact that it is a mammal. So, the "P" circle does not completely overlap the "S" circle, but it does part of it, just as being a "mammal" is part of what it means to be a horse. So, the part of the "S" circle that is colored in indicates that for the purposes of this particular proposition, we are not talking about any other trait of being a horse than the trait of being a mammal and that trait applies *to all horses*. So, the part of the "S" circle that overlaps the "P" circle is not colored in to show that it is part of the "P" circle. But note; the rest of the "P" circle is not colored in either. Why? Because, as we said earlier, not all mammals are horses, however, we are not talking about mammals, we are talking about horses, and so that is why we leave the "P" blank. We darkened the part of the "S" circle, and in this case, the class called "Horses" that is outside of the "P" circle, and not the class of mammals. Why? Because, as was stated earlier, there is more to a horse than being a mammal, and yet one thing ALL horses have in common is that they are ALL mammals. Now, the category of mammal is another problem. We did not darken in any of the "P" circle that was not also in "S" because NOT ALL mammals are horses! Therefore, one thing that all mammals do NOT share in common is being a horse! One thing all horses share in common is that they are mammals. You see the distinction. So, again, we are talking about ALL horses but we are not talking about all mammals.

Let's recap, in an "A" proposition, the subject is distributed because we have accounted for everything in the Subject, so in this case, when we say "All horses are mammals" we are accounting for all horses, we will not find a horse out there that is not a mammal! (If we did, we would claim it was NOT a horse, but something that looked like a horse. As you can see, in order to be able to communicate we have to operate within the confines of conventional definitions.) So, we darken the circle of the subject "S" to indicate that for the purposes of this argument there is NOTHING there, which is another way of saying *"There are no horses that are NOT mammals, so there would be nothing there, and to indicate that we blacken it in."* Conversely, the "P" circle is not blackened in to indicate that *there are mammals that are NOT horses.* So, in Venn diagrams, when we darken part of a circle we are claiming there is nothing there. So, now you see that the only part of "S" that is not darkened is that part that overlaps the predicate or "P", which means everything in the class "S", or in this case, "horses" belongs in class "P" or "mammals". However, note that circle "P" is not colored in at all, meaning that there are things in class "P", "mammals" that are NOT part of class "S" or "horses" meaning that not every mammal is a horse!

To conclude, therefore, the A proposition distributes the term in the SUBJECT position but not the term in the predicate position.

PROPOSITION "E" DISTRIBUTION

OK, what about the "E" proposition, the Universal Negative proposition? An E proposition might look like this:

No Horses are Cold-Blooded Animals

OK, so what do you think is distributed given what you have learned thus far about distribution? We know that this proposition is saying something about ALL horses, that is, NO horses are cold-blooded. But is it saying something about ALL cold-blooded animals? Of course, it is saying that NO cold-blooded animals are horses. Therefore, it would distribute what?

You are correct, it would distribute both the term in the subject position and the term in the predicate position. That is, there is nothing in the subject "Horses" that is a Cold-Blooded Animal, and there is nothing in the predicate "Cold-Blooded Animals" that would be a "Horse". This is another way of saying that the proposition says something about ALL horses and about ALL cold-blooded animals. OK, if we look at the Venn Diagram below we can see the two circles again, with the S for subject and the P for predicate, and the circles are overlapping again, but note, where the S overlaps the P it is shaded in, which indicates that nothing is there!

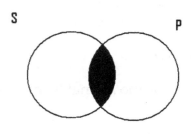

"E" Proposition

So, we can see from this Venn Diagram that indeed, the E proposition does distribute both terms. That is, NO horses are cold-blooded and NO cold-blooded animals are horses, thus accounting for everything in the class "horse" and everything in the class "cold-blooded".[22]

PROPOSITON "I" DISTRIBUTION

OK, how about the "I" proposition? It reads this way:

Some Horses are Brown (or Some H is B)

Now, does this distribute anything? Remember; ask yourself, does it tell me anything about ALL horses? No. Does it tell me anything about ALL brown things? No. All we know is that there are SOME horses that are brown. This is not a trait of all horses, nor is being a horse part of the trait of all things brown. So we would say that only some brown things are horses. When we look at the Venn Diagram, we find something a little different:

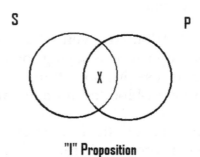

"I" Proposition

Notice that where the two circles overlap we see an "X" which is meant to indicate that there is at least one member of circle "S" that is part of circle "P". It also indicates that there is at least one thing in the circle "P" that is part of circle "S". In this case we are saying that there is at least one horse that is actually brown. (or at least one brown thing that is a horse) But note, it says nothing about all horses or about all brown things. Therefore, the "I" proposition distributes what? That's right, it distributes neither the term in the subject position nor the term in the predicate position, therefore, it distributes NOTHING! [23]

PROPOSITION "O" DISTRIBUTION

OK, how are we doing? One more propositional form remains, the "O" proposition. That proposition looks like this:

Some Horses are NOT Brown (Some H is Not B)

Again, what does this proposition distribute? Well, let's ask ourselves, does it tell me something about ALL horses? No. Does it tell me something about Brown things? Yes, if we look at the grouping of things in the subject, we know that there is nothing in the predicate group that can participate in that particular subject group, therefore, the predicate is distributed because we know that nothing in that predicate can participate in that particular subject. As a result, we are saying something about everything in that predicate class. What this means is that for the purposes of the "O" proposition we are saying that there is a particular group of brown things that does not have a horse in it. Why not distribute the subject as well? Think about it, we are just saying that at least one thing in the subject group is not part of the predicate group, we are not saying something about everything in the subject group, but we are saying something about everything in the predicate group not participating in this particular subject. One way to think of this particular subject is that it is a not-brown horse.

Let's look at it this way, if you were trying to show someone that not all brown things are horses, you would probably want to have a grouping of brown things that had NO horses in it, and then you could say, "See, no horses", the problem is, however, that you don't want to say that there are NO brown horses, so you get a grouping of brown things that includes a horse, and then you can say, "OK, see, some horses are brown…" The point is, in the "O" proposition, you are taking a grouping of brown things that does not have that particular horse because that horse is not brown, and therefore not part of the brown things! However, in the case of wanting to say that some brown things are horses, you get yourself a grouping of brown things that has a horse in it. The problem is, are you saying something about all of those brown things in the grouping that includes one horse? No, you are not. That is why the "I" proposition does not distribute anything and yet the "O" proposition distributes the predicate.

Again, let's recap. In the "O" proposition, you have a predicate class of brown things that do not include a horse. So, when you say "Some Horses are NOT Brown" you are saying something about that whole class of brown things, that there is NO horse in it. But in the case of the "I" proposition where you want to claim that there is at least one brown thing that is a horse, you will have a brown horse in amongst the other brown things, but does the "I" proposition say something about ALL those brown things in that particular class of brown things? No, thus the "I" proposition has no distribution.

This is in fact what the Venn Diagram shows us:

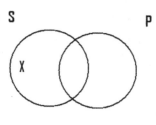

"O" Proposition

Notice that in the part of the S circle that does not overlap the P circle is the "X", this indicates that there are NO horses in the circle P, so, we would say that the "O" proposition distributes the predicate term.[24]

OK, let's recap:

A propositions distribute the Subject Term
E propositions distribute both the Subject and the Predicate Terms
I propositions distribute neither the Subject nor the Predicate Terms
O propositions distribute the Predicate Term[25]

One thing that we need to clarify, and that is when talking about distribution we are not talking about the subject "TERM" as much as we are talking about the subject "POSITION". So, a better way to define what each propositional form distributes is to state it this way:

A propositions distribute the Term in the Subject Position
E propositions distribute the Terms that are in the Subject and the Predicate Positions
I propositions do not distribute either Term
O propositions distribute the Term that appears in the Predicate Position[26]

Now, why is this so important to know? Well, let's come up with yet another draft of the Rule governing validity of a syllogism. Here is the first attempt:

Rule of Validity Draft #1
"For a syllogism to be logically valid, the minor term and the major term of the conclusion must share a similar relationship with the middle term of that syllogism."
We have to revise the rule again because something is wrong with this argument...

Most Democrats are liberal
Most Republicans are Conservative
John is a Republican
∴   John is not a liberal

This argument is flawed because it is not claiming something about ALL Democrats or about ALL Republicans, and yet it was claiming something about John that we have no right to claim. After all, could it not be possible that there might be some liberal Republicans? Or, is it not the case that there might be some Democrats that are conservative? Just ask Joe Lieberman! The problem is with distribution. Look at the first two premises of this complex argument:

Most Democrats are liberal
Most Republicans are Conservative

These are what kind of proposition? Yes, that's right, they are both "I" propositions, because saying "MOST" is NOT saying "ALL" and when we do not say "ALL" we mean "SOME" so if we re-write these propositions we get:[27]

> Some Democrats are liberal
>
> Some Republicans are Conservative

And we already know that neither of these propositions distributes anything. Do you begin to see why inductive arguments seem to be "weaker" than deductive arguments? But look at the third premise and the conclusion. How do we re-write a proposition that begins with a proper name? We treat it as if it were a universal proposition. (Later on we will also talk about how we have to treat a singular proposition as both a universal and a particular ala George Boole)[28] Thus, we would re-write them this way:

> All J is R   (J for John and R for Republican)
>
> ∴   No J is L   (J for John and L for Liberal)

Now we can see the problem, the conclusion distributes both the subject and the predicate, that is to say, the conclusion claims something about all members of the class in the subject and all members of the class in the predicate, but two of the premises do not distribute anything, or make any claim about all members of either class, and the universal affirmative (A Proposition) premise does not distribute the middle term.

So, we can now re-write the Rule of Validity Draft #2:

"For a syllogism to be logically valid the middle term must be distributed in at least one of the premises and if a term is distributed in the conclusion, it must be distributed in the premises."

OK, so let's see if we have fully defined what is needed for a syllogism to be valid. Look at this argument and tell me if you think it is valid.

> No Skyscrapers are less than 100 feet tall
>
> No Horses are Skyscrapers
>
> ∴   All Horses are less than 100 feet tall

On the surface, this looks valid, after all, "Horses" is distributed in the minor premise, and the middle term, "Skyscrapers" is distributed, actually in both premises. So what is the problem? Let's use Venn Diagrams to make our case.

This time, we have to use three circles, because we have three terms, the Subject, the Predicate and the Middle term.[29] So, we would do it this way:

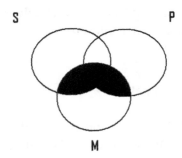

What do we have here? Remember the Venn Diagrams above for an E proposition? This Venn Diagram shows us that No M is P, that is the first premise, and that No S is M, the second premise, but what is the Venn Diagram for an "A" proposition? Remember, it looks like this:

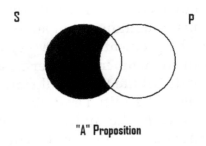

"A" Proposition

Do you see that in the Venn Diagram with the three circles? No, you do not. The problem with two negative premises is that it is telling you what is NOT the case, not what IS the case, and the conclusion being an "A" proposition is telling us what IS the case, so, if you have an affirmative conclusion, you must have affirmative premises, and if you have two negative premises, the argument is always invalid, because you cannot arrive at any kind of conclusion from two negatives. Just because no horses are skyscrapers does not necessarily mean that there are no horses in the universe that are not over 100 feet tall. (You never know!) We also pick up from this that if there is a negative conclusion, one of the premises must be negative. Remember, if we have a premise that is telling us what is NOT the case, then we have to have a conclusion that is doing the same thing. We could re-write the above silly argument this way, and end up being perfectly valid:

No Skyscrapers are less than 100 feet tall

All Horses are less than 100 feet tall

∴   No Horses are Skyscrapers

But you may object and say, "But didn't you just question whether or not there might be horses over 100 feet tall somewhere in the universe?" Yes, I could raise that objection with the previous argument because it was the conclusion, in this argument, however, we are stipulating as a premise that all horses are less than 100 feet tall which is our statement of belief based upon our limited knowledge of the universe and how we typically understand the size of a horse. Remember, in order to be able to communicate we must operate within certain accepted limits of language.

Though this argument seems silly, it is valid. Look at the Venn Diagram:

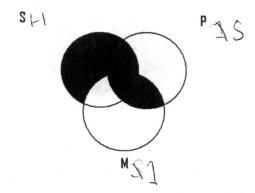

As you can see, the part of S that overlaps P is darkened, which means there is nothing there, and so we see the conclusion from the two premises. We will discuss in the next chapter how to use Venn Diagrams in determining validity of a syllogism. For now, we can rewrite our rule for a valid syllogism. The problem is, we now have several traits of a valid syllogism, instead of writing them into one definition, we will list a series of rules that govern what makes a syllogism valid.

Rules Governing Valid Syllogisms

Rule 1   A valid syllogism has just three terms
Rule 2   The Middle Term must be distributed in at least one premise
Rule 3   If a term is distributed in the conclusion, it must be distributed in the premise
Rule 4   If the conclusion is affirmative, both premises must be affirmative, and if the conclusion is negative, one of the premises must be negative
Rule 5   Both premises cannot be negative[30]

But, we are not done yet. Remember the problem with distribution? That is, if you use a proposition that distributes either the subject or the predicate and you use it to lead to a conclusion that distributes nothing, you have made a mistake. For example:

     All Cars are heavy
     All Buicks are cars
∴   Some Buicks are heavy

That seems odd. Or what about:

No animals with four legs are purple animals No A is P (A is the middle term)
All cats are animals with four legs   All C is A
∴ Some cats are not purple   ∴ Some C is Not P

Let's do a Venn Diagram to test out the two premises:

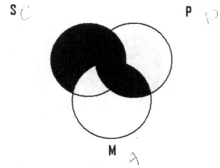

(You never chart the conclusion in a Venn Diagram, by charting the two premises only, if it is valid it will show the conclusion.)

Does this show the conclusion? No. Why? There should be an "X" in the part of M that is not part of P.

Therefore we can add a sixth rule:

Rule 6 *If the conclusion is a universal proposition, the premises must be universal. If the conclusion is a particular proposition, one premise must be a particular proposition, finally, a syllogism can never have two particular premises.*[31]

REVIEW GLOSSARY

DISTRIBUTION	A proposition says something about all members of a group in the Subject position or in the Predicate position or in both
"A" PROPOSITION	Universal affirmative proposition = All S is P (Distributes the Subject position)
"E" PROPOSITION	Universal negative proposition = No S is P (Distributes both the Subject and Predicate positions)
"I" PROPOSITION	Particular affirmative proposition = Some S is P (Does not Distribute)
"O" PROPOSITION	Particular negative proposition = Some S is Not P (Distributes the Predicate position)

Rules Governing Valid Syllogisms

Rule #1:   A valid syllogism has just three terms
Rule #2:   The Middle Term must be distributed in at least one premise
Rule #3:   If a term is distributed in the conclusion, it must be distributed in the premise*
Rule #4:   If the conclusion is affirmative, both premises must be affirmative, and if the conclusion is negative, one of the premises must be negative
Rule #5:   Both premises cannot be negative
Rule #6:   If the conclusion is a universal proposition, the premises must be universal. If the conclusion is a particular proposition, one premise must be a particular proposition, finally, a syllogism can never have two particular premises.

*If the term in the subject position (Minor Term) of the conclusion is distributed in the conclusion but not in the Minor Premise, it is also called an Illicit Minor, if the term in the Predicate Position (Major Term) of the Conclusion is distributed in the conclusion but not in the Major Premise, it is an Illicit Major.

EXERCISES

Referring to the Rules that determine whether or not a syllogism is valid, indicate whether or not the following are valid or invalid, and if invalid, which Rule do they violate?

1.　All M is P
　　All S is M
∴　Some S is P

2.　All P is M
　　All S is M
∴　All S is P

3.　No P is M　　　(answer in back of book)
　　All P is S
∴　No S is M

4.　All M is P
　　All S is M
∴　Some S is P

5.　No M is P
　　Some S is M
∴　Some S is Not P

6.　All P is M　　　(answer in back of book)
　　Some S is M
∴　Some S is P

Construct a deductive argument using two premises and a conclusion that is valid, that is, it does NOT violate any of the rules governing syllogistic validity. Write it using symbols and any of the four argument forms (A, E, I, O).

_____

_____

∴ _____

Find either a valid or invalid argument in the newspaper, and summarize it in proper syllogistic form and demonstrate how it is valid. If it is not valid, re-write the argument so that it is valid.

Chapter Three

THE CATEGORICAL SYLLOGISM:
Venn Diagrams

I n the early 20th century, John Venn (1834-1923), an English mathematician and logician, introduced a method of representing classes or categories and propositions.[32] This technique has been further developed over the years to represent propositions and deductive syllogisms. We began using them in the previous chapter and you were probably wondering what it was all about. In this chapter we will learn how to use Venn Diagrams to determine validity in an argument.

Why would we need to know about Venn Diagrams? Sometimes we need to have a graphic way of seeing the relationship between propositions and how they can work together to create an argument. Venn Diagrams also help us identify rather quickly why an argument cannot be valid, and in turn what we would have to do to that argument to make it valid. If you really want to know how dangerous and misleading invalid arguments can be, take any invalid argument and re-write it in a way to make it valid, and when you do, you can see what the person making the invalid argument is really trying to claim. Take the example from above; trying to claim someone is for certain a Republican when in fact they were using an argument which at best could only claim that John was PROBABLY a Republican.

When using Venn Diagrams to chart a three proposition argument, remember, you only chart the two premises, and never the conclusion.[33] ***The reason is simple, if your argument is valid, by charting the two premises you will have already charted your conclusion,*** thus the necessary relationship (definition of a deductive argument) between the premises and the conclusion.

Take for example the simple argument:

      No P is M

      Some S is M

∴   Some S is Not P

OK, now, let's just chart the two premises…

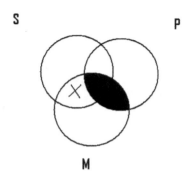

When using Venn Diagrams to chart a categorical syllogism, we have to use three circles, one for the term in the Subject Position of the Conclusion and one for the term in the Predicate Position of the Conclusion and one for the Middle Term that appears in both premises but NOT the conclusion. So, we have a circle for the "S", the "P" and the "M". Now, how do we go about charting the categorical syllogism? First, when you have both a universal and a particular premise, as we have in this argument, you ALWAYS chart the universal premise first. Why? Let's demonstrate why we have to chart the universal premise first. With the argument from above:

	No P is M	(1)
	Some S is M	(2)
∴	Some S is Not P	(3)

We see that line (1), or the Major Premise, is a Universal Negative proposition, an "E" proposition, and that line (2) is a Particular Affirmative Proposition, an "I" proposition. Let us recap what the Venn Diagram is for an "E" proposition and what a Venn Diagram is for an "I" proposition.

Now, let's take the three circles we need for the categorical syllogism:

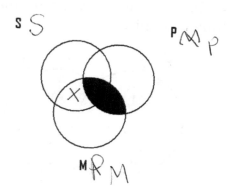

Notice that there is an "X" in the part of the circle that overlaps "S" and "M", but also note that the overlap between "P" and "M" is filled in. The "P" and "M" circles represent the "E" proposition or Major Premise in the argument and the "S" and "M" circles represent the "I" proposition or the Minor Premise in the argument. Now, why do we have to start with the universal proposition first? Look now at this diagram for the categorical syllogism before we begin to fill it out:

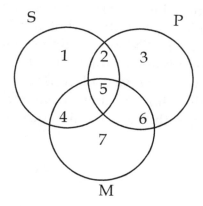

I have numbered every space that shows up on that Venn Diagram. I did this so you can remember we have to account for each of those spaces. Now, if the S and M circles represent the "I" proposition, and we remember what an "I" proposition is supposed to look like:

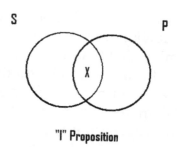

"I" Proposition

So we know that there has to be an "X" in the part of the three circle diagram that represents the "I" proposition, or the Minor Premise,

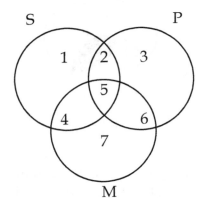

If we begin by charting the "I" proposition, where do we put the "X", in space 4 or 5? Both spaces are a case of the "S" overlapping the "M", but because of circle "P", the overlap is now divided into spaces 4 and 5. We cannot put an "X" in both spaces because there is only one "X" for an "I" proposition, because remember, what we are really saying with an "I" proposition is that there is at least ONE thing that is in both S and M, so only one X. Ok, so where does it go? If we ever see an "X" on the line separating 4 and 5, it is invalid! Ok, so what happens if we chart the universal proposition first? Right, we fill in both spaces 5 and 6, and by doing that we leave only space 4 left for the "X".

Sometimes it is difficult to follow how to chart a categorical syllogism. Taking the same syllogism we have been working with, let us break it down into two different components:

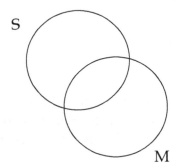 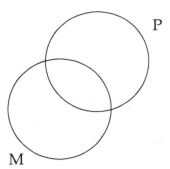

You may be thinking, Ok, this way I can easily make a Venn Diagram using circles S and M to show an "I" proposition. True, but even though I want you to see the three circles in this way, you still have to remember that S and M are intersected by P. Now, we can go ahead and chart P and M because it is a universal, and there it does not matter that P and M are intersected by S, why? Because a universal proposition is accounting for anything that intersects it, so it really doesn't matter that S intersects P and M. The reason we cannot do that same thing with particular propositions is because particular propositions do NOT account for everything that intersects it, so you have only one "X" and there has to be a clear space available in order to place it. So, if I chart the universal proposition first using the P and the M circles, and because it is an "E" proposition, it would look like this:

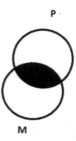

No P is M, and our Venn Diagram shows that. Let's review the Venn Diagram where I numbered all of the spaces:

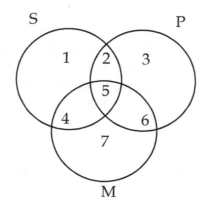

Let's fill in what we have so far by charting the universal proposition, the Major Premise, which is an E proposition. It will look like this:

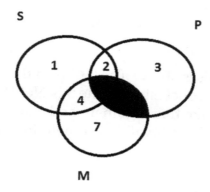

Now, you see when you get ready to chart the Minor Premise, which is a particular premise, an "I" proposition, you now know where to put the "X", space 4 is open for the "X". So now you have the completed chart for the categorical syllogism:

No P is M   (1)
Some S is M   (2)
∴   Some S is Not P   (3)

Which now looks like this:

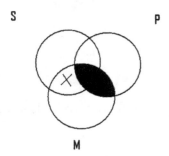

This is a valid argument. How do we know? By charting the two premises do we get the conclusion? The conclusion is "Some S is Not P" and if you look at the above Venn Diagram, isn't that what we have? If you look where the "X" is, isn't it outside of the circle "P" and isn't it inside the circle "S"? Remember what the "O" proposition looked like in a Venn Diagram?

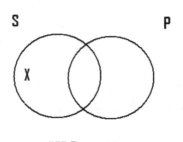

"O" Proposition

Isn't that what the two premises show? The "X" is in the circle "S" but outside the circle "P", which means it shows the conclusion, Some S is Not P, therefore it is valid.

Let's try a second example, take this argument and chart it using the Venn Diagram and you will see what I mean. This is an invalid argument in that it violates Rule 6:

All M is P
All S is M
∴   Some S is P

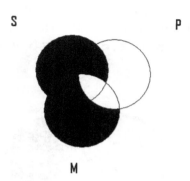

Now, do you see an "X" anywhere? No, you don't, and as you know, the conclusion is an "I" proposition that requires an "X", so, by charting the two premises, we DO NOT get the conclusion, and therefore the argument is invalid.

This is how you know, from a Venn Diagram whether or not an argument is valid. If the two premises do not give you the conclusion, then it is invalid.[34]

So, we use Venn Diagrams to help us "see" the validity or invalidity of an argument. OK, let's review how to chart a syllogism in a Venn Diagram.

First, check to see what type of propositions the premises are. Remember, the "I" and the "O" propositions are *particular* propositions, while the "A" and the "E" are *universal* propositions. If you have one universal proposition for a premise and one particular proposition for the other premise, you always chart the universal proposition first.

So, if you had a syllogism like this:

      All P is M   (major premise)
      Some S is Not M (minor premise)
∴   Some S is Not P   (conclusion)

You would FIRST chart the Major Premise (the first premise) which is an "A" proposition, a universal affirmative. So, your Venn Diagram would look like this after charting the universal premise first.[32]

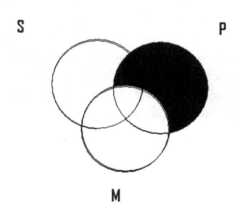

Notice that where P and M overlap, it is clearly indicating that All P is in M because the darkened part of P is all outside of M and the darkened part is the part that is empty. Now, we will chart the particular premise, Some S is Not M. Now the Venn Diagram looks like this:

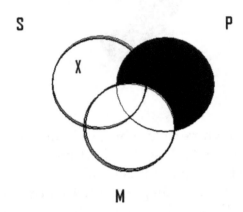

Notice the location of the "X". If we had not charted the universal premise first, we would have had three places to choose from to place the "X" as seen below:

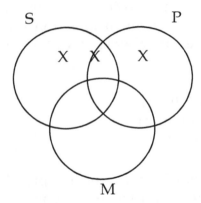

Note, there are two spaces where S is not in M, see where S overlaps P, well, that part of S is not in M, so, should the "X" go there? But that does not look right, and it is not what our conclusion claims, so we can see right away why it is important to chart the universal premise first if you have one universal premise and one particular premise. If you have two universal premises, or two particular premises, it does not matter which one is charted first.

If you have a case in which you have two choices as to where to put the "X", you have to place it on the line between the two choices, like this:

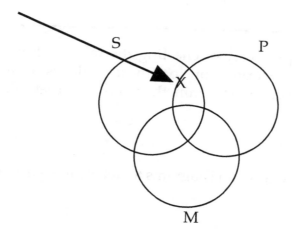

Whenever you see this, you know it is invalid!

REVIEW GLOSSARY

Venn Diagrams   A graphic way of charting the relationship among terms in either a single proposition or in a syllogism, and when used for a syllogism, to determinethe validity of that syllogism.

EXERCISES I

Now, try your hand at using Venn Diagrams to determine the validity of these syllogisms:

1.   Some P is M
        All M is S
   ∴   Some S is P

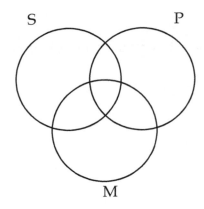

2.   No P is M
        All S is M
   ∴   No S is P

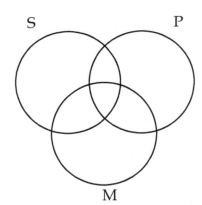

3.	All P is M
	All S is P
∴	All S is P

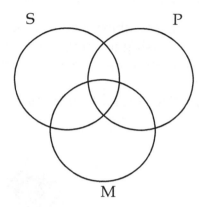

4.	Some P is Not M
	Some S is M
∴	Some S is Not P

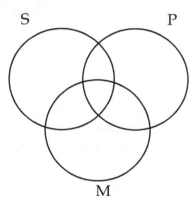

OK, now what was wrong with #4? Where do you put the "X"? No clear place to put it, is there?[36] So, you place the "X" on the line between the two possible locations for the X. What does that mean? It means that we cannot determine whether or not this argument is valid, and if we cannot determine whether or not the argument is valid, then we have to claim that it is invalid. Any time you have an argument where you are charting two particular premises, you will have an "X" which has to go on the line separating two locations where the "X" can go, thus indicating the whole argument is invalid.

Now that we have reviewed using Venn Diagrams to chart validity in a syllogism, let's do some exercises using Venn Diagrams to chart first single propositions and then syllogisms.

EXERCISES II

Using the Venn Diagram, chart the following Proposition forms, first write what the form looks like, then chart it using a Venn Diagram...for example:
Chart the "A" proposition using a Venn Diagram. First, the form itself looks like this:
All S is P
Second, the Venn Diagram looks like this:

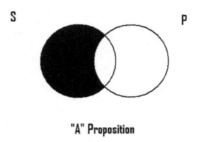

"A" Proposition

Now, using Venn Diagrams, do the same to the following propositional forms:
The E proposition...is written like this:_____
Second, the Venn Diagram for an E proposition looks like this:

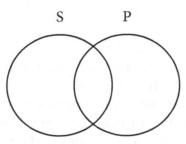

The I proposition...is written like this:_____
Second, the Venn Diagram for an "I" proposition looks like this:

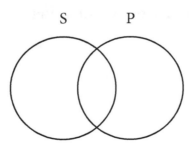

Finally, the O proposition...is written like this:_____
Second, the Venn Diagram for the O proposition looks like this:

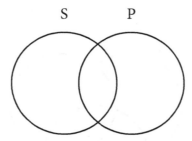

OK, now that you have done that, let's use Venn Diagrams to chart the validity of a syllogism. Using Venn Diagrams, chart the following and determine whether or not they are valid.

1.   All M is P
         All S is M
   ∴ All S is P

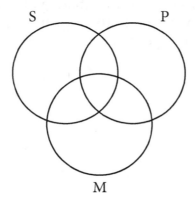

2.   No P is M   (answer in the back of the book)
         No S is M
   ∴ No S is P

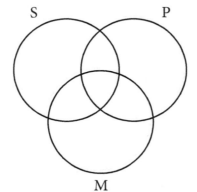

3. Some M is P   (answer in the back of the book)
    Some M is Not S
∴   Some S is Not P

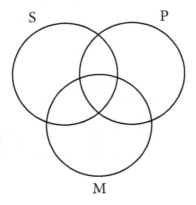

ADVANCED EXERCISE

OK, that was fairly easy, try this one…remember…you have to get any syllogism that you are charting with Venn Diagrams down to three propositions and three terms.

Just give it a try and see what happens…

All M is P
All R is M
All S is M
All S is P
All S is R
Some S is P
All P is R
Some R is not M
No M is P

Based upon what you already know, how many arguments are there here? What would be the conclusions? What are the terms?

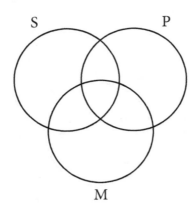

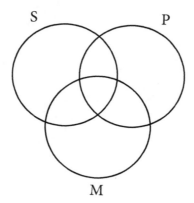

Did you figure it out?

Chapter Four

The Categorical Syllogism:
Mood and Figure: Argument Analysis

We have come a long way with just the simple three proposition syllogism. We have looked at a couple of ways to determine validity. What we have not done is to check out some of the ways in which we can determine validity rather quickly and easily. You might imagine just as there are only four propositional forms, the A, E, I, and O proposition forms, Aristotle came up with just four possible forms for syllogisms. They are referred to as the "Figure"[37] of the syllogism. They are numbered and look this way:

FIGURE 1	FIGURE 2	FIGURE 3	FIGURE 4
MP	PM	MP	PM
SM	SM	MS	MS
∴ SP	∴SP	∴SP	∴SP [38]

So, if we have an argument like this:

   All M is P
   All S is M
∴ All S is P

This would be a Figure 1 argument form.

The "mood" of the syllogism is determined by what type of propositions make up the syllogism.[39] So, if your first premise is an "E" proposition, and the second premise is an "A" proposition and the conclusion is an "E" proposition, the mood would be:

E

A

E

Now, if we take the figure number 2 and add it, we would get this:

E   No P is M (major premise)

A = All S is M (minor premise)

E ∴ No S is P (conclusion)

2

You see syllogism EAE-2 has the three types or propositions as indicated by the letters "EAE", which is the mood, and the order of the argument is determined by the figure number "2".

Now, you try it, write out the syllogism for the following mood and figures:

AAA-2

AEE-3

AAA-1

OIE-3(answer is in the back of the book)

Now, what is the point of all of this? I thought we had Venn Diagrams to help us determine validity? Well, yes, we do, but we learned earlier of the six rules which also help us determine validity of a syllogism. If we go back and review those rules, we might begin to see some patterns and the mood and figure as listed above helps us to see those patterns even faster than Venn Diagrams.

Again, what is the point? When we begin to look at regular arguments, we will want to first break them down into proper syllogisms, and by so doing, we can further abbreviate the argument by simply coming up with mood and figure. You have to admit; AAA-1 is easier to write than:

 All M is P

 All S is M

∴ All S is P

And that is easier than writing:

 All Men are Mortal

 Socrates is a Man

∴ Socrates is Mortal

And all of that is easier than taking time to draw three circles! (but we have all of these methods of testing validity to double-check ourselves in really difficult cases)

All of this works because right now we are only concerned about determining validity and that does not depend upon the content of the propositions, just the structure of the argument.

Anyway, if we can figure out what rules the various mood and figures break or keep, we can determine just by looking at the mood and figure of an argument whether or not it is valid. Let's try it...

Here are the six rules governing the validity of a syllogism.

Rules Governing Valid Syllogisms
Rule 1   A valid syllogism has just three terms

Rule 2   The Middle Term must be distributed in at least one premise

Rule 3   If a term is distributed in the conclusion, it must be distributed in the premise

Rule 4   If the conclusion is affirmative, both premises must be affirmative, and if the conclusion is negative, one of the premises must be negative

Rule 5   Both premises cannot be negative

Rule 6   If the conclusion is a universal proposition, the premises must be universal. If the conclusion is a particular proposition, one premise must be a particular proposition, and no argument with both particular premises is ever valid.

OK, now here are the distributions of the four propositional types:

"A" PROPOSITION   Universal affirmative proposition = All S is P (Distributes the Subject position)

"E" PROPOSITION   Universal negative proposition = No S is P (Distributes both the Subject and Predicate positions)

"I" PROPOSITION   Particular affirmative proposition= Some S is P (Does not Distribute)

"O" PROPOSITION   Particular negative proposition = Some S is Not P (Distributes the Predicate position)

OK, now with this information, and knowing the mood and figure, you should be able to determine, with some practice, whether an argument is valid or not just by looking at the mood and figure.

So, let's give it whirl and see how we do.

The following are all invalid, tell me why, what rule or rules do they break?

AAA-2

AAA-3

AAA-4

III-1

IOO-2

EEE-3

AEE-1

Now, using just mood and figure, the rules of validity and distribution, write down some that you believe to be valid…

I hope you have noticed our entire efforts have been focused on learning how to determine whether or not an argument is valid. All of this seems reasonable, even, dare I say it, logical! But, you and I both know people do not talk using nice neat syllogisms. If they did, we would think they talked very strangely indeed. Can you imagine the following argument at a party…

Paul says, "I would argue All Conservatives are boring, Sam is a conservative, and therefore, Sam is boring." Sam says, "I would argue Some Conservatives are boring, Sam Is a conservative, therefore, Sam is probably boring." Then Sam's wife jumps in and says, "But Sam, you are not a conservative, but you're still boring!" "No, no dear, you need to say, Some Boring People are Not Conservatives, Sam is not a Conservative, Therefore, Sam is boring," "Paul jumps in, "Sam, you have it all wrong, it should be:Some people who are not conservatives are boring, Sam is not a conservative, Sam could be boring."

Well, you get the picture. Actually, we talk more like this:

Paul said, "Ah, conservatives are boring! That's probably why Sam is boring!" Sam's wife disagrees, "Wait a minute, Sam is no conservative!" "OK, then what's his excuse?!?!?!" retorts Paul.

So, how do you make sense out of the second example of arguments made in common language?

Let's look at some other arguments.

From Tuesday, September 30, 2008 Des Moines Register Editiorial:[40]

In the midst of the economic meltdown, we must not forget the connection between money and politics. The millions of dollars given to office holders and candidates by the financial services and real estate industries have bought and paid for less regulation and less oversight, which have brought us to the grave economic crisis we face.

— Ms X, Des Moines

Let's break this argument down. What is Ms. X claiming? It seems she is seeing a direct link between the money members of the financial community contributes to politicians and office holders and the near absence of any governmental oversight of the financial industry which led to economic crisis of 2008. How would we re-write this argument in proper syllogistic form? First, we would have to determine what the final conclusion is, but in so doing, we discover several conclusions, which means there is more than one argument in the short paragraph above.

Some possible conclusions of the above argument are:

All Cases of Less Regulation and Oversight by the Government are Cases in which those who are supposed to be regulated will take advantage of the lax oversight and regulation for their own gain.

This conclusion assumes the following to be true:

Human beings given a free hand will do the greedy, selfish thing.

Another possible conclusion:

All politicians who accept large amounts of money are People who will do whatever the contributor wants them to do.

This conclusion assumes the following is true:

Human beings always feel an obligation to bow to the wishes of their benefactor.

OK, so, are there any other conclusions we could write from this "one" argument of Ms. X? Perhaps this:

There IS an economic meltdown…

And…

There IS a connection between money and politics, in the sense that politicians can be bought, which, of course, means politicians will vote the way their biggest contributors want them to vote.

I know, it seems like an awful lot crammed into one simple argument, which on the surface seemed so easy to understand. What we begin to discover, as we break down the argument into its many pieces, is a lot in her stated argument which was left unsaid. That is often the case in real life arguments; we leave out a lot of our assumptions and beliefs when stating our opinion. It is the job of the student of logic to fill in all of those blanks. When we do that we can begin to expose what assumptions the argument is based upon, which may lead us to question the soundness of the argument, even if we happen to agree with it.

Look at the argument now re-written as a series of syllogisms and see if you agree…

All Benefactors of politicians are People who expect that the politician will vote as their Benefactor wishes.

All Politicians who receive money are Politicians who have received money from a Benefactor of Politicians

∴ All Politicians who receive money are people who vote as their Benefactor wishes.

Or

All B is V
All P is B
∴ All P is V

Which leads to the next argument:

All Benefactors of politicians who are Financiers are Benefactors who wish for politicians to vote for less regulation and oversight from the government

All Politicians who receive money from Financiers are Politicians who receive money from Benefactors who are Financiers

∴ All Politicians who receive money from Benefactors who are Financiers are Politicians who vote for less regulation and oversight from the government (of Financiers and their companies)

All BF (Benefactors who are Financiers) is LR (vote for Less Regulation)
All PF (Politicians receiving money from Financiers) is BF
∴ All PF is LR

Which then leads to the next argument:

All votes for less regulation and government oversight are Cases in which Greed creates an economic disaster
Politicians who receive money from Benefactors who are Financiers are Politicians who vote for less regulation and oversight from the government (of Financiers and their companies)
∴ Politicians who receive money from Benefactors who are Financiers cause Cases in which Greed creates an economic disaster

All VR is G
All PF is VR
∴ All PF is G

But this leads to yet another argument:

All cases in which the Financier will be greedy are cases in which Financiers are not regulated by the government
All cases of financial collapse are cases in which Financiers are greedy
∴ All cases of financial collapse are cases in which Financiers are not regulated by the government

OK, I know, I know, this seems a bit much, but in fact it simply illustrates what assumptions the original argument is based upon. If we claim each of the above syllogisms to be in fact valid and "sound" (that is, the argument is valid and each of the propositions is true)[41] then my goodness but we would have to be very cynical. If in fact all of this is true and valid, then who should be in charge of Wall Street? Because apparently, if we accept the force of universal affirmative propositions, ANYONE in the same position would do the SAME thing, including the one making this argument in the first place!

Therefore, if you are willing to accept each of these arguments as both valid and true, then you would obviously want more regulation and oversight by the government, but if human beings are so easily made to be greedy, then you would want regulations to govern those who make the regulations and who provide the oversight to prevent them from taking advantage of their position of authority over the markets, thus creating yet another mess.

On the other hand, you might want to respond to Ms X's argument by asking if she is actually making an inductive argument while treating it as if it were a deductive argument. What this means is that SOME financiers become greedy with no regulation and oversight and SOME politicians who receive contributions from financiers will vote as the greedy financier wishes them to vote.

However, one can go the other way too far, that is, when deregulation was called for allowing for a true free market. The problem there was instead of using "A" propositions the politicians were using E propositions in that No financiers are actually greedy, and that even if they were, greed in a free market would be curtailed by competition. The problem with that approach was no one thought about the heights greed could reach, and how clever the greedy can be by buying up all of their competitors in such a way as to avoid the accusation of creating a monopoly.

The point is, once again, leaders want to use the force of deductive arguments when all they can truly claim is the somewhat weaker force of the inductive argument. Even if you agree with Ms. X's argument, you have to admit, the most she could really claim is less regulation and government oversight did have SOMETHING to do with the current situation, but certainly it does not address everything which has contributed to the current economic situation. In other words, the best and most sound argument concerning human behavior will most often be the middle-of-the-road position, which most people see as not demonstrating strong leadership. Therefore, it could be argued in many cases (not ALL!) people will lie and stretch the claims of their arguments because of peer pressure to demonstrate strong leadership. The problem with that approach is the world just does not operate in a black and white reality, there is just too much grey area which if ignored will allow us to be carried away in the vagaries of irrational, yet apparently strong, leadership. We will go forth in absolute confidence as we merrily trot down the bath of irrationality. How else can you explain 1932 Germany? 1950's McCarthyism? Waco?

The problem with logic is it often is rather boring and even handed. It is not very exciting when a person in leadership takes a stand that honors both sides, we tend to call them names, like "wishy-washy" or "flip floppers"! We want people who will stand for something, even when it is simply wrong. I guess we simply do not trust the power of truth and validity to take us in new and exciting directions.

REVIEW GLOSSARY

Mood=The name given the types of propositions that make up a syllogism, e.g. AAA or EIO
Figure = The number given to each of the four syllogistic forms

EXERCISES

1. Find an argument in a newspaper, perhaps the opinion page, and translate it into proper syllogistic form and determine what all of the assumptions are in making the argument in the first place by stating each of the assumptions in a proper syllogism.

Chapter Five

THE CATEGORICAL SYLLOGISM:
Translating Common Language into Syllogistic Form

OK, so how did it go, taking a real life argument and translating it? I know, you were not taught yet how to do that. Sometimes it is better to be taught something only after you have first struggled on your own to figure it out. Below are some basic rules to follow when trying to translate common language arguments.

First, determine the main conclusion to the argument as it is presented.[42] Sometimes the conclusion is not clearly stated, and so you have to come up with the conclusion as implied, for example:

"If you make someone who does not like fund raising president of a non-profit organization, it will result in a disastrous fund raising effort ...well...Sam hates fundraising, so, no wonder the public radio is broke!"

OK, there are several propositions missing here. I think anyone who would overhear this rather demeaning comment, would know what the one making the comment meant. We would automatically fill in the blanks and conclude that apparently Sam is president of a public radio station and because he hates fund raising, the radio station is broke.

So, we have to figure out the final conclusion of the argument before beginning to translate. If we know that the final conclusion of this argument is:

President Sam is the reason our public radio station is broke.

Then we can begin to build the syllogism. However, the above stated conclusion is not exactly in proper propositional form. Is it an A, E, I or O proposition? Remember, these are our only choices. If we treat it as an A proposition, how should it be re-written?

All classes of Sam being president of a public radio station are classes of a public radio station being broke.

Weird, it seems strange because the nature of a proposition is that it shows the relationship between cases or classes of things. So, we have a class or case of Sam being a president of a public radio station. That seems strange to state it that way because we are referring to a single person, President Sam, not to a general group of Presidents who do not like fundraising. However, we still have to treat President Sam as a class of "Presidents of public radio stations who do not like fundraising".[43] The same is true when referring to a specific instance of a financially broke public radio station. We have to treat the broke radio station as if it were a class of broke public radio stations. So, we might symbolize the conclusion as:

All P is B (P = President Sam; B = Broke public radio station)

Now, we begin to build the argument from the conclusion. We know from our rules that if we have an affirmative conclusion we cannot have any negative premises, so we know we can eliminate E and O propositions. Second, we know that in the A proposition the Subject Term is distributed, so we know that the subject term is known as the Minor Term, and the Minor Term appears in the Minor Premise, which is the second premise. We also know that because we have eliminated the E and O propositions, all we have left that is affirmative is the A and I propositions, but we know that we cannot use an I proposition for the Minor Premise because the I proposition does NOT distribute anything, and we know from our rules above that if a term is distributed in the conclusion it must be distributed in the premises. So, we will have to have an A proposition for the minor premise, and the Subject Term, President Sam, will need to be in the subject position in the minor premise, so we know the minor premise will have to be…

All P is _____

Can we use an "I" proposition for the first premise, or the major premise? Well, we know that the major term in the conclusion is NOT distributed, and so it would not need to be distributed in the major premise (first premise). OK, so maybe we could use an "I" proposition form…but wait, remember the rule that says the middle term must be distributed in at least one of the propositions, and if the "I" does not distribute anything, then we only have one proposition left, and that is another "A" proposition. That being said, and knowing that the only term distributed in an "A" proposition is the subject term position, we know that the middle term needs to be in the subject term position. So, we know the Major Premise, or the first Premise will look like this:

All _____ is B

We still do not know what the Middle Term is, as you can see, this is what we have for an argument so far:

All _____ is B
All P is _____
∴ All P is B

That being said, we now know what the mood and figure of this syllogism is going to have to be in order for it to be valid:

AAA – 1

OK, so let's translate the premises and conclusion:
And we know so far that the major premise (first premise) looks like this:
_____are classes of public radio stations that are broke.
And we know that the minor premise (second premise) has to look like this:

All classes of Sam being president of a public radio station are _____

And the conclusion looks like this:

All classes of Sam being president of a public radio station are classes of public radio stations that are broke.

So what is the middle term? How do we determine that? Look at the original argument;

"If you make someone who does not like fund raising president of a non-profit organization, it will result in a disastrous fund raising effort …well…Sam hates fundraising, so, no wonder the public radio is broke!"

We see here that President Sam does not like fundraising, and so we have a clue to what the middle term is, apparently it is …does not like fundraising… or something like that. Look what happens to this argument when we interject this middle term, it exposes the assumption behind this argument, an assumption you might disagree with, and as a result, disagree with the final conclusion…take a look:

All classes of Presidents of public radio stations who do not like fundraising are cases in which public radio stations go broke.

All classes of Sam being president of a public radio station are classes of Presidents of public radio stations who do not like fundraising.

∴ All classes of Sam being president of a public radio station are classes in which public radio stations go broke.

Notice how we wrote the middle term… "All classes of Presidents of public radio stations who do not like fundraising"

We had to make it clear that we were limiting our middle term to presidents of public radio stations because that was the main subject of this argument. If we had written… "All classes of Presidents who do not like fundraising…" we would have had to have yet another argument indicating that we were talking about presidents of non-profits specifically. Then construct yet another argument indicating the subject of our argument is the public radio station. See if you can construct those additional arguments here:

OK, so the assumption here is that if you have a public radio station that is broke, you have a president of that radio station who does not like fundraising. Is that true? Are there not several examples of someone doing something that they do not like doing (like this Logic class) and yet who succeed in doing it? Just because someone does not like doing something does not mean he or she will fail at it.

Might there be other reasons the radio station is broke? How about if a secretary embezzled funds from the radio station to the point that it was broke, or, how about a changing demographic that no longer supported public radio?

You begin to see the point, I hope.

OK, so what do you do with an argument like this:

Only those who proudly display the American flag are truly patriotic. Joe has never displayed an American flag, so I wonder about his patriotism…

So, how do you translate this kind of argument? Whenever you see a statement begin with the word "only" you switch the subject and the predicate and exchange "only" with the word "all",[44] so you get this…

<u>Only</u> those who proudly display the American flag are <u>truly patriotic</u>.
      ↓   Term in the subject position   term in predicate position

All who truly are patriotic are those who proudly display an American flag.

OK, so now, how about the second statement? Joe has never displayed an American flag. Certainly it is a negative statement, and remember how we treated statements that included the name of a specific person as a universal proposition. (When we get to Boolean theory, we will talk some more about "singular" statements.) So, we would have something like this...

No classes of Joe are classes of people who proudly display an American flag.

You can do that, or simply use the statement:Joes does not display an American flag... remembering that this is a universal negative proposition.

Now, how about the conclusion? What do you think it is? How would you translate:"... so I wonder about his patriotism..." Certainly, the person making the argument is implying that Joe is not patriotic, and so we might have this for a conclusion...

No classes of Joe are classes of people who are truly patriotic.

In this way, the one making the argument is not claiming that Joe is not patriotic at all, just not **truly** patriotic. Now, we could push this argument a little further and perhaps arrive at the final conclusion that only those who are truly patriotic are patriotic at all, which in turn implies that those who are NOT truly patriotic are not patriotic at all. See if you can construct those additional arguments to arrive at this further conclusion. This is how we can begin to see and analyze what people are actually trying to say in an argument.

Do you see the weakness in the argument? Wouldn't there be other reasons Joe does not display an American flag? Worse yet, is displaying an American flag all it takes to be truly patriotic?

What about this statement:
"All but employees may participate in the store's grand prize give-a-way."

What type of statement is the above? A; E; I or O? Is it universal or particular? Ask yourself a few questions about this statement. What classes are represented in this statement? There is the class of "employees" and the class of those who may participate in the grand prize give-a-way. How many of the class "employees" can participate in the grand prize give-a-way? That's right, none! So, this statement accounts for all members of the class "employees". Does it account for all members of the class those who may participate in the grand prize give-a-way? Yes, in that none of them are employees. So, it distributes both classes. Which of the four proposition types distributes both classes or the subject and predicate? That's right, an "E" proposition. So, how would we re-write this statement into an "E" proposition? Simply replace the "All but" with "No" and you get this:

"No employees are those who may participate in the store's grand prize give-a-way."

Ok, what about this statement:
"Most criminals deserve getting a second chance."

Again, we ask some questions about distribution. What are the two classes being referred to in this statement? The class "criminals" and the class "those who deserve a second chance". Does the class "criminals" account for all criminals? No. Does the class "those who deserve a second chance" account for all criminals? No. So, in this case, the statement does not distribute anything. When we say, "those who deserve a second chance" we have limited the reach of that group by the subject, "criminals" by saying "some" criminals… So, what propositional type does not distribute either the subject or predicate? That's right, the "I" proposition. So, we simply replace the "Most" with "Some" and we get this:

"Some criminals are those who deserve a second chance."

We could take the same statement from above and make it negative:

"Most criminals do NOT deserve a second chance."

Now we have an "O" proposition that would read this way:

"Some criminals are NOT those who deserve a second chance."

We know this distributes "those who deserve a second chance" simply because in this proposition we are saying among this particular group of those who deserve a second chance are not a specific group of criminals referred to in the subject.

Hopefully, you begin to see the process needed in re-writing common statements into proper propositional forms. To do so requires understanding the meaning of the statement, what the classes are and what is distributed. Often understanding what a proposition means may be difficult, so by first identifying the classes represented and what is distributed, we can begin to get an idea of what is meant. For example:

"It's not always easy to understand difficult concepts."

Ok, what does this mean? What are the classes? What does "It's" refer to? Are we referring to a disembodied reality floating out there, or are we referring to people who are having a difficult time making sense out of a difficult concept? Are we not referring to "ALL" people saying that there are times everyone may have a difficult time? Is that what is implied? Well, some might say this is an "A" proposition and some might say an "I" proposition. Let's re-write it both ways and see if we can get at the meaning of the proposition.

First, the "A" proposition re-write:

"All people are people who sometimes have a tough time understanding difficult concepts."

Ok, now let's try the "I" proposition and see what we think...

"Some people are people who have a tough time understanding difficult concepts."

Which of these two expresses what you think was originally meant? Perhaps, we should re-think our classes. Perhaps these are the classes:

"Ease of understanding" and "difficult concepts"

We could re-write it as an "I" proposition:

"Some cases of ease of understanding are cases involving difficult concepts." Or
"Some cases of ease of understanding are NOT cases involving difficult concepts."

What of these re-writes gets at the meaning of the original statement? You may object and say to me that you need more information, and I would agree. Any of these re-writes would be quite plausible given certain arguments that were being made. For example, if you were arguing with a group of extremely intelligent college students you might want to use the "A" proposition above indicating it is understandable that sometimes even very intelligent people have a tough time understanding difficult concepts.

You get the point, re-writing common statements into proper propositional form involves not only knowing the meaning of a statement, what its classes are and what is distributed, but also the context in which it appears.

EXERCISES

Translate the following into proper form (A, E, I or O forms). *(check the back for answers)*

1. Only the brave deserve the Medal of Honor.
2. Not a single employee was allowed to participate in the company's lottery.
3. Nearly everyone who smokes will die of cancer.
4. It simply is not true that any Republicans care about the poor!
5. It simply is not true that any Democrats would want to do anything to benefit small business!
6. Everyone who signs up will win a prize.
7. No one can participate except by invitation.
8. Some people really do not like sports.
9. Early detection of breast cancer saves lives.
10. Exercising daily will reduce the chance of contracting Alzheimer's.

ADVANCED EXERCISE

Translate and re-write this argument into proper form. Determine how many arguments are actually in this whole argument, and then determine whether or not they are valid.

"Democratic societies need free speech; only with it can citizens discover the truth, participate in their society's decisions, and better realize their endeavors. With free speech all people have the opportunity to understand and evaluate the issues they face. Free expression, in all its diversity, is guaranteed in the First Amendment of the Constitution, which states 'Congress shall make no law...abridging the freedom of speech.'

"John Stuart Mill believes that opinions should never be suppressed. He grounds this belief in his famous dilemma:

1. If you suppress an opinion and it is true, then you lose the chance of exchanging truth for falsity.
2. If you suppress an opinion and it is false, then you lose the opportunity of obtaining a clearer view of your own position. ("Classical Philosophical Questions", Robert J. Mulvaney, Prentice Hall, 2009, pg 431)

Chapter Six

THE CATEGORICAL SYLLOGISM:
Aristotelian Square of Opposition and Immediate Inferences

In the previous chapter we had taken regular arguments and translated them into standard form syllogisms using A, E, I or O propositional forms. As we had learned earlier, propositions are either true or false, and deductive arguments are either valid or invalid. We have also learned that arguments can be valid even if the propositions making up the arguments are not true. However, if we want a truly "sound" argument, then not only does the form of the argument need to be valid (and the FORM of the argument is really what we are calling valid), but the propositions making up the argument need to be true. Developing a "sound" argument is truly the goal of anyone studying logic, and so it is important to know whether or not a proposition is true.

This can be somewhat difficult as we are trying to translate statements into standard form. Take for example the statement:

"Not all professional athletes are overpaid."

If we accept that as a true statement, we would then translate the statement into a standard form "O" proposition by replacing the "not all" to "some" and inserting a "not" in front of the proposition "overpaid",[45] thus...

"Some professional athletes are not overpaid."

Ok, if we say this statement is true, "Some professional athletes are not overpaid." Then what is the truth value of the following statements...

All professional athletes are overpaid.
No professional athletes are overpaid.
Some professional athletes are overpaid.

On the surface it seems rather straight forward, but can we be sure? Aristotle developed what has been called the "Standard Square of Opposition" which shows us what the truth value of different propositional forms is if we know the truth value of just one.[46] The "Square" looks like this...

(The A, E, I and O refer to the four propositional forms)

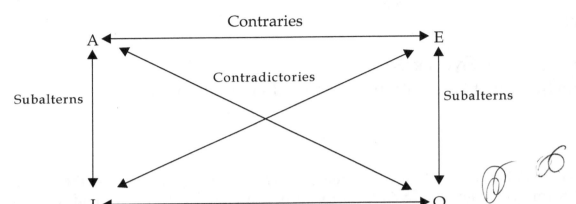

The "A" proposition is a contrary to the "E" proposition in that they CANNOT both be true, but they COULD both be false! So if I say the "A" proposition is true, then I know the "E" proposition is false. If I say the "A" proposition is false, then I have to say that the truth value of the "E" proposition is undetermined, because it is possible that they are both false (think of this example:All unicorns are white, and No unicorns are white. They are both false because there are NO unicorns!). If I say "All men are brave" is false, I cannot say that therefore "No men are brave" is true! I don't know if the "E" proposition is true or not (I would hope that it too is false!). The same is true for the "E" proposition. If I say that the "E" proposition is true then I know that the "A" proposition is false. If, however, I say that the "E" proposition is false, I do not know the truth value of the "A" proposition. For example, if I say "No horses are thoroughbreds" is false, I cannot say "All horses are thoroughbreds" is true![47]

The "I" proposition is a subcontrary to the "O" proposition because they can BOTH be true but they CANNOT both be false. So, if I say that the "I" proposition is false, then I know that the "O" proposition is true. However, if I say that the "I" proposition is true, I do not know the truth value of the "O" proposition. For example, if I say "Some dogs are huge" is true, I cannot say that "Some dogs are not huge" is false! If I say "Some dogs are purple" is false, then I know that "Some dogs are not purple" is true. The same is true if I say that the "O" proposition, "Some dogs are not spotted" is false, I know that the "I" proposition "Some dogs are spotted" is true. If I say "Some dogs are not brown" is true, I cannot say "Some dogs are brown" is false because it could be true as well.

So far we have been able to determine the relationship between an "A" proposition and an "E" proposition, and the same for the "I" and "O" propositions. What about the relationship of the "A" with the "I" and "O" or the "E" with the "O" and the "I"? As you look at the graphic above you will notice that in the center is the term "Contradictories". What that means is that if the "A" is true the "O" is always false, and if the "A" is false, the "O" is always true. And if the "O" is true, the "A" is always false, or if the "O" is false, the "A" is always true. The same is true with the "E" and "I" propositions, again, if the "E" is true the

"I" is false, and if the "E" is false the "I" is true, and if the "I" is true the "E" is false, and if the "I" is false the "E" is true.

Now, what about the subalterns? Subalternation means if the "A" proposition is true the "I" proposition is true. However, if the "A" proposition is false, the "I" proposition may be true. For example, if I say "All horses are brown" is false, "Some horses are brown" could certainly be true! If I say that the "I" proposition is true, I do not know the truth value of the "A" proposition, because again, I can flip the previous example and say that while it is true that "Some horses are brown" that does not lead to the conclusion that "All horses are brown". Now, if I say, on the other hand, that the "I" proposition is false, I cannot say that the "A" proposition might be true; because if I say "Some horses are unicorns" is false, I cannot claim that "All horses are unicorns" has any chance of being true. So, we know then, that if the "I" proposition is false the "A" proposition must also be false.

The same is true about the "E" and the "O" proposition, summarized below:

If the E is true – The O is true
If the E is false – The O is undetermined (just because "No horses are Brown" is false does not mean that "Some horses are not brown" is also false, it could be true...)
If the O is true – The E might be false, so it is undetermined (reverse the example above)
If the O is false – The E must be false

Let's create a grid to summarize all of these relationships:

We will use F for false and T for true and U for undetermined.

		A	E	I	O	
A (T)		T	F	T	F	
A (F)		F	U	U	T	
E (T)		F	T	F	T	
E (F)		U	F	T	U	
I (T)		U	F	T	U	
I (F)		F	T	F	T	
O (T)		F	U	U	T	
O (F)		T	F	T	F	

Now, why is it so important to know this? Simple, the quicker you can determine the truth value of a proposition the quicker you can determine the soundness of an argument. Before, when we were talking about mood, figure and distribution, we were talking about argument STRUCTURE, now we are talking about the truth values of the propositions making up the argument. Remember, for an argument to be sound means the argument structure must be valid and the propositions must be true. Not all propositions are as easy to know whether or not they are true as are the examples given above. Say for example, someone said to you "All quarks are smaller than protons" and stipulated that it was true. Unless you were a physicist, or have studied quantum mechanics, there is a good chance you would not know whether that is true or not, but if someone tells you, say your physics teacher, that it is true, well, you now have the basis for determining whether or not the following statement is true or false, "Some quarks are not smaller than protons." The point is, with Aristotle's Square of Opposition, you can determine whether or not statements that you may not even understand are true or false or undetermined if you know the truth value of just one statement. This comes in very handy in any kind of investigation, whether it involves a medical lab or a crime lab.

But what about the truth value of these two statements:

> No horses are reptiles
> And
> No reptiles are horses

If the first one is false, is the second one false? Do they mean the same thing? Or how about this:

> No horses are non-mammals
> All horses are mammals

Do these two propositions mean the same thing? Or how about this:

> Some dogs are brown.
> Some dogs are not non-brown

Do these two propositions mean the same thing? Or this:

> All humans are mortal
> All non-mortals are non-humans

Do these two propositions mean the same? OK, so what gives? Why bring this complication up? Because, again, remember, we do not always speak in proper syllogistic form, and so we have to translate. So what if someone, in an effort to confuse you, states...

> All non-Americans are non-conservatives

That could be translated to a simple "A" proposition:

> All conservatives are Americans

What did we just do? Something called Conversion, Obversion and Contraposition.[48] These are yet another form of what is called "immediate inferences".[49] What that means is, if you know how to convert, obvert and contrapose a complex proposition into standard form, it becomes easier to determine the truth value of the proposition, and thus the soundness of the argument. I know it will be hard to believe, but by the time we get through what might seem to you to be a complex explanation, it will actually be easier to translate propositions not stated in clear propositional forms (A, E, I or O).

Below you will see a summary of the three immediate inferences, and keep in mind, you can move from left to right or from right to left in the columns below. That is, the statement on the left means the same thing as the statement on the right except in cases of limitation. You will note that whenever you see the term (by limitation) beside an inference that means both of the statements may not mean the same thing, however, in an "A" proposition we know that all of "S" is in "P", and therefore we know that at least some of "P" is in "S", so by limitation we can convert the A proposition, though they do not quite mean the same thing. Remember in the Aristotelian Square of Opposition where we said that if the A proposition is true than the "I" proposition must be true, but that if the "I" proposition is true, we cannot conclude the truth value of the A proposition because the "I" proposition is claiming less than the A proposition is claiming. So, if I convert "All horses are mammals" to "Some mammals are horses" we see immediately that the "I" proposition does not claim as much as the A proposition, and as a result I cannot convert "Some mammals are horses" to "All mammals are horses" for obvious reasons! On the other hand, I can convert "No horses are reptiles" to "No reptiles are horses" and see that the meaning does NOT change. The same is true with the "I" proposition, "Some dogs are brown" converts easily to "Some brown things are dogs" and the meaning does not change. But you will note that we CANNOT convert an O proposition.

CONVERSION [50]

Convertend	Converse
A: All S is P	I: Some P is S (by limitation)
E: No S is P	E: No P is S
I: Some S is P	I: Some P is S
O: Some S is not P	(conversion not valid)

Remember what we said about distribution, the E proposition distributes both the S and the P and the I distributes neither, do you see a pattern here, what are the two propositions that can be converted completely without losing meaning or truth value and without limitation? Yes, the E and the I propositions.

COMPLEMENTS

Every term has its complement, that is to say, every class of things has a complement that is made up of things that are not in that class, so S has a complement of non-S, or P has a complement of non-P. On the other hand, non-S has a complement S and non-P has the complement of P. You see, it goes either way. What is the complement of "male"? "non-male" or rather "female"? And of course the complement of "female" is "non-female" or rather "male". Ok, to restate, a complement is simply the opposite, so non-S is the complement of S, and S is the complement of non-S. Just because we refer to something as a complement does NOT mean that it is negative, rather, it just means it is the OPPOSITE. Now that we understand what a complement is, *obversion is the process of keeping the same quantity but changing the quality and replacing the predicate with its complement...*

OBVERSION [51]

Obvertend
A: All S is P (means the same as)
E: No S is P (means the same as)
I: Some S is P (means the same as)
O: Some S is not P (means the same as)

Obverse
E: No S is non-P
A: All S is non-P
O: Some S is not non-P
I: Some S is non-P

Remember, the obvertend means the same as the obverse and the obverse means the same as the obvertend. You will soon see why this is very handy to know.

CONTRAPOSITION[52] is a process that actually brings together conversion and obversion. To contrapose a proposition, you simply obvert, convert, and then obvert again. So, if we obvert an A proposition we get:

No S is non-P

Then we convert it and get:

No non-P is S

And then obvert it again and get the contrapositive:

All non-P is non-S

The benefit of contraposition is that it saves you the trouble of obverting, converting and then obverting again!

As you could see from this process of obversion, conversion and obversion, we can contrapose the "A" proposition, because when we get to the "conversion" part of the process we have an "E" proposition to convert, and as we know from above, you can convert an "E" proposition directly and without losing any meaning.

Ok, so let's see what happens when we try to contrapose an "E" proposition.

First, we obvert the "E" proposition "No S is P" which becomes:

All S is non-P

Now, what happens when we convert this? We have to do it by limitation, so that it becomes:

Some non-P is S

Do you see why? Ok, now we obvert this to:

Some non-P is not non-S

Thus, we have learned that we can contrapose the "E" proposition only by limitation because at the point where we convert, we have an "A" proposition which has to be converted by limitation.

(To review, to contrapose by limitation simply means the one statement does NOT mean exactly the same as the other, and therefore you **cannot** start with "Some non-P is not non-S" and end up with "No S is P".)

Now, how about contraposing the "I" proposition. First we obvert it to...

Some S is not non-P

Now, we have an "O" proposition, but can we convert an "O" proposition? No. Therefore, we cannot contrapose an "I" proposition.

Finally, let's contrapose the "O" proposition by first obverting it to...

Some S is non-P

Then we convert this to...

Some non-P is S

And finally, we obvert this to...

Some non-P is not non-S

And this is the contrapositive of the "O" proposition.

CONTRAPOSITION [53]

PREMISS	CONTRAPOSITIVE
A: All S is P	A: All non-P is non-S
E: No S is P	O: Some non-P is not non-S (by limitation)
I: Some S is P	contraposition is not possible
O: Some S is not P	O: Some non-P is not non-S

(Note that the contrapositive for the E and the O propositions are the same, refer back to the Square of Opposition and remember that if the E proposition is true the O must be true, however, we cannot go the other way, so we can only contrapose the "E" proposition by limitation, which means that if we contrapose "Some non-P is not non-S" we will get Some

S is not P rather than No S is P simply because you cannot arrive at a universal proposition from a particular proposition.)

BOOLEAN THEORY[54]

In the 19th century, George Boole brought up an interesting question in regard to Aristotelian logic, what do you do about the fact that in the standard square of opposition, if the "A" proposition is true, the "I" proposition has to be true? Wait, I know, you are thinking, "what's wrong with that?" OK, let's try the old unicorn idea again. Would you say this statement is true:"All unicorns have a horn in the middle of their forehead."? Of course you would. But what happens when you say, "Some unicorns have a horn in the middle of their forehead."? Is it the same thing? Not really. The "A" proposition acts like a definition, and we know how to define a unicorn. The "I" proposition is not a definition, as a matter of fact, Boole claimed that the "I" proposition actually refers to **something**. Remember our Venn diagram. We said that in an "I" proposition, when you say "Some S is P" you are claiming at least one thing in the class "S" is also in the class "P". That is why we place an "X" in the proper spot, to indicate the existence of at least one thing. The problem is, in making that claim you are also claiming there IS something in class "S". In fact, Boole would claim the statement, "Some unicorns have a horn in the middle of their forehead" is actually false because there are no such things as unicorns! So what does that do to the Aristotelian square of opposition? It cuts away the subaltern relationship between the "A" and the "I" propositions, because while the "A" proposition could be true, the "I" proposition would not actually be true because as in this case, there are no unicorns. What this boils down to is no existential import in the "A" proposition. We discover that the same is true for the "E" proposition.

Now, just what is EXISTENTIAL IMPORT? Existential import simply means that the proposition claims that something exists. The "A" and "E" propositions act like definitions, but really do not claim that anything the "A" or "E" proposition is addressing actually exists. That is why we can look into any English dictionary and find a definition for "dragon" or "chimera" or even "unicorn" even though none of those things exist. "No unicorns are without a horn in the middle of their forehead." Obviously, this is true, but again, in the definitional sense. When we define a unicorn we all know a single horn in the forehead has to be part of the definition. But again, while we can find that definition in Webster's Collegiate Dictionary, it doesn't mean that unicorns exist! In fact, depending on how you wrote statements about the unicorn, every proposition, "A", "E", "I" and "O" could be false, which, of course, would be absurd, given the standard square of opposition.

So what does this do to the standard square (or Aristotelian square) of opposition? **The Boolean Square of Opposition** becomes a lot simpler, such that it looks like this:

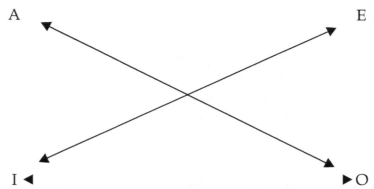

All we have left are contradictories. That is, if the "A" is true, the "O" is false, and if the "A" is false the "O" is true, and likewise in the relationship between the "E" and the "I".

Ok, confused? I shouldn't wonder. After all, I just told you depending upon how you worded the various propositions, they could all be false, and here we are claiming that not to be true. So what gives? It comes down to this, Boole realized you cannot push this situation too far because if you do, no propositions can be made about things that do not exist. So, we have to treat the universal propositions AS IF they existed. For example, instead of saying, "All unicorns are white" we would say, "If there were unicorns, they would all be white". But of course, we can also say, "If there were unicorns, they would NOT be white" is also true because once again, there are no unicorns and we can define them anyway we choose (though going against conventional definitions would make communication exceedingly difficult!) The point is, no longer is it the case that "A" propositions and "E" propositions cannot both be true or both false, why? No existential import. That is, a universal affirmative or a universal negative proposition makes no claim to actual existence. Therefore, we lose the "contrary" relationship between the "A" and the "E" proposition that we find in the Standard Square of Opposition. And because a proposition that does have existential import (an "I" and an "O") cannot be derived from a proposition that does not have existential import, then "subalternation" is lost as well. So, all we have left are contradictories.

So what does this mean? It means that in the case of CONVERSION, conversion by limitation is no longer valid. It also means that CONTRAPOSITION by limitation is not valid. However, OBVERSION remains valid for all propositional forms. So, the Boolean versions of Conversion, Obversion and Contraposition would look like this:

BOOLEAN VERSION:
CONVERSION

Convertend	Converse
A: All S is P	(conversion not valid)
E: No S is P	E: No P is S
I: Some S is P	I: Some P is S
O: Some S is not P	(conversion not valid)

OBVERSION

Obvertend	Obverse
A: All S is P	E: No S is non-P
E: No S is P	A: All S is non-P
I: Some S is P	O: Some S is not non-P
O: Some S is not P	I: Some S is non-P

CONTRAPOSITION

PREMISS	CONTRAPOSITIVE
A: All S is P	A: All non-P is non-S
E: No S is P	(contraposition is not valid)
I: Some S is P	(contraposition is not valid)
O: Some S is not P	O: Some non-P is not non-S

Why is this so important? If we want the mechanics of logic to be valid in respect to the real world, we have to take into account the Boolean theory. While the Aristotelian (Standard) Square of Opposition gives us more flexibility, the fact is, it could lead to some absurd conclusions. That in itself seems counterintuitive when applying the techniques of Logic to reality. Logic should not lead us to absurdity! However, we discover in most cases, that is, in cases of things we actually know exist, the Aristotelian Square of Opposition (Standard Square) works quite well. It is only when we begin to talk about things we do not know whether they exist or not, or things we simply don't know that the Boolean Square of Opposition becomes important.

It is similar to the situation regarding Newton's theory of gravity. It works well in the macro world, you know, the world you and I know, for example, things on earth we can see with our naked eye, and things in the heavens as well. But when you get into the sub-atomic world, Einstein discovered Newton's law of gravity did not work well at all. That is the way it is with the Aristotelian Square of Opposition, in all cases involving things we know to actually exist, it works well, but when dealing with cases we know do NOT exist, or are NOT SURE exist, it is wiser to refer to the Boolean Square of Opposition. Think about a researcher searching for a new drug to counteract a virus, wouldn't you want that researcher to be extra cautious? Of course, and so the researcher will operate within the Boolean Square simply because it limits the researcher about what he/she can claim.

Here is an example. If we stick with the Standard Square (or Aristotelian Square) of Opposition, and apply it to Conversion with limitation, then we could claim the following to both be true, "All unicorns are white" and "Some white things are unicorns". The first phrase we have no trouble with, because that is one way we define unicorns, but the second phrase...have you ever seen any white things that are actually unicorns? How about this, "All people from Mars are red" and "Some red things are Martians". Really? My guess is you would have a different attitude if we changed the wording to match the Boolean theory, "If there were people on Mars, they would be red", and we would

NOT be able to convert that statement! So, you can see, we do need the Boolean theory to make Logic more relevant to the real world when talking about things that either do not exist or we do not know whether or not they exist.

REVIEW GLOSSARY

Aristotelian Traditional Square of Opposition = A graphic illustration of an immediate inference of the truth values of propositions and how they relate to each other.

THE ARISTOTELIAN (STANDARD) SQUARE OF OPPOSITION

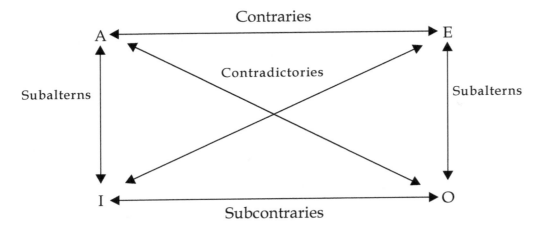

Immediate Inferences = When meaning and value can be directly inferred from one proposition to another

Conversion = The process of flipping the S and P of a standard form proposition. "A" propositions can only be converted by limitation and "E" and "I" propositions can be converted without difficulty, and the "O" proposition cannot be converted.

Obversion = The process of changing the quality of the proposition and replacing the Preposition with its complement.

Contraposition = The process of obverting, converting and finally obverting a proposition. The "A" proposition and the "O" proposition can be directly contraposed, but the "E" proposition can only be contraposed by limitation and the "I" proposition cannot be contraposed at all.

CONVERSION

Convertend	Converse
A: All S is P	I: Some P is S (by limitation)
E: No S is P	E: No P is S
I: Some S is P	I: Some P is S
O: Some S is not P	(conversion not valid)

OBVERSION

Obvertend	Obverse
A: All S is P	E: No S is non-P
E: No S is P	A: All S is non-P
I: Some S is P	O: Some S is not non-P
O: Some S is not P	I: Some S is non-P

CONTRAPOSITION

PREMISS	CONTRAPOSITIVE
A: All S IS P	A: All non-P is non-S
E: No S is P	O: Some non-P is not non-S (by limitation)
I: Some S is P	contraposition is not possible
O: Some S is not P	O:Some non-P is not non-S

Boolean Theory:deals with existential import, which means, a proposition is making a claim that something does exist. Boole pointed out that universal propositions (both affirmative and negative) do NOT have existential import, and that particular propositions (both affirmative and negative) DO have existential import, thus eliminating the possible absurdities flowing from the Standard Square of Opposition.

BOOLEAN VERSION of Conversion, Obversion and Contraposition

CONVERSION

Convertend	Converse
A: All S is P	(conversion not valid)
E: No S is P	E: No P is S
I: Some S is P	I: Some P is S
O: Some S is not P	(conversion not valid)

OBVERSION

Obvertend	Obverse
A: All S is P	E: No S is non-P
E: No S is P	A: All S is non-P
I: Some S is P	O: Some S is not non-P
O: Some S is not P	I: Some S is non-P

CONTRAPOSITION

PREMISS	CONTRAPOSITIVE
A: All S IS P	A: All non-P is non-S
E: No S is P	(contraposition not valid)
I: Some S is P	contraposition is not possible
O: Some S is not P	O:Some non-P is not non-S

The BOOLEAN (or Modern) SQUARE OF OPPOSITION

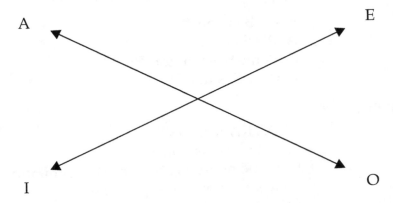

EXERCISES

Exercises using the Standard Square of Opposition. After completing using the Standard Square, answer using the Boolean Square and see what the differences are. T___(true)F___(false) U___(undetermined) *(check in the back of the book for answers)*

1. If "All horses are mammals" is true, what is the truth value of the following:

No horses are mammals   T___F___U___
Some horses are mammals   T___F___U___
Some horses are not mammals   T___F___U___

2. If "All horses are brown" is false, what is the truth value of the following:

No horses are brown   T___F___U___
Some horses are brown   T___F___U___
Some horses are not brown   T___F___U___

3. If "No horses are unicorns" is true, what is the truth value of the following:

All horses are unicorns   T___F___U___
Some horses are unicorns   T___F___U___
Some horses are not unicorns   T___F___U___

4. If "No horses are thoroughbreds" is false, what is the truth value of the following:

All horses are thoroughbreds   T___F___U___
Some horses are thoroughbreds   T___F___U___
Some horses are not thoroughbreds   T___F___U___

5. If "Some men are tall" is true, what is the truth value of the following:

All men are tall   T___F___U___
No men are tall   T___F___U___
Some men are not tall   T___F___U___

6. If "Some men are immortal" is false, what is the truth value of the following:

All men are immortal   T___F___U___
No men are immortal   T___F___U___
Some men are not immortal   T___F___U___

7. If "Some dogs are not spotted" is true, what is the truth value of the following:

All dogs are spotted   T___F___U___
No dogs are spotted   T___F___U___
Some dogs are spotted   T___F___U___

8. If "Some dogs are not mammals" is false, what is the truth value of the following:

All dogs are mammals   T___ F___ U___
No dogs are mammals   T___ F___ U___
Some dogs are mammals   T___ F___ U___

Exercises using Conversion, Obversion and Contraposition

This exercise will be using both the standard square (Aristotelian) of opposition and the Aristotelian version of Conversion, Obversion and Contraposition as well as the Boolean Square of Opposition and the Boolean version of Conversion, Obversion and Contraposition. (After answering with the Standard Square, switch and answer with the Boolean Square and see the differences in your answers)

9. If "Some historians are philosophers" is true, what is the truth value of the following? (mark an "X" in what you believe to be the correct answer)

Some philosophers are not non-historians   T___ F___ U___
All philosophers are historians   T___ F___ U___
No non-historians are philosophers   T___ F___ U___
Some non-non-philosophers are notnon-historians   T___ F___ U___

Using the four examples above, what if "Some historians are philosophers" is false, then what is the truth value of the above four (mark an "O" in what you believe to be the correct answer)

10. If "All ethicists are moral people" is true, what is the truth value of the following: Enter an "X" in what you believe to be the correct answer:

All non-moral people are non-ethicists   T___ F___ U___
No ethicists are moral people   T___ F___ U___
Some moral people are not ethicists   T___ F___ U___
Some ethicists are not moral people   T___ F___ U___
No non-moral people are ethicists   T___ F___ U___

Using the same five examples above, what if "All ethicists are moral people" is false? Enter an "O" in what you believe to be the correct answer.

11. If "Some farmers are nature lovers" is true, what is the truth value of the following: Enter an "X" in the correct answer:

Some nature lovers are farmers   T___ F___ U___
Some nature lovers are not non-farmers   T___ F___ U___
Some farmers are not non-nature lovers   T___ F___ U___
All farmers are nature lovers   T___ F___ U___

No farmers are nature lovers   T___ F___ U___
All nature lovers are non-farmers   T___ F___ U___

Using the same six examples above, what if "Some farmers are nature lovers" is false, what would be the truth value? Enter an "O" in the correct answer.

12. If "Some pilots are not drinkers" is true, what is the truth value of the following: Enter an "X" in the correct answer:

No pilots are drinkers   T___ F___ U___
Some non-drinkers are pilots   T___ F___ U___
Some non-drinkers are not non-pilots   T___ F___ U___
All pilots are drinkers   T___ F___ U___
Some pilots are drinkers   T___ F___ U___

13. If "Some pilots are not drinkers" is false, what would be the truth value of the five examples above? Enter an "O" in the correct answer.

Chapter Seven

THE DISJUNCTIVE AND HYPOTHETICAL SYLLOGISM:
Reducing the Number of Terms/Disjunctive and Hypothetical Syllogisms
❧

Now that you know how to use both the Standard Square of Opposition and Conversion, Obversion and Contraposition, and the Boolean version, let's talk about how to reduce the number of terms in an argument that may have more than the three terms of a proper syllogism. You cannot do this effectively without first understanding the Square of Opposition and Conversion, Obversion and Contraposition.

Take for example the argument:

> All humans are mortal
> All soldiers are humans
> ∴ No soldiers are immortal

OK, there appear to be four terms:humans, soldiers, mortal, immortal
We see that "immortal" is a complement of "mortal", that is, its opposite. OK, what do we get if we Obvert the major premise? That's right:

> No humans are immortal

So now, you have reduced the number of terms in the argument to three:humans, soldiers and immortal.

In addition, you may have noticed in the original argument a negative universal conclusion from all affirmative premises, and we know that is a fallacy. However, by Obverting the major premise, we now have a valid argument:

> No humans are immortal
> All soldiers are humans
> ∴ No soldiers are immortal   (EAE-1)

This is a rather straight forward approach to eliminating a fourth term if it is a complement of one of the other three terms.
What if the fourth term is not a complement, but a totally different term, for example...

> All times it rains are times there are clouds
> All times the grass is wet are times it rains
> ∴ All times the grass is wet are times I cannot mow the grass

OK, what do you do about this argument? You have these terms:

> Times there are clouds
> Times that it rains
> Times the grass is wet
> Times I cannot mow the grass

How do we resolve this case of four terms? One of two ways, we can simply say that this is an invalid argument and leave it at that, or we can say that there is more than one argument present, and several propositions that are implied but missing. I would opt for the latter simply because if we are trying to make sense out of what someone is saying to us we have to get at what is implied to better understand whether or not the person is taking us down a path toward a valid argument or making assumptions and implications that are not supportable, and perhaps invalid, and if valid, just absurd. The only way to do that is to take what we have, even if it is invalid, and do what we have to do within the bounds of Logic to make it valid. Only by doing that will we be able to uncover what may be false assumptions or claims.

So, let's go with the latter approach and create the missing arguments. Let's bring that argument back and look at it…

> All times it rains are times there are clouds
> All times the grass is wet are times it rains
> ∴ All times the grass is wet are times I cannot mow the grass

Let's create the first argument. If you look at the Major Premise (the first premise) and the Minor Premise (the second premise) we discover that we have just three terms:

> All times it rains are times there are clouds
> All times the grass is wet are times it rains

We also see that "times it rains" appears in both premises, and so must be our middle term. That means "times there are clouds" must be our Major Term, or the term in the predicate position of the conclusion, and "times the grass is wet" must be our Minor Term, or the term in the subject position of the conclusion. So, now we know what the conclusion should be for these two premises:

> All times the grass is wet are times there are clouds.

We know that the mood of this argument is AAA and the only valid figure with that mood is figure "1" so with that information we form the argument by using the term in the predicate position of the first premise as the predicate in the conclusion and the subject term in the second premise will be the subject term in the conclusion, so it would look like this:

> All times it rains are times there are clouds
> All times the grass is wet are times it rains
> ∴ All times the grass is wet are times there are clouds

Can you see that this is one of the implications of the original argument? Now, at this point you could question the entire argument just by countering and say, "there are many cloudy days when it does not rain, and so the grass would not get wet" or "you can wet grass without it raining", something to that effect. But let's continue on just to see what the next argument might be.

We are building what is called a "sorites"[55], that is, an argument actually made up of multiple arguments which are implied rather than clearly stated. In this case we will use the conclusion for one of our premises for the next argument. So, one of the premises will be:

> All times the grass is wet are times there are clouds

Now, should this be the major or minor premise? It depends on what should be the major or minor term of the conclusion. Remember the original conclusion:

> ∴ All times the grass is wet are times I cannot mow the grass

We want to be able to arrive at that conclusion. We can see that "times the grass is wet" is the subject term of the original conclusion, and we also see that "times the grass is wet" is the subject term for the conclusion of our first argument, so it will become the minor premise for this argument.

So, our second argument would look like this, thus far...

> All times the grass is wet are times there are clouds (minor premise)
> ∴ All times the grass is wet are times I cannot mow the grass (conclusion)

Now, because we have two "A" propositions, and one is the conclusion, we know that the missing premise must be an "A" proposition as well. Why do we know that? Remember, you cannot have a negative premise if you have an affirmative conclusion, and we cannot have an "I" proposition for the major premise because as we already know, the "A" proposition only distributes the subject term, and because we have distributed the subject of the conclusion, we must distribute the middle term, because we also remember the fallacy of the undistributed middle. So, that leaves only an "A" proposition, and again, as we already know, the only valid figure for the mood AAA is "1", so, the predicate of the conclusion must be in the predicate position in the major premise. We also know that the term that does not appear in the conclusion from the minor premise is "times there are clouds" and so we remember that must be in the subject position of the major premise, why? Because it is the middle term and we know the middle term must be distributed at least once in the premises. Thus the major premise would like this:

> All times there are clouds are times I cannot mow the grass.

So, now let's put the whole argument together:

> All times there are clouds are times I cannot mow the grass.
> All times the grass is wet are times there are clouds.

∴ All times the grass is wet are times I cannot mow the grass.

What is the pay-off for doing all of this? Remember the original argument with the four terms?

> All times it rains are times there are clouds
> All times the grass is wet are times it rains
> ∴ All times the grass is wet are times I cannot mow the grass

You see what happened here? We have exposed a bit of faulty reasoning by creating the premise:"All times there are clouds are times I cannot mow the grass." When in fact we know this is not always the case, and so one of the assumptions of this argument is simply false, or at least is most of the time. This is yet another example where it would be truer to say, "Sometimes there are clouds are times I cannot mow the grass." Thus, once again we see someone making an argument sound like a deductive argument when in fact it was an inductive argument.

You can see that by clearly writing down the implied argument which was missing we can better understand what the person was claiming. We can see that basically this whole argument was, shall we say, "all wet"?

We also need to review yet another kind of argument we see more often than not, the Enthymeme. *An enthymeme is any argument with a missing proposition*. There are three kinds of enthymeme:[56]

> First Order Enthymeme = The major premise is missing
> Second Order Enthymeme = The minor premise is missing
> Third Order Enthymeme = The conclusion is missing

Take for example the following argument:

All men are mortal.
Socrates is a man.

This is a third order enthymeme, in that the conclusion:Socrates is mortal, was missing.

Or this argument:

Arnold Swartzenegger was not born in the United States.
Arnold Swartzenegger cannot run for president.

This is a first order enthymeme, the first premise, "A person must be born in the United States in order to run for president" is assumed by the above argument.

Or this argument:

No mammals are reptiles

No Horses are reptiles

This is a second order enthymeme, the second premise, or minor premise, All Horses are Mammals, is missing, yet assumed by the above argument.

EXERCISES

(for answers to some of these exercises turn to the back of the book)
Reduce the number of terms to four and re-write the argument into valid form:

1.
No politicians are truthful
All people on the take are politicians
∴ All people on the take are liars

2.
All bullies are rude
Josh is a bully
∴ Josh is not polite

3.
All elderly people deserve our respect
All Retired people are old people
∴ All Retired people have a right to our respect

4.
All Non-Divine Beings are Mortal
All Human Beings are Non-Divine Beings
∴ No Human Beings are Immortal

5.
All who lay off their employees in order to give themselves a bonus are difficult to work for.
Some employers hate their employees
∴ Some Employers are Difficult to Work For

What order enthymeme are the following arguments?

1. Every person who flies a commercial airliner must pass all security checks
   Josh did not pass the security check

2. Too much easy credit causes markets to crash; as a result, the Stock Market will crash.

3. Anyone who completes this assignment is a good student, because it is difficult.

Disjunctive Syllogism[57]

There are more types of syllogism than just the categorical, which we have been covering over the last several chapters. A disjunctive proposition is an "either/or" type of proposition. "Either it is raining or it is not" is a disjunct. It is compound because we are actually making two statements:"It is raining" "It is not raining". As a result, we refer to it as a compound statement because it contains two statements in what appears to be a single statement.

The disjunctive syllogism contains a compound, disjunctive premise asserting the truth of at least one or other of the alternatives in the first premise and a second premise that asserts the falsity of one or other of the alternatives listed in the first premise. The conclusion is the statement of the alternative determined to be true. For example:

> Either John is a senator or he is a congressman. (compound disjunct)
> John is not a senator(negation of one of the alternatives)
>
> ∴ John is a congressman(statement of the alternative that was not negated)

Another example might be:

> In running the country into the ground the president is either incompetent or evil.
> The president is not evil
> ∴ The president must be incompetent

See if you can come up with your own example:

Hypothetical Syllogism[58]

Another form of syllogism is the Hypothetical syllogism. A hypothetical proposition is an "if/then" kind of proposition with the "if" term referred to as the antecedent and the "then" term referred to as the consequent.

"If the auto industry is not bailed out by the government then thousands of Americans will be out of work."

Antecedent   *consequent*

This syllogism is made up of one or more compound propositions such that the antecedent is claimed to bring about the consequent. For example, "If the auto industry is not bailed out by the government then thousands of Americans will be out of work". A pure hypothetical syllogism is made up of all compound propositions, for example:

                (1)   (2)

If the auto industry is not bailed out by the government then thousands of Americans will be out of work.   (2)   (3)

If thousands of Americans are out of work then we will have a major recession that will hurt everyone and weaken the country.   (1)   (3)

∴ If the auto industry is not bailed out by the government then we will have a major recession that will hurt everyone and weaken the country.

I have numbered each proposition so that you can see the relationship among these propositions and therefore, why the conclusion necessarily follows from the premises (definition of a deductive argument).

Note this pattern from the above argument:

                If (1) then (2)
                If (2) then (3)
Therefore: If (1) then (3)

The point is this, if proposition (1) leads to proposition (2) and proposition (2) leads to proposition (3), then it would follow that proposition (1) would lead to proposition (3). Another way of looking at it is this way…

        (1) ⟶ (2) ⟶ (3) therefore, (1) ⟶ (3)

Again, what we are after here is the structure of the argument and this structure is valid. If you want to know whether or not this argument is both valid and the individual propositions are true, then you would be testing for soundness. Right now, we are only concerned about the validity of the structure. If you want to determine whether or not this particular argument is sound, well, that is where the debating begins! However, regardless of the content, this structure will ALWAYS be valid.

There is another kind of hypothetical syllogism, and this is referred to as a MIXED-HYPOTHETICAL SYLLOGISM. The reason it is called "mixed" is because we actually only deal with one complex proposition, or that is, one "if/then" statement. The valid structure for this form of hypothetical syllogism is either to affirm the antecedent, and thus affirm the consequent, or deny the consequent and therefore deny the antecedent. If you think about it, this really helps us define what a hypothetical statement is all about. If the "if" statement in the hypothetical statement, as above:

"If the auto industry is not bailed out by the government…
actually leads to the "then" statement:
…then thousands of Americans will be out of work."

it would make sense that if we affirmed the antecedent:If the auto industry is not bailed out by the government... we would also affirm the consequent:thousands of Americans will be out of work.

But to get at the true nature of the hypothetical, let's deny the consequent:thousands of Americans will be out of work and say that thousands of Americans are not out of work, so that must mean we deny the antecedent such that the government DID bail out the auto industry. You begin to see how much a hypothetical proposition claims.

So, a mixed hypothetical syllogism will take the form of either *modus ponens* or *modus tollens*, that is to say, a compound hypothetical proposition is followed by the affirmation of the antecedent thus leading to the affirmation of the consequent (*modus ponens*) or a denial of the consequent thus leading to the denial of the antecedent (*modus tollens*).[59]

Take another example (*modus ponens*):

> If John ran for the senate then John won the senate race
> John ran for the senate
> ∴ John won the senate race

What will NOT work is if you affirm the consequent, which is referred to as the FALLACY OF AFFIRMING THE CONSEQUENT.[60] For example:

> If John ran for the senate then John won the senate race
> John won the senate race
> ∴ John ran for the senate

Wait a minute, could it not be possible that John was a write-in candidate?

Or, to bring forward an example hot in the news today, and something politicians are debating rather vigorously, to demonstrate the fallacy of affirming the consequent we get this argument:

> "If the auto industry is not bailed out by the government then thousands of Americans will be out of work."
> Thousands of Americans are out of work.
> ∴(therefore) The auto industry was not bailed out by the government

There will be many politicians who would argue that there are still thousands of Americans out of work even though the government DID bail out the auto industry. So, you see the fallacy.

An example of (*modus tollens*):

> If John ran for the senate then John won the senate race
> John did not win the senate race

∴ John did not run for the senate

An example of the FALLACY OF DENYING THE ANTECEDENT:[61]

If John ran for the senate then John won the senate race
John did not run for the senate
∴ John did not win the senate race

But once again, we use the bailout argument to demonstrate the fallacy of denying the antecedent:

"If the auto industry is not bailed out by the government then thousands of Americans will be out of work."
The auto industry was bailed out by the government.
∴ (therefore) Thousands of Americans are Not out of work

However, there will ALWAYS be thousands of Americans out of work no matter how good our economy is, so we can easily see the fallacy of denying the antecedent in order to deny the consequent.

(Ok, side-bar:you might have been confused by this argument, because I was denying the antecedent, well, the antecedent stated that "If the government did NOT bail out the auto industry…" so, to DENY that statement I must say, "The government DID bail out the auto industry…" Likewise, with the consequent, to deny the consequent:"then thousands of Americans will be out of work." I would have to write:Thousands of Americans are NOT out of work."

But we have already seen from above that with the fallacy of affirming the consequent claiming that John won the senate race confirms that John ran for the senate leaves out the possibility that John did not run but was a write-in candidate. In this case of denying the antecedent fails to take into account that even if John had not run for the senate he might have still won the senate race as a write-in candidate.

You may think to yourself that it is very likely that if he did not run he did not win, but keep in mind, we are using deduction which means that the conclusion necessarily follows from the premises, and so as a result, we have exposed the fallacy of affirming the consequent and denying the antecedent.

Perhaps the "bailout" example more clearly demonstrates these fallacies.

REVIEW GLOSSARY

Complement = The negative of a term, as in "non-A" is the complement of "A" and "A" is the complement of "non-A"

Disjunctive Proposition =An "either/or" proposition. For example, "Either Sam is wise or Sam is foolish"

Disjunctive Syllogism=A syllogism in which you deny one element of the Disjunctive proposition in order to affirm the other element of the Disjunctive proposition. For example:

> Either Sam is wise or Sam is foolish
> Sam is not foolish
> ∴ Sam is wise

Enthymeme = An argument having a missing but implied proposition.

First Order Enthymeme = An argument in which the major premise is missing.

Second Order Enthymeme = An argument in which the minor premise is missing.

Third Order Enthymeme = An argument in which the conclusion is missing.

Hypothetical Proposition = An "if/then" proposition in which the "if" element is referred to as the "antecedent" and the "then" element is referred to as the "consequent". It is a proposition in which the consequent is claimed to follow due to the antecedent. For example:"If we do not bail out the banks then the economy will fall into a recession"

Pure Hypothetical Syllogism = An argument made up of three compound hypothetical propositions such that the antecedent of the first premise becomes the antecedent of the conclusion, and the consequent of the first premise becomes the antecedent of the second premise, and the consequent of the second premise becomes the consequent of the conclusion. For example:

> If we do not bail out the banks then the economy with fall into a recession.
> If the economy falls into a recession then millions of people will be out of work
> ∴ If we do not bail out the banks then millions of people will be out of work

Mixed Hypothetical Syllogism = An argument in which either the antecedent is affirmed, thus affirming the consequent of the hypothetical proposition as the conclusion (modus ponens) or the consequent is denied thus denying the antecedent as the conclusion (modus tollens)

Modus Ponens = Affirming the antecedent, thus affirming the consequent.

Modus Tollens = Denying the consequent, thus denying the antecedent.

Fallacy of Affirming the consequent = Affirming the consequent in order to affirm the antecedent.

Fallacy of Denying the antecedent = Denying the antecedent in order to deny the consequent.

Sorites= An argument in which is embedded several implied arguments. An example of a sorites is when you find an argument that has four different terms, thus there is more than one argument. Another example is when you find an argument that has more than one conclusion, meaning again there is more than one argument. Another example is when you have an argument that has more than two premises, which usually means you have more than one argument. All of these would be called a sorites.

EXERCISES (*see the back of the book for some answers*)

1. Solve the following sorites:
    All murderers deserve the death penalty
    Alex is a murderer
    Alex does not deserve leniency
    Alex is a terrorist
    ∴ All terrorists deserve the death penalty

(There are several arguments here, you will need to fill in the missing premises and build all of the arguments; HINT:start with the conclusion and build backwards; remember the basic form of arguments, and the rules that govern valid arguments in order to build the missing arguments. *See the back of the book for one solution to help get you started.*)

Determine whether the following are valid and whether they are pure hypothetical arguments, mixed hypothetical arguments or disjunctive arguments.

2. If I would have asked for your opinion then I wanted it, I did not ask for your opinion therefore I did not want it!

3. The flight was late or she missed her flight, the flight wasn't late, so she must have missed her flight!

4. If Joe did not do it, then Sam must have done it. If Sam did it, then Joe could not have been there. So, if Joe did not do it, then Joe could not have been there.

5.. If I notified you, then I would have wanted you to know. I do want you to know, therefore, I did notify you!

6.. If the death penalty does not curb violent crimes, then the death penalty is ineffective. If the death penalty is ineffective, then the only reason to have the death penalty is about vengeance. Therefore, if the death penalty does not curb violent crimes, then the only reason for having the death penalty is to get even.

7..   Either Jim mowed the lawn or Josh did.
Jim did not mow the lawn.
Therefore, Josh did.

8..   If the cow jumps over the moon then I am a monkey's uncle.
I am NOT a monkey's uncle.
Therefore, the cow did NOT jump over the moon.

9..   If the price of gas goes up much more then electric cars will become more popular.
The price of gas is going up much more.
Therefore, electric cars will become more popular.

10.   If the price of gas goes up much more then electric cars will become more popular.
Electric cars are becoming more popular.
Therefore, the price of gas is going up much more.

Chapter Eight

FALLACIES:
Fallacies of Relevance, Presumption and Ambiguity

We have spent quite a bit of time becoming familiar with the structure of arguments by studying various types of syllogism. Now that we understand basically how a syllogism looks and works, and how it is valid, it is time to turn our attention to the fallacy. Remember, in the beginning of this course we discussed at length how ambiguous language can be. Now we are ready to look directly at some of the ways the ambiguity of language can be used to make fallacious arguments appear to be valid. What makes an argument fallacious is not that it is invalid, because in many ways it can have a valid form, rather, what makes a bad argument fallacious is that it *appears* to be a perfectly valid and good argument, when in fact it is false and fallacious. In other words, fallacies are "tricks" used to fool us into thinking we are looking at a valid and good argument.[62]

It was important to first learn the proper structure for a valid argument as in the various types of syllogisms, and now you can translate a common language argument into standard form to better get at what the author is really saying in the argument. As we saw in the previous chapter, many arguments are actually a sorites, that is, what appears to be a single argument but is actually several arguments most of which are implied. By exposing the implied arguments we are better able to understand what is actually being claimed in the original argument. This kind of work is aided by our knowledge of the various fallacies. In other words, as we translate arguments into standard form, we can better spot fallacies.

There are three categories of fallacies in informal logic: fallacies of relevance, fallacies of presumption and fallacies of ambiguity.

FALLACIES OF RELEVANCE [63]

An argument suffers the fallacy of relevance if the premises simply do not lead to the conclusion, or rather are not related to the conclusion. There are eight different fallacies of relevance (again, with our thanks to Aristotle):

1. **Argument *Ad Ignorantiam***
2. **Argument *Ad Verecundiam***
3. **Argument *Ad Hominem Abusive***
4. **Argument *Ad Hominem Circumstantial***
5. **Argument *Ad Populum***
6. **Argument *Ad Misericordiam***
7. **Argument *Ad Baculum***
8. **Argument *Ignoratio Elenchi***

1. Argument *Ad Ignorantiam*[64]

"No one has proved that there is no man in the moon, therefore, there must be a man in the moon." "Can you prove to me that Big Foot does not exist? OK, then certainly he must exist." "No one can prove evolution, I mean, were you there? So, evolution must not be true."

These are all arguments suffering from the fallacious process of reasoning referred to as "Argument *Ad Ignorantiam*" Another way to refer to this fallacy is to call it Argument from Ignorance. The nature of this fallacy is simple, if something has not been proven true, then it must be false, or if something has not been proven false, then it must be true.

This is a fairly common fallacy. Think for just a minute how many times you have heard a teenager say to his parents, "Did you actually see ME at the party or will you take the word of Josh over me? So how can you say that I was there?" This is a fallacy most often demonstrated in television programs involving suspects, crime, and a crime investigation. The defense lawyer might say to the star witness for the prosecution, "Did you actually see my client kill the woman?" "No, but I did see him come out of her apartment." At that point the defense lawyer might argue that the only evidence against his client is circumstantial. In other words, if you didn't see my client do it, then he didn't do it. The defense lawyer wants the jury to accept his reasoning, and of course it is the job of the prosecution to bring forth more evidence that does more than simply place the suspect at the scene of the crime. However, the fallacy of ignorance has also been used effectively in prosecuting innocent people. Turn the above argument on its head, and the prosecutor might seek to cross examine the star witness and say, "While you did not actually see the defendant kill the victim, you did see him leave the apartment at approximately the time death occurred, which was between 10:30 and 11:30PM?" "Yes, I did." "So, you can't say that he didn't kill the victim?" "No, I can't say for certain that he did not kill the victim, I just don't know." Then the prosecutor might say to the jury, the witness cannot say that the defendant did not kill the victim, therefore… This is precisely why it is important that a defendant is innocent until proven guilty, to avoid conviction from ignorance.

How do you avoid this fallacy? Never be satisfied with any argument that claims one thing because you can't prove the alternative.

2. Argument *Ad Verecundiam*[65]

"Some people think you have to be a rocket scientist in order to pick out the best flat screen TV. Well, I am a rocket scientist, and ….."

Any argument that appeals to inappropriate authority is an argument *Ad Verecundiam*. It is an appeal to false or inappropriate authority. Why would you appeal to a rocket scientist about a flat screen TV? What would they know about such technology, unless that is what they designed? Then, you would have to be concerned about who was paying the scientist to make the commercial. Any testimonial about the quality of a product, or its utility made by someone who would not have any particularly special knowledge about that product, like a rocket scientist and flat screen TVs, is such a fallacy.

Of course, we see this quite a lot in commercials. Different celebrities are hawking different products, something about which they know no more than you. We also see this fallacy used when trying to convince you of the value of some product by telling you that people you know have bought the product already, so therefore, you can trust that this is a good product. Really?

Perhaps one of the most pernicious examples of this fallacy is something on the internet called "Wikipedia". Why? Isn't the information on that site reliable? Not when you consider that anyone can insert content into anything, whether they are an expert or not. The problem is, it looks like an encyclopedia, and reads like an encyclopedia, and so one is lulled into thinking that it is as reliable as an actual encyclopedia that goes through a peer review of actual experts in every field of material covered. The only refereeing by experts in Wikipedia is voluntary, which means, you cannot always be sure it has actually been refereed. So, we could be easily duped into thinking that we are reading authoritative information when in fact we may not. That is not to say that all of the information on Wikipedia is unreliable. As a matter of fact, a lot of material on Wikipedia is fairly reliable, but that just leads to the greater problem, lulling you into thinking that it is ALL reliable.

So, how do you avoid such a fallacy? Require that whatever claim is made is backed up by an expert in that particular field or product. In the case of Wikipedia, if you are researching something in Wikipedia, follow it up with a refereed journal or published work in hard copy on the same topic. If you want to know about what product is the best to purchase, read *Consumer's Report* and other such magazines which actually test products and are reviewed by people who are experts and have nothing to gain from the company that produces that product. Which is why *Consumer Reports* does not allow any company whose product they are reviewing in the magazine advertise in the same magazine, to avoid the appearance of a conflict of interest.

3. Argument *Ad Hominem Abusive* [66]

Perhaps one of the more commonly used fallacies of relevance in a political campaign. In the 2008 presidential campaign Barak Obama was accused of being a closet Muslim, a friend of a terrorist, not really born in America, and we heard reference to John McCain's age. None of these things had anything to do with either candidate's ability to lead the country, and yet we were bombarded with these images throughout the campaign. Even in today's political climate, Obama is being called a "socialist" which conjures up the specter of Communism! But look at what is being said today about Michelle Bachman and her migraine headaches and Mitt Romney being Mormon and Tim Pawlenty stealing the thunder from the American Olympic Hockey team! Why? In politics image seems to be everything, and when one side is not clear on the issues, or has a position that is not popular on the issues, that side will often resort to using the argument known as *Ad Hominem Abusive*, that is, trying to misdirect the attention of the public from the issues and focus instead on character flaws of their opponent, whether true or not.

Take another example from the courtroom. The defense attorney might be concerned about the testimony of the witness against her client, and will try to find some character flaw of that witness to misdirect the jury's attention from the testimony itself;

"Miss Jones, you have testified today that my client, Mr. Roberts, did attack you and robbed you? Miss Jones, is it not true that you are a prostitute?" "I…I…" "Come now, Miss Jones, you are under oath, you must answer the question." "I…guess…I…am" "What is that, Miss Jones, would you speak up please?" "Yes, I am." "OK, so you are a prostitute. Ladies and Gentlemen of the jury, I would want you to consider carefully the testimony of a known hooker and drug addict who has made it a habit to lie to the police…" Of course, the prosecutor would raise an objection, but the damage has been done. Just because she is a prostitute has nothing to do with whether or not Miss Jones was attacked and robbed by Mr. Roberts, but you can see how the jury might be swayed to at least consider Miss Jones' testimony with some suspicion.

This is a fallacy used most often when one has no real argument against their opponent. How do you avoid such a fallacy? Or how do you avoid committing such a fallacy? Know the issues well; pay no attention to the character attacks, and when you hear character attacks, suspect an attempt to avoid the real issues and demand to hear the issues addressed or the evidence of the abusive claims.

4. Argument *Ad Hominem Circumstantial* [67]

This fallacy will often be used in many of the same ways as *Ad Hominem Abusive*, the difference is, with *Ad Hominem Circumstantial* the focus is to accuse the person by association. For example, "Why would you take the word of a preacher whose car is parked near the local bar every week?" Now, never mind that the preacher is visiting a nursing home that happens to be across the street from the bar, but the person making the accusation has no interest in being fair and impartial! Or, take the example of the parent who gets furious with his son who was found on the same street at the same time that a liquor store was robbed, again, does the father take time to listen to the son explain that he had a flat tire two blocks away and was walking to the nearest garage, which was two doors down from the liquor store. It is the case of guilt by association.

We also saw this fallacy used in the 2008 presidential race, when Barak Obama was accused of supporting terrorism because one of his neighbors was a social terrorist in the 60's and their children went to the same school. Or the fact that Obama went to a church whose preacher made some outlandish remarks against the United States, again, guilt by association. We also saw several images of John McCain with President Bush, trying again to make it clear that to elect McCain was to continue the Bush years; guilt by association. On the other side of it, or the fallacy of claiming something positive for yourself, is also known as the fallacy of Division, an example of which would be Tim Pawlenty trying to gain popularity by associating with the American Olympic Hockey team. He has even gotten a couple of the former members of that team to speak on his behalf.

Why a fallacy of relevance? Simple, none of these cases of accidental association have anything to do with the character or quality of the person. How to avoid such a fallacy? Respond to the accusations with the truth. On the other hand, when someone levels this fallacy at you it is clear they have no interest in fairness, and so one knows to avoid people like that when possible. Of course, one of the problems is, this fallacy can carry a lot of weight with many people. Let's face it, what would you think if you saw your preacher's car near a bar? What would you think if you saw one of your friends standing with some people who were accused of torching a house? But of course, on the other side of it,(fallacy of Division) if you see someone always hanging out with the best, the smartest, and the sharpest around, you might tend to think they are as smart as well, when in fact that may not be the case at all. You see the problem.

5. Argument *Ad Populum* [68]

This is a fallacy in which one uses emotional words to sway the argument when solid, rational evidence simply is not present. Adolf Hitler was a master at fomenting the crowds with his inflammatory rhetoric. We hear the same thing when we hear the cry to be patriotic. If you want to sway people to your side, make certain they see that your way leads to supporting the traditional Motherhood, apple pie, and the American flag. Nationalism is itself an exercise in the argument *Ad Populum*, that is, the appeal to emotional language to motivate masses of people to do what they would normally not be willing to do.

This is a difficult fallacy to uncover, because it can be as subtle as how we word things. For example, those who oppose abortion refer to themselves as being "Pro-life" while their opponents refer to them as "Anti-abortion". Those who favor abortion refer to themselves as "Pro-choice" while their opponents refer to them as "Pro-abortion". You can see the emotive difference in how we refer to things. Or take for example how questions are worded when running a survey. How do you think people would respond if they were asked the question, "Do you believe in the right of a person to kill a baby?" Now, how do you think people would respond to the question, "Do you think a woman has a right to decide whether or not to be pregnant?" One could argue that they are asking basically the same thing, but in clearly different ways. That is why one has to be extremely careful how questions are worded in a survey if they want a valid sample and a valid opinion. Obviously, if you were given the first question to answer, who would answer yes to killing a baby? So, those who oppose abortion could use this question in a survey to show that the vast majority do not support abortion, while the other side using the other question might come up with quite different results from the same people, claiming the vast majority supports a woman's right to an abortion.

How to avoid this fallacy? Listen carefully for what is being said and not how it is being said. This requires an ability to rise above the emotionalism that can ensnare us all and focus on what is really being claimed.

6. Argument *Ad Misericordiam* [69]

This is the fallacy that appeals to the emotion of compassion and caring of the audience. Take for example the woman who was traveling 30 mph over the speed limit and was pulled over by a state patrolman. "Officer, I'm so sorry, I was so upset about the fact that I just lost my job, and my boyfriend just left me, and I can't afford the rent, and I am on my last tank of gas. Please, don't give me a ticket today, not the way this day has been…" Never mind that the woman was exceeding the speed limit by 30 mph, never mind that she was endangering people around her, her personal problems are simply not relevant in this situation, yet, who has not tried to appeal to the mercy of a patrolman?

We have seen this fallacy used when someone is trying to gain the advantage over others. Con men often use this ploy in tricking people into giving them their money. Or how about the defense attorney defending his client who killed both of his parents in cold blood say to the judge, "Your honor, we ask for leniency, for after all, he is now an orphan!"

How to avoid this fallacy? This is a good example where one has to forgo emotion as much as possible when dealing with a serious situation. When you hear such an argument from another, you have to ask yourself what that person wants from you, apart from the emotion, and decide on its own merits whether or not you wish to participate. To avoid using this fallacy yourself, try living a life with NO excuses!

7. Argument *Ad Baculum* [70]

"You can disagree with me, if you want, and you can also look for another job, doesn't matter to me." Do you hear the thinly veiled threat? This is the fallacy of an argument *Ad Baculum*, that is, an argument using force to bring one to the desired conclusion. If you ever find yourself in a position where force is being applied to you in order to get you to agree with the conclusion being promoted by the one exerting the force, you are the unfortunate recipient of the argument *Ad Baculum*. The Nazis were famous for this during the Nazi Regime in Germany from 1932 to 1945. If you were not a subscriber to the party newspaper someone would come around and say something to the effect, "We are so sorry that you have allowed your subscription to lapse, we know it was unintentional, and that you will re-subscribe today, after all, we would hate to have anything happen to your family."

This is a fallacy often employed by those who have either a position of power over you or has something on you that they can use to coerce you into agreeing with their conclusion, and thus doing what they want you to do.

How do you avoid such a fallacy? If you are the one in the weaker position, you have to decide what it is worth to you. We are all free, but at what cost? To avoid using it yourself requires a commitment to never take advantage of others through coercion.

8. Argument *Ignoratio Elenchi* [71]

This is an attempt by one to refute the argument of the other, but misses the point of the original argument, and in essence refutes nothing from the argument they are trying to refute. Take for example, someone begins to argue against the war in Iraq, and another refutes it by speaking in general terms about patriotism, protecting our liberties, fighting terrorists, etc. Basically, nothing is stated regarding the specific argument against the Iraq war, therefore, the one refuting this argument misses the point of the argument. It could very well be that the person arguing against the war in Iraq agrees with his opponent that we need patriotism, we need to protect our liberties, and we need to fight against terrorists, but what has this got to do with a war in which, it could be argued, none of these issues are part of this war at all.

Many politicians have used this fallacy very effectively when trying to respond to arguments against their policies or against decisions they have made. Instead of addressing their assailant's specific arguments against them, they might say something like "Well, there you go again, sounding like some kind of puffed up politician." In other words, you might see some of the previous fallacies used in such a way as to miss the point of the argument one is trying to refute.

Another way to refer to this fallacy is called the "Straw Man" fallacy. That is where you rephrase the issue being discussed making it weaker and then attacking the weakness and as a result sounding like you refuted the argument. Back to the Iraq War example, rephrasing the argument to be something like, "Not to support our men and women in the military when they are in Iraq is unpatriotic. Are you unpatriotic?" Now, it sounds like a refutation of someone arguing against the Iraq War, but is it? Not at all because the rephrased argument does not address the original dispute of whether or not the war was legitimate and justified.

How to avoid this fallacy? Be willing to challenge the one committing this fallacy by asking directly what that has to do with the subject in question.

FALLACIES OF PRESUMPTION [72]

How often is it the case that we assume much more than we know? Whenever we assume anything we are setting ourselves up to commit a fallacy of presumption. In other words, we presume too much in our arguments without substantial support for our claims. We often "jump to conclusions" such that we think we have made a reasonable claim, when in fact we have made the mistake of assuming a connection where there really is not one at all. The following are fallacies of presumption:

1. **Complex Question**
2. **False Cause**
3. **Begging the Question:***Petitio Principii*
4. **Accident**
5. **Converse Accident**

1. Complex Question [73]

Someone has accused you of rape, and you are innocent. The prosecutor asks you, "Did you smoke after you raped the victim? Please answer yes or no?" OK, do you see the problem here; the prosecutor has asked you a complex question. What makes it complex? He asks you a question about smoking, which by itself is a simple harmless question, but when placed in the context of what you are accused of doing forces you to actually admitting to the rape when you thought you were answering a question about smoking! That is what a complex question does; it sets you up so that no matter how you answer, you have just admitted to what the questioner was really after in the first place. Or, take for example, this question, "Why are men so much more easy-going than women?" You see, in this question, it is assumed that men are more easy-going than women, and so in answering this question one is falling into the assumption being made by the one asking the question.

How to avoid this fallacy? Listen carefully to what is being said and do not rush to respond. If you believe it to be a complex question, your opening response should be, "You have posed a complex question which I can only assume you have done in order to trap me into agreeing with your base assumption..." Or, if you happen to be on trial, you better hope your attorney knows his/her logical fallacies!

2. False Cause [74]

Another common mistake we make is to assume that just because one thing follows another chronologically, therefore, the former event caused the latter event. In many cases we practice a form of superstition, for example, a baseball player wears a certain pair of socks and hits two home runs and a double in one game, so he wears the same socks, unwashed, in every game after that. One could argue in a case like this, psychologically the player benefits from this little game of "luck". There are far more serious examples of false cause. Many complained that attacking Iraq because of the terrorist events of "9-11" was an example of false cause. The leadership of Iraq, and the Iraqi people themselves had nothing to do with the tragic deaths caused by terrorists on "9-11", yet thousands have lost their lives as a result of the U.S. invasion of Iraq. We continue to hear that we would rather battle against terrorism overseas than here in our own country. One could hardly argue with that sort of thinking, except, why are we in Iraq if that is what we are doing?

Another example of false cause can be found in the arguments against same-sex marriage, claiming that allowing same-sex marriage would undermine and destroy heterosexual marriages. Where is the causal connection, and yet just by making the statement raises the concern that there *might* be a causal connection.

We have to be careful with this fallacy, simply because it is so common and so, apparently, easy to believe. The Nazis successfully blamed all the bad things happening to Germany on the Jews, because after WWI many Jews took control of the monetary businesses in Germany, thus fomenting an attitude in Germany at the time that they needed to rid the country of their scourge. In fact, the financial industry in Germany was probably saved from collapse by many who took it over, including those who were Jewish. Germany was in bad shape partly due to the Treaty of Versailles, not because of the Jews. Are we beginning to see the same thing in this country right now in regard to Hispanics and Latinos and Latinas? If an argument of false cause supports our prejudices, it is easy to believe it to be a valid argument. We have witnessed this in this country on the issues of race when the black man was blamed for anything bad happening to a society. There are still white supremacist groups in the U.S. that believe the country is doomed now that they have elected an African American president.

Fear is often the mother of arguments of false cause. We will often lay blame on that which frightens us or that which we are not familiar with. When someone is gripped with fear all of the logic in the world will not change that person's mind. Fear has a way of shutting down our reasonable abilities to think clearly. It makes sense, then, to be suspicious of those who use fear to promote their agendas.

Another way we are sucked into using this fallacy for ourselves is if we are defending ourselves in a situation for which we are responsible. We often try to redirect blame for something we did to how we were raised, what our life was like when we were growing up, or the problems with the system! These can all be examples of false cause.

This fallacy plagues researchers much of the time. A researcher is often trying to establish some sort of causal connection between two events. If we can discover what causes pancreatic cancer, there is a good chance of finding a cure. But what does "cause" pancreatic cancer? How do we sort through the millions of bytes of information to determine what is a possible "cause" and what is not? The same problem arises when we think we have found a cure for a particular disease. We have to run blind tests, that is, we have to give some people a placebo (sugar pill) and some the actual medication we think may be the cure, making sure both groups suffer the same symptoms, and do not know whether they are receiving the placebo or the actual drug. This has to be an extensive test, because the researcher has to rule out if the person taking the placebo is getting better due to a psychosomatic affect.

How do we avoid this fallacy? Being honest and humble with ourselves when we are the ones who might employ this fallacy, and being alert to what is actually being implied by the argument if presented by someone else. If we are a researcher, demand the highest standards of testing and analysis by first clearly stating our prejudices and assumptions, and follow it up with blind testing. (Thus, the researcher's use of the Boolean Square of Opposition!)

3. Begging the Question: *Petitio Principii* [75]

This is a fallacy whose form will always be valid, but worthless. Why? Because the argument will contain as premises the conclusion reworded allowing one to prove the conclusion by using the conclusion. On the surface this would seem to be obvious, but how often do we use it to our advantage? What mother has not said to their child, "What mommy says is right because what mommy says is right." More significantly, though, is this example, "Everyone knows children function much better if they have clear boundaries, because clear limits on what one can and cannot do is just what children need to grow up better."

This fallacy is easier to fall into than one might think. Even in the area of philosophy, to claim inductive reasoning is an effective way to make decisions due to the fact that what has happened in the past will happen in the future, falls into this fallacy because such a claim is based upon assuming the reason the future will be like the past is because it always has been. You see the problem? Any time you claim something is just because it is, you are using the conclusion as your premise to reach your conclusion! It is also known as a circular argument.

How do you void this fallacy? Make certain when making an argument, the conclusion is not part of its own justification.

4. Accident [76]

You are driving down the road and you are just passing a pond when you happen to notice someone appears to be drowning in the middle of the pond. You stop your car, jump out and rush to the aid of the drowning person. You rescue them and then call 911 for assistance. You have saved the person's life, but after the police arrived and the ambulance took the near drowned victim to the hospital, you are issued a ticket because there was a "No Trespassing" sign at the edge of the pond and you broke the law. How would you feel upon receiving the citation? Would you think it was a bit unfair? Why?

What you have just experienced, as you were assisting an "accident" victim, is that you yourself have just become a victim of the fallacy of "Accident", that is, the police officer has applied to you the law of "No Trespassing" and applied it to you regardless of the circumstances. Accident is the fallacy when you apply what is generally the case to every individual case regardless of the circumstances. It is what some might refer to as "going by the book", as in the case of the police officer. Another example of the fallacy of "Accident" might be a student who has to miss the last six classes due to the fact that he is in the hospital, and the professor fails the student because his attendance policy states clearly, "any student who misses six class periods or more will fail", the student in the hospital would think the failing grade was simply not right due to the fact that the student couldn't get to class regardless of his efforts. (I suspect the Academic Dean would support the student in this case.) This is a very obvious case because everyone would see this as an example of "Accident".

How to avoid the fallacy of "Accident"? Always be alert to any exceptions to a law or policy, recognizing there are circumstances which exist or come up that no one could predict when establishing the law or policy. Being alert to exceptions means first of all you believe there are exceptions to every law and/or policy. Getting to that point may be the greatest move to avoiding this fallacy. What it comes down to is this, follow policies, but always remember policies are designed to address most general circumstances and not ALL circumstances. So, when applying policy always keep in mind the individual circumstances.

5. Converse Accident [77]

"All Japanese are short!" "White men can't jump!" "George Burns smoked a cigar everyday of his adult life and he lived to be 100, see, cigar smoking is not hazardous to your health!" These are all examples of the fallacy of "Converse Accident", that is, moving from the example of a single case or a few cases and generalizing about a whole race, culture, or human health. While it is true that George Burns did live to be 100 and did smoke cigars, the overwhelming evidence is that cigar smoking is hazardous to your health, who knows how long old George might have lived if he hadn't smoked? Of course, there are always exceptions (see above!). While it is true, most Japanese people you meet are less than 5'8" tall, one might conclude that all Japanese are short. That is, until you meet a Japanese Sumo wrestler who might stand at 6'5" tall. You can see how this fallacy commits a similar mistake as the fallacy of "Accident" in that one assumes there are no exceptions to your generalization. This fallacy is often expressed through "prejudice".

How to avoid this fallacy? Be careful never to make a generalization about something or some group of people when talking about your experiences. However, this fallacy, while obvious, has been used in commercials (as in "everyone does...." How can it be true that "everyone" actually does that? Do you know everyone?) Marketing is done based upon some general assumptions made about groups of people, the young, the baby-boomers, women, men, etc. While this may work for marketing purposes, and may seem rather harmless, keep in mind, some of the same methods are used in "profiling" where the stakes are a bit higher and more is at risk. This fallacy is another example of why many do not like the concept of "profiling", which actually applies the traits of a few to all members of a group if not used properly.

In some ways this fallacy is an example to treating an inductive argument as if it were deductive. What I mean is, in racial profiling, we use inductive methods to claim that in general people who look a certain way will tend to act a certain way. The mistake is made when we actually believe anyone looking a certain way will ALWAYS act a certain way. That is converting racial profiling from addressing a probable form of expected behavior to a necessary form of expected behavior.

FALLACIES OF AMBIGUITY [78]

This is the fallacy that most clearly demonstrates the ambiguity of language. This fallacy depends upon the ambiguity of language. This fallacy most often appears when the one utilizing it seeks to confuse the one to whom they are speaking, or make an implication by using words that have multiple meanings. In this fallacy, the conclusion is erroneously reached by the ambiguity of the meaning of words.

1. **Equivocation**
2. **Amphiboly**
3. **Accent**
4. **Composition**
5. **Division**

1. Equivocation [79]

"He was a great fighter pilot; therefore, he would make a great president!" "'I see,' said the blind man as he picked up his hammer and saw." These are examples of using words in more than one way in the same sentence. In the first example, the term "great" is in reference to his being a fighter pilot, and perhaps he was a great fighter pilot, the problem is, just because he was a great fighter pilot does not mean you can use the same sense of the word "great" in reference to anything else he would do, including being president. In the second example, the word "see" and "saw" are used in two different ways and yet because we know the person is blind, we think this is a strange thing to say because one use of the word "see" is reference to understanding something, whereas the other meaning has to do with eyesight. The word "saw" in this context obviously refers to the tool you cut wood with, yet in this context it seems odd because it can also refer to someone having "seen" something.

When we use a word in two different ways in an argument we commit the fallacy of Equivocation. We have seen many instances similar to our first example stated above. It is often assumed that if someone is a good scholar that he would be a good teacher. Or, if someone is a good politician she would be a good president.

How to avoid this fallacy? Know your language, and be alert to any cases in which the multiple meanings of the word are being used to arrive at a false conclusion.

2. Amphiboly [80]

This is a fallacy committed when the statement used as a premise is stated such that its interpretation as a premise makes it true but the conclusion makes it false, it is amphibolous. In other words, a statement is made in such a way that it seems like nonsense. Jay Leno every Monday night gave example after example of amphibolies when he read "Headlines" from local newspapers. The reason we laughed is because the statements themselves sounded ridiculous. For example:"10th Annual Southeastern Guide Dog Barbecue", you know them guide dogs sure make great barbecue!

How to avoid this fallacy? Pay attention! This is a fairly easy fallacy to spot, because we often find ourselves laughing!

3. Accent [81]

This is a fallacy in which a statement is taken out of "context" to make an argument against someone. For example, in the 2008 presidential election, it was said that Barak Obama was going to raise taxes, but never was it clarified upon whom Obama was going to raise taxes, just that he was going to raise taxes. The argument was put forward not before groups of wealthy people, but to groups of middle and lower middle class people implying that they would receive the tax hikes. In fact, Obama did say he was going to raise taxes, but only on people who made more than $250,000 per year. An independent group which was following the tax plans of the presidential candidates made it clear that most people would benefit far more from Obama's tax plan than from McCain's tax plan. The same thing is being said today against "Obamacare" (the name "Obamacare" is an example of the fallacy of Ad Populum), that people are suffering from it, when in fact, the average person is benefitting from the fact that all pre-existing conditions must be covered by insurance, and all diagnostic tests are now covered 100% by the insurance companies.

There is another sense of Accent which we cannot overlook. How we say something, the way we emphasize our words can make all the difference in what is conveyed. For example, "I didn't say you could do that." What does it mean if I emphasize the words this way, "I didn't say you could do that" which could imply what you are doing is OK because someone must have said you could do that. Or "I **DIDN'T** say you could do that" or "I didn't **SAY** you could do that" implying that again, you could still do it simply because you chose to do it without asking permission. You begin to see how we can change the meaning of a phrase by just how we say the words, how we emphasize different words.

How do we avoid such a fallacy? Knowledge about the subject will help a great deal. Also, being clear about our own assumptions and seeking factual information to either confirm or reject our assumptions.

4. Composition [82]

This is a fallacy in which we apply to the whole the attributes of the individual parts which make up the whole. For example, just because each soldier is physically strong does not mean we have a strong army; or, just because every individual part of a machine is lightweight that the machine itself is lightweight; or, because each part is well made the whole machine is well made. Another type of Composition fallacy has to do with applying the attributes of a part of a collection with the whole of the collection. For example, to say that semi-trucks burn more fuel than automobiles on the one hand sounds right, yet when we realize there are several hundred cars for every semi-truck on the road, we begin to see that automobiles as a collective, burn more fuel than semi-trucks as a collective.

While both of these types of Composition seem to be similar if not the same, they are not. In the first type, we are talking about a whole being given the attributes of its parts, thus an automobile would be such a whole, whereas, when we talk about the Collective being given the attributes of the individual parts of the collection, we are not talking about a whole when talking about a Collective. A junk yard is a collective of car parts, but it is not a car. A house is a whole; a pile of bricks is a collective. The first type of Composition would apply to the house the attributes of the parts that make up the house, whereas the second type of Composition would apply to the collective pile of bricks the attributes of each brick.

How to avoid this fallacy? Never accept the attempt at giving to a whole the qualities of its individual parts, or to the collective the qualities of its individual members. In other words, always remember that just because the football team may have very strong talented players does not necessarily mean it is a strong and talented team!

5. Division [83]

Division is Composition in reverse. We had two types of Composition; we have two types of Division. We have the type in which we claim what is true for the whole is also true for its parts. We commit this fallacy any time we claim that because the car is heavy each of its parts must also be heavy, or because the college is a well known college with the reputation of being the best in the land, then Joe Smith, one of its college students, must also be the best college student in the land. (This takes us back to Ad Hominem Circumstantial in that while there is "guilt" by association, there is also good reputation by association, which is also a fallacy.) The second type of fallacy of Division has to do with applying to the individual parts of a collective the attributes of the collective itself. To say that Wal-Mart employees work three shifts is not to say that every Wal-Mart employee works three shifts, but rather the collective of employees together work a total of three shifts. While it is true to say that college students major in Art, Chemistry, Forensics, Athletic Training, Psychology, Biology, Mathematics, it is not true to say that each college student majors in all of those.

How to avoid this fallacy? Never accept an argument claiming one part of a whole or one person of a collective has the same qualities as the whole or collective just because of the association. Demand additional proof, for example, check out the academic records of the student going to a great university with a great academic reputation if you really want to know what kind of student he/she is.

REVIEW GLOSSARY

FALLACIES OF RELEVANCE

1. Argument *Ad Ignorantiam*
2. Argument *Ad Verecundiam*
3. Argument *Ad Hominem Abusive*
4. Argument *Ad Hominem Circumstantial*
5. Argument *Ad Populum*
6. Argument *Ad Misericordiam*
7. Argument *Ad Baculum*
8. Argument *Ignoratio Elenchi*

FALLACIES OF PRESUMPTION

1. Complex Question
2. False Cause
3. Begging the Question: *Petitio Principii*
4. Accident
5. Converse Accident

FALLACIES OF AMBIGUITY

1. Equivocation
2. Amphiboly
3. Accent
4. Composition
5. Division

EXERCISES *(check for some answers at the back of the book)*

Indicate which fallacy is committed in each of the following:

1. Every time I walked a certain way, a rooster would crow, so it must be that if I walk that certain way, a rooster will crow, I think I will call it the Rooster walk!

   _____

2. "When you robbed the liquor store, were you wearing a ball cap? Answer yes or no!"

   _____

3. Has anyone ever proved that there is no God? Then how can you deny that He exists?

   _____

4. Why would you ever take the word of a child molester?

   _____

5. How could you have nothing to do with the robbery, witnesses have seen you hanging around the boys who were caught in the robbery.

   _____

6. I know I have missed class a lot, but I just haven't been feeling like going to class, I mean, I have been depressed, and am having trouble with my boyfriend. I hope this doesn't hurt my grade!

   _____

7. Everyone on that football team can bench press over 400 pounds, so they are the strongest team out there, so why aren't they number one in the polls?

   _____

8. That football team has won 18 straight games, that is clearly the best team out there, and so each of their players must be the best player for their position out there!

   _____

9. Please, do as I say, because you really would not want to upset me!

   _____

10. Local high school dropouts cut in half.

_____

11. The New York Giants must have the best players in the NFL, after all, they won the Superbowl!

_____

12. The Vizio television must be a good TV, after all, Ellen DeGeneres promotes it on her television program

_____

13. Drunk gets nine months in violin case.

_____

14. Children who are taught at an early age how to behave through strict boundaries are always better adjusted, because we know that children get along much better if they know their limits, and they can't know their limits if they are not taught through strict boundaries.

_____

15. Two sisters reunited after 18 years in checkout counter.

_____

16. Most birds can fly. Tweety the Penguin is a bird. Therefore, Tweety can fly.

_____

17. "We hear that a writer has just filed a two million dollar lawsuit against the Coors beer company for pickling his brain. It seems that he had been consuming large quantities of Coors' 3.2 beer, containing only 3.2 percent alcohol and so supposedly non-intoxicating, at his local tavern. But, the suit contends, the stuff was insidiously marinating his mind; and as a result he has been unable to finish writing his second novel. The author may have a point. But we have to wonder whether the damage was caused by the beer, or by the current fad of product liability suits." Wall Street Journal (02.14.79).

_____

18. The United States policy toward mainland China was surely mistaken because Shirley McLaine, the well-known actress, said, at the time, she had grave misgivings about it.

_____

19. Water is liquid, therefore the molecules that make it up are liquid.

_____

20. Every song on the CD lasts less than an hour, so the CD must last for less than an hour.

_____

21. If you don't accept that the Sun orbits the Earth, rather than the other way around, then you'll be excommunicated from the Church.

_____

22. Most people believe in God, therefore, God must exist.

_____

23. Trinitarianism holds that three equals one. Three does not equal one. Therefore: Trinitarianism is false.

_____

Chapter Nine

Logic Puzzles and Riddles

Perhaps one of the more interesting aspects of logic can be found in solving logic puzzles and riddles. When Sherlock Holmes was on the scent to the solution of a crime, he was in the process of unraveling a complex riddle. Television audiences' everyday enjoy watching a CSI crime show, or a crime show featuring clairvoyants, the same thing, trying to unravel a complex riddle. Often, what characterizes such riddles is a dearth of information, which often leaves the audience wondering "who done it"? We are thrilled but mystified when the hero or heroine looks at something, or hears something, and they get this look on their face that they have suddenly figured it out. They became privy to a little bit of information that was not available to the audience, and as a result, figured out the riddle or crime. We wait with baited breath thinking we might have it figured out, but often do not have a clue until we hear or see what that little bit of information was we did not have before.

A good puzzle or riddle should give you just enough information to make it possible to figure out and solve the riddle. However, to be a really good puzzle, it cannot give you too much information or it would make it too easy and as a result not challenge you to use your imagination forcing you to organize your thoughts in a logical fashion in order to fill in the blanks and come up with the solution.[84]

Here are some steps to help you solve a logic riddle or puzzle:

Step One:
Do not read too much into the information you have been given, in other words, you only know what information has been given you. For example, if a puzzle says that the perpetrator had a daughter, and one of the suspects is listed as a bachelor, while it is possible that a bachelor can father a child, we have to assume that being a bachelor would rule them out, simply because it is the rule of thumb that bachelors do not have daughters, though it is true some do, you simply do not know whether this particular bachelor is one of those who just happened to have fathered a child. (Remember distribution in a previous chapter?)

Step Two:
Organize your thoughts on paper to keep track of every variable involved in the riddle. For example, if there are five individuals you list them in a vertical column on the left, then across the top, all of the characteristics listed in the information that is given. For example:

Step Three:

As you are filling out the grid you have created, make sure to draw a circle ◯
in the box that indicates that is the person with that characteristic and if one person has that characteristic, you know no one else does, so you mark an X in all the other boxes. For example, say that we know that John is a bachelor, because the information tells us that, so we would do this:

	Bachelor	Husband	Grandfather	Uncle	Brother
John	◯	X	X	X	X
Ralph	X				
Joe	X				
Jim	X				
Ron	X				

But we also know that John is none of the others, because the riddle tells us that each characteristic belongs to only one of the persons listed. So, we add X's to John's line as seen above. So from one little bit of information, "John is a bachelor" we have filled out 9 of the 25 squares. OK, so what happens if another clue is that the "Brother" and Jim are great friends, and then we see another clue that says Jim and Ralph have never met. Those two bits of information help us fill out our grid quite a lot. Look what we can do now...

	Bachelor	Husband	Grandfather	Uncle	Brother
John	◯	X	X	X	X
Ralph	X				X
Joe	X				
Jim	X				X
Ron	X				

We know right away that Jim must not be the brother, because the Brother is his best friend. So we add an X for Jim under Brother. If Ralph has never met Jim, then Ralph cannot be the Brother, so we add another X for Ralph under Brother. (Ok, I know, they might have been separated at birth and never met, but again, we are going with what is generally the case.)

Now we know that either Joe or Ron is the Brother. What if another clue is that Ron is married to John's sister? That must mean that Ron is the Husband, so we put an ○ for Ron as the Husband, but that eliminates him as the Brother, so now, the grid looks like this:

	Bachelor	Husband	Grandfather	Uncle	Brother
John	○	X	X	X	X
Ralph	X	X			X
Joe	X	X			
Jim	X	X			X
Ron	X	○	X	X	X

OK, now we know that Joe must be the Brother, so now the grid looks like this:

	Bachelor	Husband	Grandfather	Uncle	Brother
John	○	X	X	X	X
Ralph	X	X			X
Joe	X	X	X	X	○
Jim	X	X			X
Ron	X	○	X	X	X

Now we are down to trying to figure out whether the Grandfather is Ralph or Jim. What happens if the last clue is:"Jim's last birthday allowed him to buy alcoholic beverages legally."

OK, I know it is possible, though not probable, that a 21 year old man could be a grandfather, but let's face it, not likely. So, we have to say that Jim is not the Grandfather; Ralph is, so our final grid looks like this:

	Bachelor	Husband	Grandfather	Uncle	Brother
John	○	X	X	X	X
Ralph	X	X	○	X	X
Joe	X	X	X	X	○
Jim	X	X	X	○	X
Ron	X	○	X	X	X

And by the process of elimination, we know that Jim is the Uncle, as indicated above. Now, let's list the clues, and see how much information we had:

There are five men, John, Ralph, Joe, Jim and Ron. One is a Brother, one an Uncle, one a Grandfather, one a Husband and one a Bachelor. Given the following information, who is what?

Clue #1	John has never married
Clue #2	The Brother and Jim are great friends
Clue #3	Jim and Ralph have never met
Clue #4	Ron is married to John's Sister
Clue #5	Jim's last birthday allowed him to buy alcoholic beverages legally

Now, as just a list of clues, at first glance one might not be able to see the solution. By having a grid where we can lay everything out, we can begin to fill in the boxes and by a process of elimination, come up with the solution:

John	Bachelor
Ralph	Grandfather
Joe	Brother
Jim	Uncle
Ron	Husband

Now, try your hand at the following riddle:

J's Gas and Shop just opened with an Owner, Night shifter, Day shifter, Weekender, and Manager. The five people who work there are, in no special order, Jim, Jack, Joe, Jill, and Jon. The Owner is the Manager's next-door neighbor; the Manager is the Weekender's brother; the Day shifter is dating the Weekender, the Night shifter is married to the Owner's daughter. Jon does not live in the same town as any of the other people at the Gas and Shop. Jon has never been married. Jim just graduated from high school and this is his first job. Joe got his job at the Gas and Shop from his next door neighbor. Jon lives too far away to work during the week. Jill cannot work weekends. Jim cannot work in the day time.

	Owner	Manager	Weekender	Day Shifter	Night Shifter
Jim					
Jack					
Joe					
Jill					
Jon					

EXERCISES:(*see back of book for some answers*) Here are a couple more puzzles:

1. **Who Lives Where?**

There are six friends who decided they would try to keep in touch after graduating Simpson College. They promised to send each other their addresses. The problem is, when sending the addresses they forgot to indicate whose address was whose! Jennifer decided she knew her friends well enough she could figure it out. So, here are the six addresses:

1504 West Indies DR, San Diego, CA
785 North D ST, Indianola, IA
30 Place RD, County Down, Northern Ireland
7830 Westover ST, Cambridge, MA
2340 Dresden RD, Zanesville, OH
119 W 63rd ST, New York, New York

Here are the six friends in no apparent order:
Jennifer, Sadie, Madelyn, Gwen, Paula, Adriana

Here is what Jennifer knew about each of her friends:
Sadie:Being very musically inclined, and having majored in a BM in music, violin, had decided she wanted to live near a major Symphonic Hall.
Madelyn:Had always wanted to teach at her Alma Mater, and so decided she would remain in the town where their college was located.
Gwen:Was planning on seeking a graduate degree at an Ivy League University.
Paula:Having studied veterinarian science had decided she wanted to start a farm near her hometown. Jennifer couldn't remember right off the name of her hometown, but she knew it was East of the Mississippi River.
Adriana:Had dreamed of moving to her ancestral country to live, at least for a few years before getting married.

WHERE DOES JENNIFER LIVE? _____

2. **WHO KILLED SAM?**

It seemed somehow appropriate that Sam was killed on April 15, seeing how he had spent ten years in prison for tax evasion. He was killed between 1 and 3am just outside Chicago. There were five suspects called in for questioning. All of them former gang members with Sam. Each of the five made three statements, two were true and one was false.

Sony:	Me and Sam were best buddies.	T	F
	Joe killed Sam	T	F
	I don't even own a gun.	T	F

Joe:	Sony lied when he said I killed Joe.	T	F
	Sony does not own a gun.	T	F
	Jake wasn't near Chicago on Tax Day.	T	F
Jake:	I did not kill Sam.	T	F
	I was in New York on the 15th.	T	F
	Jason hated Sam.	T	F
Jason:	Jake lied when he said I hated Sam.	T	F
	Sam and me were best buddies.	T	F
	Sony was jealous of our friendship.	T	F
Jimmy:	I did not kill Sam.	T	F
	I would never hurt Sam let alone kill him.	T	F
	Sony and Sam were best buddies.	T	F

WHO KILLED SAM?_____

3. The employees of a small bank are Mr. Smith, Mr. Black, Mrs. Harrison, Miss Ambrose, Mr. Kelly, and Miss Earnshaw. The positions they occupy are manager, assistant manager, cashier, stenographer, teller, and clerk, though not necessarily in that order. The assistant manager is the manager's grandson, the cashier is the stenographer's son-in-law, Mr. Smith is a bachelor, Mr. Black is twenty-two years old, Miss Ambrose is the teller's step-sister, and Mr. Kelly is the manager's neighbor. Who holds each position?

4. Alice is known for losing her car keys, and a group of her friends met with Alice at a local restaurant just for fun. Jill, Jan, Julie, Jasmine and Joy have conspired to take Alice's keys and one of them hold them and make Alice guess who has her keys. Alice comes back from the powder room and Jan announces, "Alice, we all know how you have such a tough time keeping track of your keys." (eye-roll from Alice) "So, we have taken your keys and one of us is holding them. Each of us will make three statements, two of the statements are false and one is true. We will not leave here until you figure out who

has your keys..." Alice responds, "Oh, good grief! Okay, get on with it!" After they are done laughing, Jill makes the first three statements.

Jill	a.	I would never take your keys.	T	F
	b.	Joy took your keys and gave them to Jasmine!	T	F
	c.	Jasmine then gave the keys to Jan!	T	F
Jan	a.	Jill lied when she said I had your keys.	T	F
	b.	Joy took your keys and gave them to Jasmine.	T	F
	c.	Jasmine then gave your keys to Julie.	T	F
Julie	a.	Jan lied when she said Jasmine gave me your keys.	T	F
	b.	Jasmine gave the keys to Jan.	T	F
	c.	Jan then gave the keys to Joy.	T	F
Jasmine	a.	I do not have your keys.	T	F
	b.	Julie was right, Jan did give the keys to Joy.	T	F
	c.	Jan then gave the keys to Joy.	T	F
Joy	a.	I do not have your keys!	T	F
	b.	Jill was telling the truth that Jan has your keys!	T	F
	c.	Jasmine did give the keys to Jan!	T	F

WHO HAS ALICE'S KEYS?_____

Chapter Ten

Symbolic Logic or Formal Logic

To this point we have been analyzing deductive syllogisms using language and the basic elements of Aristotelian logic. What we have discovered is that the use of language can be problematic simply because language is itself often vague and prone to several different interpretations. Therefore, our analysis of deductive syllogisms cannot be as precise as we would like. In addition, it is often difficult to show the actual deductive relationship in a syllogism without doing a lot of translating and re-writing to get the argument into proper form. To overcome some of these difficulties, logicians came up with a system of symbols and connectives to be used in such a way as to clearly indicate the deductive relationships found within deductive arguments. In other words, by developing symbols of connection, and defining their truth values, it helps one to see without much thought the actual connection among the propositions within an argument. That is why I referred earlier to the concept of an architect's design for a building. When you can see the actual structure of the building, you will also see in the architect's detailed drawings how everything fits together and is held together.

Remember, we are now entering into what is called "Formal Logic" which simply means we are entering into Symbolic Logic. Formal logic is understood to not involve language but using only symbols to avoid the ambiguity caused by language.

In logic, if you remember, we are all about distinguishing good arguments from bad, valid arguments from invalid arguments, and sound arguments from unsound arguments. While we have been trying to do that in the previous chapters, in this and the succeeding chapters, we will be able to see much more clearly whether or not an argument form is valid or invalid, sound or unsound. We can do that by eliminating the use of language and replacing the language with symbols. Let's begin with the symbols for the different connections among the elements of a deductive argument.

SYMBOLIC CONNECTIVES [85]

The Symbol for a Conjunctive:	•
The Symbol for Negation:	~
The Symbol for a Disjunctive:	v
The Symbol for a Conditional:	⊃
The Symbol for a Tautology:	≡
Proper Punctuation:	( ) [ ] { }
The Symbol for Therefore:	∴

You will find the use of these symbols in what we call "compound" propositions.[86] There are two types of propositions, simple and compound.[87] A simple proposition would be:

Socrates is a man

A compound proposition would be:

Socrates is a man and he is short

There are actually two propositions in this one sentence, the claim that Socrates is a man and the claim that Socrates is a short man. It is this kind of proposition, the compound proposition, which we will be studying when defining the different symbolic connectives. The use of the sign ∴ is to indicate the conclusion that has been arrived at, or "therefore".

1. Conjunction [88]

What is a conjunction? It is any time you have two components of a proposition joined in such a way that they reflect the meaning of "both/and". For example, "The car has four doors and it is red." If I were to break this compound proposition down, I would see that "The car has four doors" and "The car is red" are two components of the compound proposition. If I was to use the symbol for a conjunctive, and replaced the words with symbols such that:

p = The car has four doors
q = The car is red

The compound proposition would look like this:

p · q

What does this connective mean? When we use the term "mean" in this context, we are actually referring to its truth-value. If we know whether or not the compound proposition is true, we have to know its truth values and we can get at that through the truth table. The truth table will help us understand what this relationship means. A truth table simply helps us to see the truth value of each component or statement in a compound proposition and as a result, the truth value of the entire compound proposition. As we have heard before, statements or propositions are either true or false, and so to help us get at the truth value of a conjunctive we have this truth table:[89]

p	q	p · q
T	T	T
T	F	F
F	T	F
F	F	F

What this truth table means is simply IF p is True and q is True, then the compound conjunctive proposition is also True, or if the p is T and the q is F, then the compound conjunctive proposition is false, etc.

Notice the only line where you see that "p · q" is true is when both "p" and "q" are true. That is the meaning of "both/and". So, if I say, "I'm moving to Phoenix and am a monkey's uncle" we are looking at a false statement, because one of the components of the compound statement is not true. (You can guess which!)

The importance of the conjunctive form "p · q" is that any two components can be connected in a conjunctive and so long as both are true, the compound statement is true. But remember, each component has to be such that to replace it would not alter the nature of the compound statement. For example, "Josh and Joe are friends" is not a conjunctive, because "Josh and Joe" are not two components of a compound proposition, rather it is a simple statement of a relationship. However, the compound proposition: "Paris is the capital of France and London is the capital of England" is a compound sentence and it is true because both components are true.

However, one thing that "p · q" does not mean is something like, "He got up and he got dressed." While this may look like a compound proposition, it is actually a statement of chronological events, "He got up" and then "He got dressed". I doubt you would want to say, "He got dressed and he got up", that would seem odd. So, the connective for a conjunct simply claims that the compound statement is true only if both components are true.

If you think about it for a moment, you should come to understand that it is far more likely that a conjunct will be false than it will be true simply because a conjunctive compound proposition can only be true in one case, and false in all others. So, if as we move further along in symbolic logic, you see an argument with a lot of conjunctives in it, there is a good chance the compound propositions might be false and the whole argument then might be invalid. But, that is for a later chapter.

2. Negation [90]

The negation of a statement in English is often preceded by a "not", but for the purposes of symbolic logic, the symbol for negation is the "tilde" or ~. The negation of a statement is its contradictory or its opposite. Therefore, if I use the symbol "J" to stand for "John is a teacher" then to symbolize "John is not a teacher" I would write this:~J. Keep in mind, however, that "J" is the negation of "~J" just as "~J" is the negation of "J". The truth table for negation is:[91]

p	~p
T	F
F	T

You may remember back when we were discussing syllogisms we talked about "complements" that is, "John is not a teacher" is the complement of "John is a teacher". Why do we use different terms? We were using classical logic when discussing syllogisms, and now we are using modern symbolic logic, and so we use the term "negation", but in fact, they are the same thing. So, I could say the " ~p" is the complement of "p", or "p" is the complement of "~p".

3. Disjunction [92]

A disjunctive is formed when two components of a compound proposition are joined by the connective "or". There are two different uses of the connective "or", one inclusive and the other exclusive. If you were to say, "Class absence will be excused for sickness or a college function requiring your absence." This is the inclusive sense, because it means that either alternative could be true or both could be true. On the other hand, when you go into a restaurant and the menu reads, "Salad or soup included with the meal" that is the exclusive sense of the connective "or" simply meaning that you can have one or the other but not both. Often, the words "but not both" will be added for clarification.

For the purposes of symbolic logic we will be using the weak sense of the connective "or", that is, either alternative could be true or they both could be true, *but they both cannot be false.* We use the "v" (wedge) to symbolize disjunction because the first letter of the Latin word for the weak meaning of "or" is a v (*vel*). We refer to this symbol as the "wedge".

The truth table for a disjunctive is:[93]

INCLUSIVE TRUTH TABLE

p	q	p v q
T	T	T
T	F	T
F	T	T
F	F	F

As you can see from this truth table, something rather interesting comes to our attention, if it is the fact that we are using the "inclusive" sense of "or" and yet we have a truth table that appears to look something like the "exclusive" use of the term "or"…

EXCLUSIVE TRUTH TABLE

p	q	p v q
T	T	F
T	F	T
F	T	T
F	F	F

Do you notice that in the "exclusive" use of the term "or" the only difference between the truth tables is that in the "exclusive" use of the term "or" when both alternatives p; q are true, the truth value of the disjunctive is False! So, we see that when in the "inclusive" truth table either one of the alternatives is true, the disjunctive is true. How do we account for this?

Simple, normally, when using the "v" we mean the inclusive sense of the term, but when you have a disjunctive syllogism, like this:

> Either John is guilty or the baker did it.
> John is not guilty.
> The baker did it.

This represents the "exclusive" meaning of the connective "or", because in a disjunctive syllogism, by negating one of the alternatives, it is the same as saying "but not both". So, what that means for us is simply this, whenever we are using the "v" we use it in the "inclusive" sense of the term. However, when we have a case in which it is made clear that "not both" is meant, like in a disjunctive syllogism, then we know it is the "exclusive" sense, and because the truth table for the "inclusive" sense has three out of four truth values which can be applied to the "exclusive" truth table, we can actually use both meanings for the "or", what will help determine which meaning is being used will be the context of the compound proposition.[94]

In other words, we will use the inclusive truth table simply because in logic the only time we are concerned about the exclusive sense of disjunction is when we have a clear disjunctive syllogism that denies the truth of one of the disjuncts. Only in that case do we use the exclusive sense of the "v". We can still use the inclusive truth table because it expresses the proper truth values of the disjunctive in all other cases.

4. Conditional (Material Implication) [95]

Perhaps the most defining symbol in all of symbolic logic is the horseshoe, "⊃", which simply denotes the relationship of "if/then" between two components of a compound proposition (yes, this is the symbolic version of a compound hypothetical proposition). In the compound conditional…

If Rachel studies hard, then she will pass the test.

The first component of the compound conditional:"Rachel studies hard" is referred to as the antecedent and the second component of the compound conditional:"she will pass the test" is referred to as the consequent.

The reason I refer to the horseshoe "⊃" as the defining symbol for symbolic logic is simply because in any symbolic logic compound argument, if the premises are true, the conclusion must be true or the whole argument is invalid. Remember toward the beginning of this course we learned that propositions are either true or false and deductive arguments are either valid or invalid. It just so happens that the truth table for the truth value of a compound conditional matches the table of validity for a deductive argument. Below is the truth table of the compound conditional proposition:[96]

p	q	p ⊃ q
T	T	T
T	F	F
F	T	T
F	F	T

As you can see, the "p" is the antecedent and the "q" is the consequent. Any time the antecedent is true and the consequent is false, the compound conditional proposition is false. However, any time the antecedent is false, the compound conditional proposition will always be true regardless of the truth value of the consequent. Likewise, any time the consequent is true, you know the compound conditional proposition is also true!

The only time a compound conditional proposition is false is when the antecedent is true and the consequent is false. This is the same in determining validity of an argument. If the premises are true and the consequent is false, it is invalid.

What does the "if/then" statement mean? It is an implication of the relationship between the antecedent and the consequent such that if the antecedent is true then the consequent is true. It does not mean that the antecedent and the consequent are actually true; it simply asserts that IF the antecedent is true then the consequent must be true. That is why, if in fact the antecedent is true and the consequent false, then the whole thing is false.

How do we demonstrate the meaning of this implication? We refer back to the truth values of the conjunctive, $p \cdot q$, and realize that the only time $p \supset q$ is **false** is the same as saying $p \cdot \sim q$ is true. OK, what did I just do? We already know that the only time $p \supset q$ is false is when "p" is true and "q" is false. So, if the truth value of "q", in this particular case, is false, then $\sim q$ would be true. So, $p \cdot \sim q$ would therefore be true. [97]

Now, if on the other hand, we are saying that $p \supset q$ is **true**, then we are saying that the "p" is true and the "q" is true, and if that is the case, then $p \cdot \sim q$ would be false, because then $\sim q$ would be the negation of q, and if q is true then $\sim q$ is false. If that is the case, then $p \cdot \sim q$ is false. How can we make $p \cdot \sim q$ true? We negate the whole conjunction. How do we do that? We put the conjunction, $p \cdot \sim q$ inside parentheses () and then put a $\sim$ on the outside of the parentheses thus changing the truth value of the whole conjunction. So, $\sim(p \cdot \sim q)$ would be true. We have learned now, in this particular case, the $\sim(p \cdot \sim q)$ has the same truth value as $p \supset q$ if $p \supset q$ is true.[98]

There are at least three different ways to understand the "if/then" phrase. We can understand it as the consequent logically following from the antecedent:

If all warm-blooded animals are mammals, and a horse is a warm-blooded animal, then the horse is a mammal.

We can also understand the "if/then" phrase as a definition:

If the water is a solid and is at a temperature below 32° then the water is ice.

We can also understand the "if/then" phrase as something that requires empirical testing to determine its truth:

If you put this dried up old plant into water, then it will immediately bloom into a beautiful flower!

And finally, there is a sense of some "if/then" statements in which there is no definitional or logical connection between the antecedent and the consequent, and there is no amount of empirical testing that would make any difference, rather, we see that the nature of the antecedent and the consequent is such that the person making the compound conditional statement is talking about a decision he would make if something happened:

If the Cleveland Browns win the next Super Bowl, then I'll eat my hat!

But there is yet another meaning of the "⊃", and that is "material implication". Material implication simply put, means there is no case in which the consequent is false that the antecedent can be true. For example:

If the Cleveland Browns win the 2016 Super Bowl then I'm a monkey's uncle!

It is clear that I am not a "monkey's uncle" and therefore it is also clear that the Cleveland Browns will not win the Super Bowl (Not even made it to the playoffs!)

All of these meanings are wrapped up in the horseshoe "⊃" symbol. You may think that this is a bit ambiguous, well, you are right, so far as the meaning of the language is concerned. What is NOT ambiguous is the truth value of the conditional itself. That is the point of symbolic logic; we simply rid ourselves of the ambiguity of language and focus instead on the truth value of the compound propositions, and in turn on the validity of the arguments containing those compound propositions.

5. Tautology (Material Equivalence) [99]

When we speak of a tautology, we are talking about "material equivalence" which is to say that two statements are "materially equivalent" when they share the same truth value. This means that each statement materially implies the other, that is, "p" is true if and only if "q" is true, or "p" is false if and only if "q" is false. What this means, in short, is that $p \equiv q$ is materially equivalent to $q \equiv p$. Thus, one can call the statement form $p \equiv q$ a biconditional, that is, it holds the same truth value regardless of whether it is $p \equiv q$ or $q \equiv p$. The truth table for material equivalence looks like this:

p	q	$p \equiv q$
T	T	T
T	F	F
F	T	F
F	F	T

Notice the only time a material equivalent is false is if both sides do not share the same truth value. So, if both the "p" and the "q" are true, the material equivalence is true. If both the "p" and the "q" are false, the material equivalence is true.

6. Proper Punctuation [100]

You may have wondered, when I used this as a partial definition of the "⊃", ~(p · ~q), what was going on? Because of the nature of compound propositions, and the way arguments are stated, we have to have a way to separate out one compound proposition from another when forming an argument in symbolic logic. Take for example:

"If the United States does not attack Iran or pulls out of Iraq then some far right wing conservatives will claim that the United States is soft on terrorism"

How would you symbolize this argument? Let's determine first what symbolism we will use:

A = United States does not attack Iran
I = United States will pull out of Iraq
C = far right wing conservative will claim that the U.S. is soft on terrorism

Using proper punctuation, it would look like this:

$(A \lor I) \supset C$

We used parentheses around the first compound proposition that was in a conditional relationship with a second proposition, or another way of stating it, the parentheses is placed around the "IF" statement or the antecedent, all that comes before the "then", because all that comes after the "then" is the consequent.

OK, so how would we use proper punctuation to symbolize this complex argument?

"If Russia attacks Georgia then Russia is aggressively involved in expansionism and will renege on their agreement made twenty years ago regarding the breakup of the Soviet Union. If that happens, then the United States will need to review their standing treaties with Russia. If the United States condemns Russia for its unprovoked aggression against Georgia, then the cold war will probably resume."

If we assign the following symbols:R = Russia Attacks Georgia; E = Russia is involved in expansionism; B = reneging on their agreement made at the time of the breakup of the Soviet Union; T = US will review standing treaties with Russia; C = the US condemns Russia for its unprovoked aggression against Georgia; CW = resumption of the COLD WAR.

The symbolic argument would look like this:

ANTECEDENT   CONSEQUENT
$\{[(R \supset E) \cdot B] \supset [(R \supset E) \cdot B] \supset T\} \supset (C \supset CW)$

It appears more complicated than it actually is. If you re-read the argument as stated, the final conditional compound proposition, "If the United States condemns Russia for its unprovoked aggression against Georgia, then the cold war will probably resume" is predicated on the truth of the series of compound propositions that preceded it.

We know that $[(R \supset E) \cdot B]$ is the symbolic form of:If Russia attacks Georgia "$\supset$" **then** Russia is aggressively involved in expansionism **and** "•" will renege on their agreement made twenty years ago regarding the breakup of the Soviet Union. So why did I use it again in the second half of the antecedent? Because the simple phrase "If that happens" is referring to [(R ⊃ E) · B].

Now, here is a translation of the complex symbols:

{[(R ⊃ E) · B] ⊃ [(R ⊃ E) · B] ⊃ T} ⊃ (C ⊃ CW)

If Russia attacks Georgia "⊃" **then** Russia is aggressively involved in expansionism **and** "•" will renege on their agreement made twenty years ago regarding the breakup of the Soviet Union. THEN If Russia attacks Georgia "⊃" **then** Russia is aggressively involved in expansionism **and** "•" will renege on their agreement made twenty years ago regarding the breakup of the Soviet Union THEN the US will review standing treaties with Russia. THEN if the US condemns Russia for the unprovoked aggression against Georgia, THEN the Cold War will resume.

You will note that when we begin to use punctuation, that is parentheses (), brackets [ ] and braces { }, we start first with parentheses and move out next using brackets and end up with braces. We used braces around {[(R ⊃ E) · B] ⊃ [(R ⊃ E) · B] ⊃ T} because the whole phrase represented the antecedent in this complex argument. The presence of the braces indicates that all of these compound propositions belong together in order to help us understand the argument and its conditional relationship with the consequent:(C ⊃ CW).

REVIEW GLOSSARY

1. The Symbol for a Conjunctive: ·   This symbol means "both/and", the truth value of this compound proposition is on true when both components of this conjunctive are true. The two components connected by the " · " are called the "conjunctives".

2. The Symbol for Negation: ~   This symbol indicates the contradictory, denial or complement of a proposition

3. The Symbol for a Disjunctive: v   This symbol indicates the "inclusive" meaning of "either/or", but can also encompass the exclusive meaning of either/or but not both. The truth value of this symbol is only false if both alternatives are false. The two components that are joined by the "v" are called "alternatives"

4. The Symbol for a Conditional: ⊃   This symbol indicates the "if/then" relationship between two components of a compound proposition. There are several interpretations of that relationship, but the one most often referred to with this symbol is that of "material implication" which simply means that if the consequent is false the antecedent cannot possibly be true. Thus, the only time a conditional is false is when the antecedent is true and the consequent is false. The component of the compound conditional that appears before the "⊃" is referred to as the "antecedent" and the component that appears after the "⊃" is referred to as the "consequent".

5. The Symbol for a Tautology: ≡   This symbol refers to material equivalence which simply holds that any two statements are materially equivalent if they share the same truth value. This can further mean that any two statements that are materially equivalent also imply each other due to their shared truth value.

6. Proper Punctuation: () [ ] { }   Parentheticals (); Brackets [ ]; Braces { } These marks of punctuation are used to separate out the compound proposition found in a complex argument. The parentheticals are used first, followed further out by the brackets and finally the braces.

7. Truth Tables[101]   An instrument used in determining the truth value of a compound proposition. When setting up a truth table use the formula of 2^n, that is, multiply 2 times the number of variables to determine how many lines will be in the truth table. If you have p and q, that would require four lines, if you just had "p" that would only require two lines. Always start with T in the left hand column. We will cover in more detail the construction of complex truth tables in a later chapter.

EXERCISES

EXERCISE I *(check at the back of the book for some answers)*
Using the truth tables of " · "; "v"; " ⊃ ", determine the truth values of the following compound propositions (circle the correct answer):

1. Columbus is the capitol of Ohio or Pierre is the capitol of South Dakota.   T   F
2. ~(Columbus is the capitol of Ohio and Pierre is the capitol of South Dakota)   T   F
3. Juneau is the capitol of Alaska and Lawrence is the capitol of Kansas.   T   F
4. Sacramento is the capitol of California or San Diego is the capitol of California.   T   F
5. Austin is the capitol of Texas and Jackson is the capitol of Mississippi.   T   F
6. If Colorado City is the capitol of Colorado, then I'm a monkey's uncle!   T   F
7. If Helena is the capitol of Montana, then Honolulu is the capitol of Hawaii   T   F
8. If Las Vegas is the capitol of Nevada then Seattle is the capitol of Washington.   T   F
9. If Baton Rouge is the capitol of Georgia then Tallahassee is the capitol of Florida. T   F
10. ~(Columbia is the capitol of Missouri and Columbia is the capitol of South Carolina. T   F

EXERCISE II

If P and Q is true and R and X is false, what is the truth value of the following complex propositions? (Circle the correct answer)

1. P ⊃ X
2. P · Q   T   F
3. P v X   T   F
4. (P · R) ⊃ (R v X)   T   F
5. [(R v Q) v (P · X) · ~[(R · P) v (Q ⊃ X)]   T   F
6. {[(Q ⊃ R) ⊃ (P · X)] v [~(P · R) ⊃ ~(P v Q)]} v (P ⊃ X)   T   F
7. ~{~[(P ⊃ Q) v (P · X)] ⊃ [(P · X) · (Q ⊃ X)]}   T   F
8. ~{~[~(~P · ~X) ⊃ ~(~X ⊃ ~R)] · ~[~(P · X) · ~(Q ⊃ X)]}   T   F
9. {~[(Q v R) v (X · R)] v ~[(P v X) · (X v R)]} ⊃ ~{~[~(P · R) ⊃ ~(Q ⊃ P)] · ~[~(P · X) v ~(Q ⊃ R)]}   T   F
10. (P ⊃ R) v ~(~P ⊃ ~R)   T   F

EXERCISE III
Translate the following into symbols and the correct compound proposition using proper punctuation:

1. Either Santa Fe is the capitol of New Mexico or Austin is the capitol of Texas.

2. If Salt Lake City is the capitol of Utah and Oklahoma City is the capitol of Oklahoma then Carson City is the capitol of Nevada.

3. If the US government does not bail out the three big auto makers then the recession will get worse and if the recession gets worse, then more people will lose their jobs and if more people lose their jobs, then the recession could decline into a depression and the number of homeless would begin to escalate.

EXERCISE IV
Additional Exercises:
Determine the truth values of the following:

If P and Q are true, and X and Y is false, and Z is unknown, what are the truth values of the following:

1. {[(X ⊃ Q) ⊃ (Z ∨ P)] · [(P ∨ Y) · (X · Z)]}

2. [(~P ⊃ ~Z) ∨ ~(X ⊃ Z)] ∨ ~(Q ⊃ P)

3. {[(Z ∨ ~Z) · (X ⊃ Y)] ⊃ ~[~(P ⊃ X) ⊃ (Z · ~Z)]} ⊃ {~[~(X ⊃ Z) · (Q ∨ Z)] ⊃ ~[~(~X · Y) · ~(~Z ∨ Z)]}

Determine the truth value of the following complex compound propositions if you know that the P is true and the Q is false but you do not know the truth value of X, Y or Z:

4. {[~(Q ⊃ X) ⊃ (~Y ∨ Y)] ⊃ ~[~(~Z ⊃ P) ≡ (X · ~X)]} ≡ ~{~[~(X ≡ ~X) ⊃ ~(P ⊃ Q)] ⊃ [(X ⊃ Y) v (Z v X)]}

5. [(X · ~X) ⊃ (Y v ~Y)] ≡ ~[~(Y ⊃ P) · (X ⊃ Z)]

6. {~[~(X · Z) ⊃ (Y v X)] ⊃ ~[(Q ⊃ P) ⊃ (X · Q)]} ∨

7. $\{\sim[(X \cdot \sim X) \supset (Z \supset Y)] \supset [\sim(Z \vee Y) \vee (X \supset Y)]\}$

We do not know the truth-value of any of the variables, is the following true or false?

$\sim\{[\sim(X \vee \sim X) \supset \sim(\sim(P \cdot Q)] \vee [(Z \supset W) \equiv (\sim P \cdot Q)]\} \supset \{[(X \cdot Y) \cdot (P \cdot Q)] \vee [(Z \cdot Y) \supset (W \vee X)]\}$

We know that the truth-value of P is false, but we do not know the truth-value of any of the other variables. Is this compound complex statement true or false?

$\sim\{\sim[\sim(\sim P \vee Q) \supset \sim(\sim Z \vee X)] \vee \sim[\sim(\sim Q \vee \sim P) \equiv (Z \cdot \sim Z)]\} \cdot \{ \sim[\sim(Q \supset \sim P) \supset (X \cdot Z)] \supset \sim[\sim(\sim Z \equiv \sim V) \equiv (\sim Q \vee Z)]\}$

Chapter Eleven

FALLACIES:
Truth Tables & Assigning Truth Values

To test for validity is a key process in deductive logic. Using truth tables is an effective way to test for the validity of a deductive argument. One will find, however, that building truth tables can be somewhat cumbersome, but that is another issue. As we discussed in the previous chapter, the validity of a deductive argument has the same truth values as a true compound conditional proposition, that is, if the antecedent is true the consequent must be true, if the antecedent is true and the consequent is false, then the compound conditional proposition is itself false. As for a deductive argument, if the premises are true and the conclusion is false, the whole thing is invalid.

As we used truth tables to determine the truth value of a compound proposition (the conjunct; the conditional; the disjunct; the material equivalent; the negation) so we can use truth tables to determine the validity of a deductive argument using compound propositions. In the review glossary of the previous chapter I pointed out how to create a proper truth table by using the formula 2^n, which simply means, you take 2 times however many variables there are. So, in the following complex argument:

$$(P \vee Q) \cdot (Q \vee R)$$
$$(P \vee Q)$$
$$\therefore \quad (Q \vee R)$$

There are three variables, P, Q and R. So, the formula would be 2^3, which would be 2 x 2 x 2 or 8 lines. That would look like this:[102]

	P	Q	R	(P v Q)	(Q v R)	(P v Q) · (Q v R)
1	T	T	T	T	T	T
2	T	T	F	T	T	T
3	T	F	T	T	T	T
4	T	F	F	T	F	F
5	F	T	T	T	T	T
6	F	T	F	T	T	T
7	F	F	T	F	T	F
8	F	F	F	F	F	F

Note how I assigned the first four lines under "P" a "T" and the second four lines under "P" an "F", then look at the column under "Q", I assigned the first two lines a "T" then the next two lines an "F" then again another two lines with the "T", and finally the last two lines an "F" again, and finally the column under the "R" you will note it begins with a "T" and then it is "F""T""F""T""F""T""F". Do you see the pattern of assigning "T" and "F"? If your truth table has two variables, there will be just four lines, and in that case under the first column the first half of the lines (2 lines in this case) will be assigned a "T" and the second half an "F", then the next column will cut that in half. So, if I have 3 variables as I do above, I assign the first four lines under the first column all "T"s and the last four lines under that first column all "F"s. Then when I go to the next column, I assign the first two lines a "T" and the second two lines an "F" and then two lines a "T" and two more lines an "F". The final column will be assigned every other line beginning with the "T". That is the pattern of assigned truth values. If you had sixteen lines you would have four variables, and so in the first column you would assign the first eight lines a "T" and the second eight lines an "F", and in the second column the first four lines would be a "T" then the second four lines an "F" then the third four lines another "T" then the last four lines an "F". Under the third column you would assign the first two lines a "T" then the next two lines an "F" and so on. In the final or fourth column you would begin by assigning the first line with a "T" then the second line an "F" and then every other one would be a "T" after that. So, note the pattern, the first column is half and half, then the second column is in fourths and then the third column is eighths and finally the fourth column is every other one.

Ok, now, let's take a look and see how we can determine validity of this argument. Note that (P v Q) · (Q v R) is the first premise and (P v Q) is the second premise, and (Q v R) is the conclusion. Now, on the truth table above, is there any line in which (P v Q) · (Q v R) and (P v Q) are both true and (Q v R) is false? How do you start to look? Just check out any instance where (Q v R) is false and then check to see if (P v Q) · (Q v R) and (P v Q) are both true. Check out line 4, where (Q v R) false, are either (P v Q) · (Q v R) or (P v Q) false? Yes, (P v Q) · (Q v R) is false, therefore, that line is OK. Now the only other place that (Q v R) is false is the last line, line 8. Again, are either (P v Q) · (Q v R) or (P v Q) false? Yes, (P v Q) is false, therefore that line is OK, so we can honestly say that this argument form is valid.

	P	Q	R	(P v Q)	(Q v R)	(P v Q) · (Q v R)
1	T	T	T	T	T	T
2	T	T	F	T	T	T
3	T	F	T	T	T	T
4	T	F	F	T	F	F
5	F	T	T	T	T	T
6	F	T	F	T	T	T
7	F	F	T	F	T	F
8	F	F	F	F	F	F

The formula 2^n yields the following number of lines for number of variables:

#variables	#lines
2	4
3	8
4	16
5	32
6	64
7	128

etc

Now, what did I mean by argument "form"?[103] We call this an argument form simply because it does not matter what the letters stand for, or if you used completely different letters, the form would remain the same. For example:

(p v q) · (q v r)   (X v Z) · (Z v Y)
(p v q)   Is the same as: (X v Z)
∴   (p v q)   ∴   (Z v Y)

That is, the form is the same. You are now beginning to see the benefit of symbolic logic; we construct argument forms rather than arguments. The argument can be developed from this form, but we are focused on discovering valid argument forms. It does not matter what the letters stand for, this form will always be valid. Our truth table demonstrated that constancy in validity.

Understanding the "forms" of an argument is important to help you begin to see more clearly whether or not an argument is valid. Below are some exercises to help you distinguish specific substitution instances of arguments for the forms. (A substitution instance is a specific argument; an argument form is not specific but can be used with any content.)[104]

The argument forms are the forms developed from the connectives:" · "; " v "; " ⊃ "; " ≡ ".

Determine what substitution instances on the left side match the argument form on the right side: (see the back of the book for answers)

[(A · B) v (C · D)] · (D v E)   p ≡ q

P ≡ ~~P   p v q

X · (P v Q)   p ⊃ q

(R · Z) ⊃ (Q v X)   p · q

Z v [(P · Z) v (Q ⊃ R)]

REVIEW GLOSSARY

Truth Tables	A graphic instrument to determine the validity of an argument. To construct a proper truth table use the formula 2^n, that is 2 x the number of variables.
Argument Forms	The basic argument form derived from the four symbolic connectives.
Substitution instance	A specific argument made up of compound propositions that can be reduced to the argument forms.

EXERCISES

Using truth tables, construct and determine the validity of each of the following arguments:

1. P ⊃ Q
    ~P
∴   ~Q

2. (P · Q) v (Q v R)
    ~(P · Q)
∴   (Q v R)

3. P
    Q
    ∴ P v Y

4. (P ⊃ Q) · (Q ⊃ R)
    ~ (P ⊃ Q)
    ∴ (Q ⊃ R)

Assigning Truth Values [105]

We have now covered building truth tables to prove validity. There is, however, an easier way. We know that an argument cannot be valid if it has all true premises and a false conclusion. That is why we use the conditional P ⊃ Q as our definition of validity for an argument, because if the antecedent "P" is true and the consequent "Q" is false, the whole thing is false. Thus, we know that if the premises are true and the conclusion is false, the argument is invalid.

What has this to do with a formal proof of validity? Simple, if we can find any argument form in which the conclusion is false and all the premises are true, then we know that argument form is invalid. But we have already looked at Truth Tables and have recognized how cumbersome Truth Tables can be, so how can this be any kind of "short cut" for determining validity?

What are we looking for in a Truth Table? We are looking for that one line where we find all true premises and a false conclusion, and if we find that line, we know that argument form is invalid regardless of what the other lines show. So, what we have to try and do is replicate that line by having a false conclusion with all true premises. We start with an argument form and then assign the truth values to the individual variables in order to make the conclusion "false", and then see if by assigning truth values *consistently*, we can assign the truth value of "true" to each premise while having a false conclusion.

For example:

1. P · X

2. R ⊃ Q

3. X v R

4. (P ⊃ R) v (X · Q)
    ∴ X ⊃ Q

Now, what do we have to do to show that the conclusion X ⊃ Q is false? What is the only way that a conditional proposition is false? Right, if the antecedent is true and the consequent is false, so the truth values of the letters X and Q are clear, the X is true and the Q is false, so we would list them this way:

X = T
Q = F

Now we know the truth values of two of the variables or letters. All of the variables or letters in the above argument are:

P
Q

R

X

We now know this much:

P =?
Q = F
R =?
X = T

Now, how do we determine the truth value of the other variables or letters (P and R)? Remember, in order to prove validity, we have to be able to show that this argument form cannot have a false conclusion without at least one premise being false, so we are trying to make all of the premises true to find out if it is invalid. However, if we discover that no matter what truth values we give P and R the premises cannot all be true, then we know that the argument is valid. But we must try to assign truth values so that we end up with all true premises and a false conclusion to show the argument form is invalid. However, keep in mind; we must assign the truth values consistently. In our efforts, we may discover that the argument form is actually valid because we end up with at least one false premise no matter what we do. So, let's begin.

We know what makes each of the propositions true, so we will try to do that now.

1. $P \cdot X$
2. $R \supset Q$
3. $X \vee R$
4. $(P \supset R) \vee (X \cdot Q)$
   $\therefore X \supset Q$

Ok, let's take the first premise:$P \cdot X$, what would it take to make that one true? We have already assigned the truth value of True to the "X" due to making the conclusion false, therefore, for this proposition to be true; the "P" must also be true. So now we know this much:

P =   T
Q =   F
R =   ?
X = T

Ok, what we have left is the "R" variable. What truth value does it need? Where does it appear? The first place it appears is in the second premise:$R \supset Q$. We already know that the "Q" is false, so in order for this premise to be true the "R" must be false as well.

So now we have the truth values assigned:

P =   T
Q =   F

R =   F

X =   T

Now let's apply those truth values consistently in the argument:

1.   P · X   T
2.   R ⊃ Q   T
3.   X v R   T
4.   (P ⊃ R) v (X · Q)   F
    ∴ X ⊃ Q   F

What we have discovered is that the fourth premise, (P ⊃ R) v (X · Q) is false based upon the truth values we have assigned to each variable. We already know that we cannot provide any other truth values for any of the variables in order to keep the other premises true. So, we have to conclude that this argument form is in fact valid, because with a false conclusion at least one premise has to be false, and in fact we find that to be the case.

Let's try another one;

1.   (P v Q) v (S ⊃ Z)
2.   (S · X) · (Y v Z)
3.   Y ⊃ Z
4.   [(P ⊃ Z) v (Y v S)] · ~[(R ⊃ X) ⊃ ~(Y v Q)]
    ∴ Z ⊃ Y

Once again, we have a conditional for a conclusion, so we know the "Z" must be true and the "Y" must be false in order for us to have a false conclusion, because remember, we are trying to find all true premises and a false conclusion to see if this argument form is invalid, however, if we cannot find all true premises and a false conclusion, then we know it is valid.

Here are the variables (or letters) in this problem:

P

Q

R

S

X

Y

Z

Right now we know the truth values of two of the variables:

P = ?
Q = ?
R = ?
S = ?
X = ?
Y = F
Z = T

Looking at the argument again, we will start with the first premise to determine the truth values of each of the variables in that premise, and so on.

1. $(P \lor Q) \lor (S \supset Z)$
2. $(S \cdot X) \cdot (Y \lor Z)$
3. $Y \supset Z$
4. $[(P \supset Z) \lor (Y \lor S)] \cdot \sim[(R \supset X) \supset \sim(Y \lor Q)]$

   $\therefore Z \supset Y$

We know that Z is true, and in the first premise, with a v all we need is one side of the v to be true to make the whole thing true. With the Z in the consequent position of the conditional $S \supset Z$ the S can have any value, either true or false for $S \supset Z$ to be true. So, let's just pick S to be true, (we will see later why we went that way).

Now how about P and Q? With $S \supset Z$ being true, it does not matter what P and Q are because the first premise is already true. So, we may have to look at where else P and Q appear. They do appear in the fourth premise $[(P \supset Z) \lor (Y \lor S)] \cdot \sim[(R \supset X) \supset \sim(Y \lor Q)]$. Now what would it take to make this premise true?

OK, we already know that Z is true, S is true and Y is false, so let's apply those values and see what we are left with. We will start inside the brackets on the left side of the " $\cdot$ "; $[(P \supset Z) \lor (Y \lor S)]$. Now we know that for a premise that is conjoined by a " $\cdot$ " both sides have to be true. So we will start with $[(P \supset Z) \lor (Y \lor S)]$. This part of the premise being a "v" we know that just one of the parentheticals has to be true. So, if Z is true it does not matter what P is because a true consequent in a conditional will always make that conditional true. We also know that the Y is false but the S is true, so Y v S is true, so both sides of the v are true, and we still do not know the truth value of P. Let's pick one, how about False just for some variety? (Is this an arbitrary selection? Yes, because sometimes you have to try trial and error in cases like this.) So now our variables have the following truth values:

P = F
Q =?
R =?
S = T

X =?
Y = F
Z = T

OK, we still do not know the truth values of Q, R or X. Let's look at the bracketed statement to the right of the "·" in the fourth premise:~[(R ⊃ X) ⊃ ~(Y v Q)]. Now we know that when a tilde ~ appears it negates whatever it applies to, so we want the statement inside the brackets [ ] to be false so that with the ~ the statement is then true. OK, so we see the consequent of the bracketed statement:~(Y v Q) and realize that the statement inside the parentheses should be true so that with the ~ it becomes false. Why? Remember, we need to make the whole bracketed statement false so that with the ~ it becomes true, and we know that with a conditional ⊃ if the consequent is false and the antecedent is true, the conditional is then false, which is what we want. If the Y is false, then we have to make the Q true, that way Y v Q would be true, but with the ~ on the outside of the parentheses makes it false. Now we have a false consequent, we just have to make the antecedent true. We do not have truth values assigned yet to R or X. If we look at the other premises, where else do R and X appear?

1. (P v Q) v (S ⊃ Z)
2. (S · X) · (Y v Z)
3. Y ⊃ Z
4. [(P ⊃ Z) v (Y v S)] · ~[(R ⊃ X) ⊃ ~(Y v Q)]

    ∴ Z ⊃ Y

(We see that X appears in the second premise, and with it being a "·" statement on the left of the "·" for the whole premise, and we know that both sides of a "·" have to be true for the whole thing to be true, and so if the S is true the X must be true. So we will assign the truth value of true to X. To recap, here is where we are right now in truth value assignments:

P = F
Q = T
R =?
S = T
X = T
Y = F
Z = T

With the X being true, and as the consequent in the parenthetical antecedent of the bracketed statement:~[(R ⊃ X) ⊃ ~(Y v Q)] we know that it does not matter what the truth value of R is because it does not appear anywhere else, so we will assign the truth value of false just for some variety.

P = F
Q = T
R = F
S = T
X = T
Y = F
Z = T

Now we have assigned all of the truth values, now let's see if we have all true premises and a false conclusion.

1. $(P_F \lor Q_T) \lor (S_T \supset Z_T)$ T
2. $(S_T \cdot X_T) \cdot (Y_F \lor Z_T)$ T
3. $Y_F \supset Z_T$ T
4. $[(P_F \supset Z_T) \lor (Y_F \lor S_T)] \cdot \sim[(R_F \supset X_T) \supset \sim(Y_F \lor Q_T)]$ T
    $\therefore Z_T \supset Y_F$ F

Please note that I have indicated what truth value we have assigned to each variable by listing them like this: We assigned the truth value of False to the variable "P" and so have P_F, and so on.

We have shown that this argument form is invalid, because we were able to create all true premises and a false conclusion while assigning truth values consistently to each variable.

The basic concept in assigning truth values to prove validity is to assign those truth values to each variable that will result in all true premises and a false conclusion. If you cannot do that, if no matter how you assign truth values (and you have to assign them consistently) you end up with at least one false premise along with the false conclusion, then you know the argument form is valid.

EXERCISES
Now try these out and see which are valid and which invalid:

1. $(P \cdot Q) v (R \supset X)$
    $X v Y$
    $\sim(X \cdot R) v (P v Q)$
    $\sim[\sim(P \supset Q) \cdot (R v Y)]$
    $\therefore \quad P \supset Q$

2. $\{[(P \cdot Q) v (Z \supset Y)] \supset [(R \supset X) \cdot (Z \supset P)]\} v \{[(Q \supset X) \cdot (R \supset Z)] v [(P \cdot R) \cdot (Q \cdot Z)]\}$
    $P \supset Q$
    $Z \supset Y$
    $(R \supset X) v (P \cdot Q)$
    $\therefore X v Y$

3. $X v Y$
    $P \supset Q$
    $Z \cdot R$
    $(R \supset X) v (P \cdot Q)$
    $\therefore X \supset P$

4. $(P \supset Q) v (X \cdot Z)$
    $(R \supset Q) \cdot (P \supset Z)$

X v Z

R · P

(P ⊃ R) ⊃ (X ⊃ Z)

∴ R · P

5. [(P · Q) ⊃ (X v Z)] v [~(Z v X) · (W · Y)]

~[(P · Q) ⊃ (X v Z)]

∴ ~ [~(Z v X) · (W · Y)]

REVIEW GLOSSARY

Truth Values =	The two truth values are "T" for true and "F" for false.
Assigning Truth Values =	Beginning with the conclusion, assigning truth values of either True or False to try and have a false conclusion with all true premises in order to prove invalidity.
Valid Argument Form =	Any argument form that does NOT have all true premises and a false conclusion.

Chapter Twelve

Formal Proofs of Validity: The Elementary Valid Argument Forms (EVAF)[106]

While the truth table is a very handy and effective tool in proving validity, one can easily see that with the formula 2^n the size of a truth table would quickly become unwieldy. We have already seen that with three variables there are eight lines, and with four variables there would be sixteen lines and with five variables there would be thirty two lines. The problem is most arguments rarely have as few as three variables! So, what else can we do? Earlier in this book we discussed four different valid argument forms when we were discussing syllogisms. Remember what they were?

> Disjunctive Syllogism
> Pure Hypothetical Syllogism
> Mixed Hypothetical Syllogism: Modus Ponens & Modus Tollens

If we were to write these in symbolic form we would have the following:

> Disjunctive Syllogism
> p ∨ q
> ~p
∴   q

> Pure Hypothetical Syllogism
> p ⊃ q
> q ⊃ r
∴   p ⊃ r

> Mixed Hypothetical Syllogism: Modus Ponens
> p ⊃ q
> p
∴   q

> Mixed Hypothetical Syllogism: Modus Tollens
> p ⊃ q
> ~q
∴   ~p

How does this help us come up with formal proofs for a deductive argument? If we can show these forms exist within the argument, and because we know that these forms are always valid, and we can arrive at the conclusion of the argument using these and other valid argument forms, then we know the argument itself is valid.

So, if we take the argument:

> If Louise was hired then she went to Des Moines.
> If she went to Des Moines then she bought a house there.
> If she bought a house there then she would have a Des Moines address.
> She does not have a Des Moines address.
> Either Louise was hired or they hired someone else.
> Someone else was hired.

If we were to translate this into symbolic form:
L = Louise was hired; D = she went to Des Moines; B = she bought a house in Des Moines; A = Des Moines Address; H = Hired someone else

1. L ⊃ D
2. D ⊃ B
3. B ⊃ A
4. ~A
5. L v H
   ∴ H
6. L ⊃ B 1, 2 Pure Hypothetical Syllogism (H.S.)
7. L ⊃ A 6, 3 H.S.
8. ~L 7, 4 Modus Tollens (M.T.)
9. H 5, 8 Disjunctive Syllogism (D.S.)

Thus, we now have a formal proof of the validity of this argument. Because we were able to reach the conclusion "H" by using valid argument forms, we have shown that this argument itself is valid. How did we do this, take a look at the above argument as we applied the different valid argument forms:

1. L ⊃ D
2. D ⊃ B
3. B ⊃ A
4. ~A
5. L v H
   ∴ H
6. We arrived at L ⊃ B by applying H.S. to lines 1 and 2 so that it would look like this:
   1. L ⊃ D
   2. D ⊃ B
   ∴ L ⊃ B

7. We then applied H.S. again, but this time to lines 6 and 3, so that it looked like this:

    6.   L ⊃ B
    3.   B ⊃ A
    ∴   L ⊃ A

8. Then we applied Modus Tollens (MT) to lines 7 and 4 to come up with this:

    7.   L ⊃ A
    4.   ~A
    ∴   ~L

9. We can now arrive at the conclusion H by applying Disjunctive Syllogism, DS to lines 5 and 8 to get this:

    5.   L v H
    8.   ~L
    ∴   H

So how did I know what valid argument forms to apply? The way it works, for example, take premises 1 and 2. You look at them and you see what looks like the two premises of a pure hypothetical syllogism, but what is missing? Right, the conclusion, which in this case becomes line 6. Then, if we take line 6 and look at line 3, what do we see? Exactly, another set of premises for a hypothetical syllogism, and what is missing is the conclusion, which becomes line 7. Now, we see ~A in line 4, and we know that we now have L ⊃ A in line 7, and you put these together and you have Modus Tollens. When you apply Modus Tollens to line 7 and 4 respectively, you get line 8. Now, look at line 5, and you know you want to isolate the "H" for your conclusion, so what could you do? Well, line 5 is a disjunctive, and we know we can have a disjunctive syllogism which would isolate the "H" if only we had a ~L, but we do, in line 8. That yields line 9 which is our conclusion thus proving this argument form is valid.

If the four logically valid argument forms can help us determine the validity of complex arguments, are there other valid argument forms that can be proven with truth tables to always be valid? Yes, there are.

The first of these additional valid argument forms is called **"Constructive Dilemma"**[107] or C.D. This is the form of that valid argument:

    (p ⊃ q) · (r ⊃ s)
    p v r
∴   q v s

The definition of a Constructive Dilemma is this: An argument form in which the first premise is made up of two compound conditional propositions in a conjunct followed by a second premise made up of the antecedents of the two compound conditional propositions placed in a disjunctive relationship which then implies the conclusion which is made up of the disjunction of the consequents of the first premise.

Let's break this valid argument form down:

$(p \supset q) \cdot (r \supset s)$

If you have two conditionals in a conjunct, like the above, and then you have as one of the premises of the argument the two antecedents of these two conditionals in a disjunct:

$p \vee r$

Then the conclusion can be the two consequents in a disjunct:

$\therefore \quad q \vee s$

This is always valid, and if you constructed a truth table you would find that you never have a line in the truth table where you have a false conclusion and all true premises, because it is always valid.

The next of the additional valid argument forms is called **"Absorption"**[108] or Abs. This is the form:

$$p \supset q$$
$$\therefore \quad p \supset (p \cdot q)$$

The definition of Absorption (Abs) is this: Any compound conditional proposition implies the conditional made up of the antecedent and the consequent in a conjunction as the consequent in a conditional with the original antecedent. Below is the truth table to prove the constancy of validity of this argument form:

p	q	$p \cdot q$	$p \supset q$	$p \supset (p \cdot q)$
T	T	T	T	T
T	F	F	F	F
F	T	F	T	T
F	F	F	T	T

As you can see, the only case in which the conclusion $p \supset (p \cdot q)$ is false, the premise is also false. Thus, we know that in every instance, this argument form known as Absorption is always valid.

The next additional valid argument form is referred to as **"Simplification"**[109] or Simp. This is the form:

$$p \cdot q$$
$$\therefore \quad p$$

This means that if you have a conjunct you can isolate the left side of the conjunct, as in this case, the "p" was on the left of the • and thus we could isolate it.

Again, the truth table will demonstrate that this is always a valid argument form:

p	q	p · q
T	T	T
T	F	F
F	T	F
F	F	F

You can see that every time "p", the conclusion, is false, the premise p · q is also false, thus always valid.

The next valid argument form is referred to as **"Conjunction"**[110] or Conj. This is the form:

       p

       q

∴   p · q

If you have two variables in an argument, or two compound propositions in an argument, you can conjoin them as a conjunct. So, if you had the following:

P ⊃ Q

X ∨ R

You could conjoin them to be:(P ⊃ Q) • (X ∨ R)
The truth tables demonstrate the validity of this argument form as well:

p	q	p · q
T	T	T
T	F	F
F	T	F
F	F	F

As you can see, any time the conclusion p · q is false one or both of the premises is false.

The final elementary valid argument form is referred to as **"Addition"**[111] or Add. This is the form:

       p

∴   p ∨ q

This is one of those odd valid argument forms that appear to add a component out of thin air! Where did the "q" come from? It does not matter; the following truth table demonstrates that this is indeed a valid argument form:

p	q	p ∨ q
T	T	T
T	F	T
F	T	T
F	F	F

The point of this valid argument form is that it does not matter what the truth value of the mysterious "q" is, this will always be valid. In other words, this particular valid argument form comes in very handy in an argument you are trying to solve where the letter you need is missing, if you can isolate a single variable in the argument "tree" then you can add the letter you need by Addition.

Now to summarize the nine **Elementary Valid Argument Forms (EVAF)**:[112]

1. Modus Ponens (M.P)
2. Modus Tollens (M.T.)
3. Pure Hypothetical Syllogism (H.S.)
4. Disjunctive Syllogism (D.S.)
5. Constructive Dilemma (C.D.)
6. Absorption (Abs.)
7. Simplification (Simp.)
8. Conjunction (Conj.)
9. Addition (Add.)

How to Provide a Formal Proof of Validity for a Complex Argument

At the beginning of this chapter we talked about formal proof of validity and proceeded to give a rather simple argument that was not complete, that is, it was enthymematic. Remember we had gone over a few chapters ago about enthymemes, that is, an argument with missing propositions, either premises or the conclusion. In symbolic logic, we will have arguments that will have the conclusion but will be missing several premises that would help us reach that conclusion. If we can use valid argument forms to create those missing premises and thus arrive at the conclusion, then we know we have a valid argument even if some of it is missing.

How do we go about doing this? First, it helps a great deal if you have memorized the nine Elementary Valid Argument Forms (EVAF), memorizing them will assist you in recognizing them in the body of the complex argument to give you an idea of where to start. Take this argument for example:

1. A ⊃ B
2. B ⊃ C
3. ~C
4. A v D
∴ D

Now, how do we get to "D" from the four premises? Is it immediately obvious? Not really. But take a look at lines 1 and 2 and what do you see? Do you see part of a pure hypothetical syllogism? If you did, then what would be the outcome of that hypothetical syllogism? If you said A ⊃ C, you would be correct. So, we write that down as line 5 and indicate how we arrived at that by listing the lines, in proper order, and indicate by the letters H.S. that we used the Elementary Valid Argument Form referred to as Hypothetical Syllogism. So, our formal proof would look like this, so far…

1. A ⊃ B
2. B ⊃ C
3. ~C
4. A v D
∴ D
5. A ⊃ C 1, 2 H.S.

Now, look at lines 5 – 3, do you see another possible Elementary Valid Argument Form? Do you see Modus Tollens? If you did, did you get ~A as the result? If so, then you know that you listed line 5 first and then line 3 to get line 6 using M.T., so our formal proof of validity would now look like this…

1. A ⊃ B
2. B ⊃ C
3. ~C
4. A v D
∴ D
5. A ⊃ C 1, 2 H.S.
6. ~A   5, 3 M.T.

But why did I go for line 5 instead of line 2? It is called strategy. I knew that I needed to isolate the "D" which is found in a disjunctive in line 4, and what I needed was a disjunctive syllogism, which means, for me to get the "D" meant I needed a ~A, which I could get using MT with lines 5 and 3, NOT lines 2 and 3. Could I have solved the problem using lines 2 and 3 in MT? Yes! It would have taken a few more steps, but try it yourself and see if you can find the alternate solution. We always try to find the solution that requires the fewest number of steps. The fewer the steps the more elegant the solution.

Now, do you see the final step in this formal proof of validity? Do you see a disjunctive syllogism? If you did, then you know you have completed the formal proof of validity. You knew to take line 4 and line 6 and come up with the conclusion. So now our formal proof of validity would look like this:

1. A ⊃ B
2. B ⊃ C
3. ~C
4. A v D
∴ D
5. A ⊃ C 1, 2 H.S.
6. ~A   5, 3 M.T.
7. D   4, 6 D.S.

Let's add another wrinkle to this process with this next example:

1. B ⊃ C
2. Q ⊃ Z
3. B
4. ~C
∴ Z v X

Ok, now what is going on here? It may be difficult to see any EVAF right off, because if you look at lines 1 and 2, that is not what you need for a Hypothetical Syllogism, and if you look at lines 3 and 4, you could create a Conjunction, but for what purpose? It will not get you closer to the conclusion which appears to come out of nowhere. You have to be thinking here that you will probably be using such things as Addition and Constructive Dilemma. Now why am I saying that? What do I see? I see line 3, the "B" standing there isolated. Now, I could use lines 1 and 3 to have Modus Ponens and end up with "C", but what would I gain from that move because we already have a "~C" in line 4 and that would create a contradiction, and I don't want that. So that must not be the way to go. Now, if I made lines 1 and 2 a Conjunction, then used addition with line 3, I could end up with a Constructive Dilemma, like so…

1. B ⊃ C
2. Q ⊃ Z
3. B
4. ~C
∴ Z v X
5. (B ⊃ C) · (Q ⊃ Z) 1, 2 Conj..
6. B v Q 3, Add
7. C v Z 5, 6 C.D.

Remember, with Constructive Dilemma I need to have the two conditionals in a conjunct, and so I conjoined lines 1 and 2. Now I need a disjunct of the two antecedents, and because the B is the antecedent of the first conditional I know I can use Addition to add the Q and so get the disjunct B v Q. Now why did I go this way? I know that if I can isolate the Z I can add the X to the Z to get the conclusion. I just have to isolate the Z. To do that, because I already have a ~C in my argument, I know that if I can get a disjunct like C v Z, then by applying the ~C in a disjunctive syllogism, I can isolate the Z. I can get that disjunct through C.D. by putting the two consequents in a disjunct as a result of having the disjunct already of the two antecedents. Let's look at the graphics of this process:

This is what I want to construct to get my conclusion...

$(B \supset C) \cdot (Q \supset Z)$
$B \vee Q$
$\therefore C \vee Z$

Can you see in the body of the original argument the elements we need for this C.D.? Look again:

1. $B \supset C$
2. $Q \supset Z$
3. B
4. $\sim C$
$\therefore \ Z \vee X$

So far so good, I have now C v Z and if I look at line 4 I have a ~C which combined with line 7 will give me a Disjunctive Syllogism, so it would look like this...

1. $B \supset C$
2. $Q \supset Z$
3. B
4. $\sim C$
$\therefore \ Z \vee X$
5. $(B \supset C) \cdot (Q \supset Z)$ 1, 2 Conj..
6. $B \vee Q$ 3, Add
7. $C \vee Z$ 5, 6 C.D.
8. Z 7, 4 D.S.

But wait, I'm not quite done yet, the conclusion is Z v X, where did the "X" come from? While it may seem strange, you can use the EVAF known as "Addition" to finally arrive at your conclusion by simply adding in a "v" relationship the "X" you are needing, so now the final solution looks like this...

1.   B ⊃ C
2.   Q ⊃ Z
3.   B
4.   ~C
∴ Z v X
5.   B v Q 3, Add.
6.   (B ⊃ C) · (Q ⊃ Z) 1, 2 Conj..
7.   C v Z 6, 5 C.D.
8.   Z 7, 4 D.S.
9.   Z v X 8, Add.

Let's try one more, let's see how many of the nine of the Elementary Valid Argument Forms we can use in the following complex argument:

1.   P ⊃ Q
2.   Q ⊃ R
3.   Q ⊃ P
4.   Q
5.   ~P
∴ P · R

What do you see right away? Several options. Look at lines 1 and 2, Hypothetical Syllogism, or lines 3 and 5, Modus Tollens, or lines 2 or 3 and 4, either combination would lead to Modus Ponens. However, the answer we want is P · R. Now there are several ways of getting to this conclusion.

The simplest would be to isolate a P and an R and then through Conjunction, you have your proof. We could do that through a series of Modus Ponens, like below…

1.   P ⊃ Q
2.   Q ⊃ R
3.   Q ⊃ P
4.   Q
5.   ~P
∴ P · R
6.   P 3,4 M.P.
7.   R 2, 4 M.P.
8.   P · R 6, 7 Conj.

OK, that is one way, but remember, we want to use as many of the Elementary Valid Argument Forms as possible for this exercise, so, let's try another route. What this will show you is that in some complex argument forms there is more than one way to provide a proof. While it is true the more elegant proof is the one that takes fewer steps, for now, we are just interested in using as many different Elementary Valid Argument Forms as possible.

So, let's try the following:

1. P ⊃ Q
2. Q ⊃ R
3. Q ⊃ P
4. Q
5. ~P

∴ P · R

6. P ⊃ R   1, 2 H.S.
7. P ⊃ (P · R) 6, Abs. (You can now see our sought after conclusion, but how to isolate the "P"?)
8. ~Q 3, 5 M.T.
9. Q v P 4, Add. (why did I add the P to the Q? That's right, to isolate the P through D.S.)
10. P 9, 8 D.S.
11. P · R 7, 10 M.P.

Now, granted, this is not as elegant as the one that took only 8 lines, but it does show how the same argument can be proven to be quite valid with two completely different approaches.

REVIEW GLOSSARY

The Nine Elementary Valid Argument Forms (EVAF)

1. Modus Ponens (M.P)

$$p \supset q$$
$$p$$
$$\therefore \quad q$$

2. Modus Tollens (M.T.)

$$p \supset q$$
$$\sim q$$
$$\therefore \quad \sim p$$

3. Pure Hypothetical Syllogism (H.S.)

$$p \supset q$$
$$q \supset r$$
$$\therefore \quad p \supset r$$

4. Disjunctive Syllogism (D.S.)

$$p \vee q$$
$$\sim p$$
$$\therefore \quad q$$

5. Constructive Dilemma (C.D.)

$$(p \supset q) \cdot (r \supset s)$$
$$p \vee r$$
$$\therefore \quad q \vee s$$

6. Absorption (Abs.)

$$p \supset q$$
$$\therefore \quad p \supset (p \cdot q)$$

7. Simplification (Simp.)

$$p \cdot q$$
$$\therefore \quad p$$

8. Conjunction (Conj.)

$$p$$
$$q$$
$$\therefore \quad p \cdot q$$

9. Addition (Add.)

$$p$$
$$\therefore \quad p \vee r$$

EXERCISES *(See the back of the book for some answers)*

Using the EVAF's, provide a formal proof for the following:

1.　　1.　P

　　　　2.　Q
　∴　　P · Q　　　　(this should only require one step)
　　　　3.

2.　　1.　　P ⊃ Q

　　　　2.　　Q ⊃ R
　　　　3.　　R ⊃ X
　　　　4.　　P
　∴　　　X　　　　　　(How many steps do you suppose this could take?)

3.　　1.　　(A ⊃ B) v (X ⊃ D)

　　　　2.　　B
　　　　3.　　B ⊃ X
　　　　4.　　~(A ⊃ B)
　　　　5.　　D ⊃ B
　∴　　　X · D　　　　(How many steps do you suppose this could take?)
　　　　6.
　　　　7.
　　　　8.
　　　　9.

Fill in the blanks provided how I arrived at each step using the EVAF:

4.　　1.　　P ⊃ Q

　　　　2.　　~Q
　　　　3.　　R ⊃ S · Q ⊃ S
　　　　4.　　P v R
　∴　　　S
　　　　5.　　R ⊃ S　　　　_____
　　　　6.　　(P ⊃ Q) · (R ⊃ S)　_____
　　　　7.　　Q v S　　　　_____
　　　　8.　　S　　　　_____

5. 1.   X ⊃ T
    2.   R ⊃ X
    3.   R v X
    ∴   (R · X) v (X · T)
    4.   R ⊃ (R · X)   _____
    5.   X ⊃ (X · T)   _____
    6.   R ⊃ (R · X) · X ⊃ (X · T)   _____
    7.   (R · X) v (X · T)   _____

6. 1.   (P ⊃ Q) · (S v T)
    2.   (Q ⊃ R) · (Z ⊃ Y)
    3.   P
    ∴   P · R
    4.   (P ⊃ Q)   _____
    5.   (Q ⊃ R)   _____
    6.   (P ⊃ R)   _____
    7.   P ⊃ (P · R)   _____
    8.   P · R   _____

7. 1.   (P ⊃ Q) · (S v T)
    2.   (Q ⊃ R) · (Z ⊃ Y)
    3.   P
    ∴   R
    4.   (P ⊃ Q)   _____
    5.   (Q ⊃ R)   _____
    6.   (P ⊃ R)   _____
    7.   P ⊃ (P · R)   _____
    8.   P · R   _____
    9.   R · P   _____
    10. R   _____

Provide a formal proof for this argument:

8. 1.   (F ⊃ G) · (H ⊃ I)
    2.   J ⊃ K
    3.   (F v J) · (H v L)
    ∴.   G v K

Chapter Thirteen

FORMAL PROOFS OF VALIDITY: THE RULES OF REPLACEMENT[113]

W hile the nine EVAF's are very handy, and do help us a lot, what do you do if you
have this problem?

$$P \lor R$$
$$\therefore \quad R \lor P$$

None of the nine EVAF's will help you on this one, as simple as it may appear. Or, how
about this one?

$$\sim(P \lor Q)$$
$$\therefore \quad \sim Q$$

Again, none of the nine EVAF's will help you with this problem, even though it is easily
proven to be valid.

Or how about this one?

$$P \equiv Q$$
$$\sim(\sim P \cdot \sim Q)$$
$$\therefore \quad P \cdot Q$$

Intriguing, isn't it? The point is, we have just barely begun to find ways of demonstrating a
formal proof of validity. The rules of replacement are simply this, we can infer any statement
by replacing that statement with a logically equivalent statement. For example: Double
Negation. We know that the negation of "p" is "~p", but if we use Double Negation; ~~p,
we realize that ~~p is the same as "p".

The following are the ten **rules of replacement**, that is, each of the statements listed is
accompanied by its logically equivalent replacement, which means, you can replace one
with the other. The ± is a symbol which simply means what is on one side means the same
thing as what is on the other side, so if you start with what is on the left you can use what
is on the right and vice versa.

1. De Morgan's Theorems (De M): ~(p · q) ± (~p ∨ ~q)
                                                   ~(p ∨ q) ± (~p · ~q)
2. Commutation (Com):   (p ∨ q) ± (q ∨ p)
                                                   (p · q) ± (q · p)

3. Association (Assoc): $[p \lor (q \lor r)] \pm [(p \lor q) \lor r]$
$[p \cdot (q \cdot r)] \pm [(p \cdot q) \cdot r]$

4. Distribution (Dist): $[p \cdot (q \lor r)] \pm [(p \cdot q) \lor (p \cdot r)]$
$[p \lor (p \cdot r)] \pm [(p \lor q) \cdot (p \lor r)]$

5. Double Negation (D.N.) $p \pm {\sim}{\sim}p$

6. Transposition (Trans) $(p \supset q) \pm ({\sim}q \supset {\sim}p)$

7. Material Implication (Impl) $(p \supset q) \pm ({\sim}p \lor q)$

8. Material Equivalence (Equiv) $(p \equiv q) \pm [(p \supset q) \cdot (q \supset p)]$
$(p \equiv q) \pm [(p \cdot q) \lor ({\sim}p \cdot {\sim}q)]$

9. Exportation (Exp) $[(p \cdot q) \supset r] \pm [p \supset (q \supset r)]$

10. Tautology (Taut) $p \pm (p \lor p)$
$p \pm (p \cdot p)$

The use of the nine EVAF's is different than these rules of replacement. **In the EVAF's, you can only apply the Elementary Valid Argument Form to the whole line in the argument**, *whereas with these ten rules of Replacement, you can apply them to only part of the line.*[114] For example:

1. $(Q \cdot P) \supset (X \supset R)$
2. $P \cdot Q$
∴ $X \supset R$

Ok, so how would you provide a formal proof of this argument's validity? It sort of looks like Modus Ponens, doesn't it? But there is something wrong, isn't there. Look at line 2, it reads $(P \cdot Q)$ and that is not what is in line 1. That reads $(Q \cdot P)$, so what would we have to do? It would look like this:

1. $(Q \cdot P) \supset (X \supset R)$
2. $P \cdot Q$
∴ $X \supset R$
3. $(P \cdot Q) \supset (X \supset R)$ 1, Com
4. $X \supset R$ 3, 2 M.P.

As you can see, we applied Commutation to only part of line 1, but it was enough to provide the proof we needed.

The point of the Rules of Replacement is simply this, we can substitute $(P \cdot Q)$ for $(Q \cdot P)$ because they are logically equivalent, that is, they mean the same thing. There is no loss in meaning by replacing one with the other.

The best way to learn how to use the Rules of Replacement is simply to give them a try. Here are a few examples:

Provide a Formal Proof for the following by using the Rules of Replacement as well as the nine EVAFs:

1. P ≡ Q
2. ~(P · Q)
3. P
∴   ~(P v Q)
4. (P ⊃ Q) · (Q ⊃ P) 1, Equiv
5. P ⊃ Q 4, Simp
6. Q 5, 3 M.P.
7. ~P v ~Q 2, De M
8. ~Q v ~P 7, Com
9. ~P 8, 6 D.S.
10. (Q ⊃ P) · (P ⊃ Q) 4, Com
11. Q ⊃ P 10, Simp
12. ~Q 11, 9 M.T.
13. ~P · ~Q 9, 12 Conj
    ~(P v Q) De M

OK, did you follow the logic of this proof? When we see the P ≡ Q we know right away that we can replace that with two compound conditional propositions in a conjunctive; (P ⊃ Q) · (Q ⊃ P) by way of Material Equivalence. This is something we want to do simply because there is a lot we can do with this particular conjunctive. It is simply a good idea to use Material Equivalence any time we can. We also see ~(P · Q), which we also recognize as De Morgan's Theorem, and so we would naturally try to use that as well. In other words, as you see what looks familiar in either the EVAF's or the Rules of Replacement, we need to pursue those. We see that the conclusion looks also a lot like De Morgan's Theorem, and so we want to see if there is any way we can isolate a ~P and a ~Q, because if we can, then we can put those two together in a conjunction, which looks like the other side of ~(P v Q) in De Morgan's Theorem. So, that also helps us with our strategy.

Strategy is important in trying to decide how to proceed. The difficulty with developing a good strategy is the need to know all of the EVAF's and the Rules of Replacement. That is a total of 19 rules we need to know. We need to know them well enough we can "see" them in a problem we are working on in order to help develop a strategy in providing a formal proof of validity.

For example,

Let's go back to the problem above:

1. P ≡ Q
2. ~(P · Q)
3. P
∴   ~ (P v Q)

We always want to start with the conclusion. Why? Simple, the conclusion will point us in the direction we want to go to find the solution. The first thing we want to do is re-write the conclusion in as many ways as we can using the Rules of Replacement. Why will we do that? Again, simple, by looking at all of the equivalent ways of writing ~(P v Q) one of the ways we will re-write it will probably show us what we need to do to find the solution.

So, what are all the ways we can re-write ~(P v Q)? Using DeMorgan's Theorem we get (~P · ~Q). We know (~P · ~Q) is logically equivalent to ~(P v Q). This helps us realize if we could isolate a ~P and ~Q then we could use conjunction to get (~P · ~Q) and then use DeMorgan's Theorem to get the conclusion ~(P v Q). Knowing that, we can go back up and re-write all of the premises, which we did in the above example.

Now, if we continue with this same example, how else could you write line 2 above? (~P v ~Q) by DeMorgan's Theorem. Now with ~P v ~Q I could use line 3 and have a Disjunctive Syllogism. Now I know this is not how I solved it in the first example, but there are often more than one way to show a formal proof of validity. So, it would look like this:

1. P ≡ Q
2. ~(P · Q)
3. P
∴ ~(P v Q) (re-writing the conclusion to be (~P · ~Q) by way of DeMorgan's Theorem)
4. ~P v ~Q   2, D.M.
5. ~Q   4, 3 DS
6. (P ⊃ Q) · (Q ⊃ P) 1, Equiv
7. (P ⊃ Q)   6, Simp
8. ~P   7, 5 MT
9. ~P · ~Q   8, 5 Conj
10. ~(P v Q)   9, DM

We have a formal proof of validity, and it is more elegant than the first time we tried it above.

REVIEW GLOSSARY

Rules of Replacement

1. De Morgan's Theorems (De M): $\sim(p \cdot q) \pm (\sim p \vee \sim q)$
   $\sim(p \vee q) \pm (\sim p \cdot \sim q)$

2. Commutation (Com): $(p \vee q) \pm (q \vee p)$
   $(p \cdot q) \pm (q \cdot p)$

3. Association (Assoc): $[p \vee (q \vee r)] \pm [(p \vee q) \vee r]$
   $[p \cdot (q \cdot r)] \pm [(p \cdot q) \cdot r]$

4. Distribution (Dist): $[p \cdot (q \vee r)] \pm [(p \cdot q) \vee (p \cdot r)]$
   $[p \vee (p \cdot r)] \pm [(p \vee q) \cdot (p \vee r)]$

5. Double Negation (D.N.) $p \pm \sim\sim p$
6. Transposition (Trans) $(p \supset q) \pm (\sim q \supset \sim p)$
7. Material Implication (Impl) $(p \supset q) \pm (\sim p \vee q)$
8. Material Equivalence (Equiv) $(p \equiv q) \pm [(p \supset q) \cdot (q \supset p)]$
   $(p \equiv q) \pm [(p \cdot q) \vee (\sim p \cdot \sim q)]$

9. Exportation (Exp) $[(p \cdot q) \supset r] \pm [p \supset (q \supset r)]$
10. Tautology (Taut) $p \pm (p \vee p)$
    $p \pm (p \cdot p)$

The Nine Elementary Valid Argument Forms (EVAF)

1. Modus Ponens (M.P)
   $p \supset q$
   p
   $\therefore \quad q$

2. Modus Tollens (M.T.)
   $p \supset q$
   $\sim q$
   $\therefore \quad \sim p$

3. Pure Hypothetical Syllogism (H.S.)
   $p \supset q$
   $q \supset r$
   $\therefore \quad p \supset r$

4. Disjunctive Syllogism (D.S.)
   $p \vee q$
   $\sim p$
   $\therefore \quad q$

5. Constructive Dilemma (C.D.)
   $(p \supset q) \cdot (r \supset s)$
   $p \vee r$
   $\therefore \quad q \vee s$

6. Absorption (Abs.)
   $p \supset q$
   $\therefore \quad p \supset (p \cdot q)$

7. Simplification (Simp.)
   $p \cdot q$
   $\therefore \quad p$

8. Conjunction (Conj.)
   p
   q
   $\therefore \quad p \cdot q$

9. Addition (Add.)
   p
   $\therefore \quad p \vee q$

(Check the back of the book for some answers)

Provide a formal proof using both EVAF's and the Rules of Replacement.

1. 1. Q
   2. S
   ∴ [P ⊃ (Q ⊃ S)]

2. 1. P ⊃ Q
   2. Q ⊃ R
   3. X ⊃ P
   4. P ⊃ ~X
   ∴ ~P · ~X (What's another way to write this using DeMorgan's?)

EXERCISE II

3. 1. P ⊃ Q
   2. P
   ∴ ~(~P v ~Q) (How would you re-write this?)
   3.
   4.
   5.

4. 1.   Q ⊃ R
    2.   ~P ⊃ X
    3.   P ⊃ Q
    4.   R ⊃ Z
  ∴ ~X ⊃ Z
    5.
    6.
    7.
    8.
    9.

5. 1.   (P · Q) ⊃ R
    2.   ~(Q ⊃ R)
    3.   X ⊃ P
    4.   Z ⊃ R
  ∴ X ⊃ (X · R)   (Another way to re-write the conclusion is: X ⊃ R by Abs.)
    5.   P ⊃ (Q ⊃ R)   1, Exp
    6.   ~P   5, 2 MT
    7.   ~P ∨ R   6, Add
    8.   P ⊃ R   7, Impl
    9.   X ⊃ R   3, 8 HS
    10.   X ⊃ (X · R)   9, Abs.

6. 1.   P ⊃ Q
    2.   ~Q
    ∴P ≡ Q
    3.
    4.
    5.
    6.

EXERCISE III

7. 1.   Q ⊃ P
    2.   P ⊃ R
    3.   R ⊃ Z
    4.   Z ⊃ X
    ∴ Q ⊃ X
    5.
    6.
    7.

8. 1.   P ⊃ (Q ⊃ R)
    2.   ~R
    3.   P
    ∴ ~Q

9. 1. $P \supset (P \cdot Q)$
   2.   P
  ∴ $\sim Q \supset Z$

10. 1. $\sim P \lor (Q \cdot R)$
   2. $(\sim R \supset \sim P) \supset (Z \supset X)$
   3. $(Z \supset X) \supset \sim Y$
  ∴ $Y \supset Z$
   4.
   5.
   6.
   7.
   8.
   9.
   10.
   11.
   12.

11. 1. $(P \cdot Q) \cdot R$
   2. $(\sim P \supset X) \supset Z$
      ∴ $P \cdot Z$

12. 1. $(D \supset F) \cdot (P \supset N)$
   2. $D \lor P$
   3. $(D \supset \sim N) \cdot (P \supset \sim F)$
      ∴ $F \equiv \sim N$

13. 1.   M ⊃ ~C
   2.   ~C ⊃ ~A
   3.   D ∨ A
       ∴ ~M ∨ D

14. 1.   (~V ⊃ W) • (X ⊃ W)
   2.   ~(~X • V)
       ∴ W
   3.   ~~X ∨ ~V   _____
   4.   X ∨ ~V   _____
   5.   ~V ∨ X   _____
   6.   W ∨ W   _____
   7.   W   _____

15. 1.   J ∨ (~J • K)
   2.   J ⊃ L
       ∴ (L • J) ≡ J
   3._____ Abs.
   4._____ Comm.
   5._____ Dist.
   6._____ Simp.
   7._____ Comm.
   8._____ Add.
   9._____ Comm.
  10._____ Assoc.
  11._____ DeM.
  12._____ Impl.
  13._____ Conj.
  14._____ Equiv.

Chapter Fourteen

QUANTIFICATION THEORY OR PREDICATE LOGIC

Thus far we have covered Aristotelian Logic, also known as Informal Logic, and modern logic, or Symbolic Logic otherwise known as Formal Logic. We have learned what is required for a Categorical Syllogism to be valid, and we have also discovered how to determine validity for complex arguments in Symbolic Logic. Is there a connection between these two disciplines in logic? They both share something in common; they are limited in what they can claim about any argument and are limited to determining validity of deductive arguments. In addition, there is no distinction made between actual individuals and generalizations. We treat complex compound propositions as single propositions, and the simple propositions "A, E, I and O" as found in Categorical Syllogistic logic do not fully express the internal structure of what is claimed in each proposition.

Remember the difficulty George Boole discovered concerning the A, E, I and O propositions? Boole discovered that when it came to making statements about things that did not exist, the A and E propositions seemed to not change in truth value. For example, we can make the statement "All unicorns are horses with a horn in the middle of their forehead" without any difficulty, because that is how we define a unicorn, even though unicorns do not exist. We can also say, "No unicorns are black" again because it is agreed in our common meaning of the term "unicorn" that there are no black unicorns even though there are NO unicorns at all! Yet, when we go to particular propositions, "Some unicorns are horses with a horn in the middle of their forehead", something happens to the original meaning of the proposition. Why? Because particular propositions, the "I" and the "O", claim that SOMETHING exists, while "A" and "E" propositions do not. While we may agree with this, it is not clear from the outset why this is. The reason it is not clear is because the four propositional forms do not fully express their inner structure.

The reason the "A, E, I and O" propositions do not clearly show their internal structure is because up to this point we have had no way of showing that internal structure. With quantification theory (thanks to Gottlob Frege)[115] we are now saying that we must apply the tools of logic to the real world. Quantification theory, also known as Predicate Logic, will enable us to do so by graphically demonstrating the internal structure of all propositions.

Let's begin with the common categorical syllogism:

All men are mortal
Socrates is a man
∴ Socrates is mortal

We see the internal structure of the argument, but not of the individual propositions. What are we actually saying when we state:"All men are mortal"? Because we know the "A" proposition distributes the subject position, we know we are saying something about all men. So, we are saying "If it is a man, then it is mortal". But we want to make certain one understands this applies to ALL men, not just to most, so we need a "quantifier" to indicate, in this case, the universality of application of this predicate, "mortal". So, in quantification theory, we use capital letters for the predicate, in this case, "M" for mortal, and lower case letters for the subject, which in this case would be "h" for human[116]. So, it would look like this:

Mh

But, we want it understood that we are referring to ALL men, so we need a universal quantifier, and in this case it would be (x), indicating that all that is human is ...
So now we have symbolized "All humans are mortal" as:

(x) Mh

We can now borrow from the field of logic and quantification and say that all letters from "a" to "u" can be used in the lower case to refer to individual instances, and that the letters "v, w, x, y and z" can be used as general place holders.[117] What that means is, if we are talking about this proposition:

Socrates is mortal

We treat it as an A proposition, and would rewrite it with a quantifier like this:

(x) Ms

Remember, we talked a lot about "structure" and not about content, and so we are here again saying that when you see (x) Ms, it does not matter what content the letters M and "s" stand for, we know when we see this symbolization that anything "s" has the predicate "M" regardless of what M stands for and what "s" stands for, so what we have is a *statement function.*[117] In other words, we have a general form of an "A" proposition.

We can now apply general variables to demonstrate the type of proposition form we are talking about. We keep the (x) and replace the "M" with Φ and the "s" with any of these letters:v, w, x, y or z. For our purposes we will replace the "s" with "x" and get this statement function:

(x) Φx

Now, we know (x) Ms is a substitution instance for (x) Φx, that is (x) Ms is referring to a specific individual while (x) Φx is referring to anything that is "x" having the predicate Φ.
But this is still not quite expressive enough of the internal meaning of the "A" proposition. As we stated earlier, "Socrates is mortal" is a way of saying, "If it is Socrates, then it is

mortal". Or, if we are talking about All humans are mortal, "If it is human, then it is mortal". How shall we demonstrate this internal structure?

First, because it is universal we begin with the universal quantifier, (x), and because it is stated as a conditional, we need to show a conditional. So, we will symbolize it this way: ***Quantification of the "A" proposition***[118](x) (Φ y $\supset$ ψy)

Here the (x) makes it universal, the Φ refers to any subject and the ψ refers to any predicate. What does the "y" refer to in this quantification of the A proposition? That is what refers to a specific instance. So, if we were using this form of quantification to indicate "All Humans are Mortal" it would look like this:(x) (Hy $\supset$ My) the "y" is referring to a specific instance of being both human and mortal.

Now we can see the inner structure of the "A" proposition, and as such, can see more of what the "A" proposition is claiming. It is a conditional, and as such, it is just claiming, in the case of unicorns, "IF" there are unicorns, THEN they are horses with a horn in the middle of their forehead. Now we can see the "A" proposition will be true even though there are no unicorns. Why? Because we know that if the conditional has a FALSE antecedent, it is always TRUE! (Remember the truth-table of a conditional.)

Ok, that was the A proposition, how about the E proposition? Again, because it is a universal, we will continue to use the universal quantifier, (x). If I say, No unicorns are black, we would begin with (x) to indicate that I am referring to ALL unicorns, and the predicate in this case is B for black, and because I said No unicorns are black, and use the "u" for unicorn, it would look like this:

(x) ~Bu

But again, it does not demonstrate the internal structure of the E proposition, and so because it is a universal, it too is a conditional, and so I would re-write it this way, keeping the "B" for black and the "u" for unicorns to look like this:

(x) (Ux $\supset$ ~Bx)

This now reads, IF there are things "x" that are Unicorns, then the things "x" are NOT black. Now we will apply the general characters to demonstrate the E proposition regardless of what is being referred to:

Quantification of the "E" proposition:[119]   (x) (Φ x $\supset$ ~ψx)

Now that we have quantified the "A" and the "E" propositions, we need to quantify the "I" and the "O" propositions. When we see this statement, "Some unicorns are horses with a horn in the middle of their forehead" what are we claiming? We are claiming there is at least one thing that is both a unicorn and is a horse with a horn in the middle of their forehead. We know (x) is a universal quantifier, but we are now referring to particular propositions. Remember, Boole said particular propositions had "existential import"[120], and so when it comes to quantifying a particular proposition, we use an "Existential" quantifier, and in logic it looks like this:

∃x.[121]

This is the same thing as saying, "There is at least one thing…" So, if we symbolize "Some unicorns are horses with a horn in the middle of their forehead" and use "u" for unicorn and "H" for "horse with a horn in the middle of their forehead" we would symbolize it this way:

(∃x) Hu

Again, the problem is, it does not fully demonstrate the inner structure of the "I" proposition. Remember, the "I" proposition is claiming that there is at least one thing that is both a unicorn and a horse with a horn in the middle of its forehead. So, we would rewrite it this way:

(∃x) (Ux • Hx)

This is now saying, there is at least one thing "x" that is both a unicorn and a horse with a horn in the middle of its forehead. Now, if we replace the U for unicorn with Φ to refer to anything, and replace the H for horse with a horn in the middle of its forehead with Ψ to refer to any predicate, then we get the quantification of the "I" proposition:

Quantification of the "I" proposition:[122]   (∃x) (Φx • Ψx)

Do you remember the truth-table for a conjunction? Yes, both sides of the • have to be true for the whole thing to be true, therefore, because unicorns do not exist, the variable on the left side of the • is false thus rendering the whole thing false. This explains why Boole could argue that when speaking about things that do not exist, the "A" proposition could be true while the "I" proposition is false.

The "O" proposition, "Some horses are not unicorns", where we use "h" for horses and "U" for unicorns, would look like this:

(∃x) ~Uh

This is the same thing as saying, there are some things "x" that are NOT both horses and unicorns. Another way of symbolizing this would be:

(∃x) (Hx • ~Ux)

If we replace the H for horses with the Φ and the U for unicorns with Ψ we get this quantification of the O proposition:

Quantification of the "O" proposition:[123]   (∃x) (Φx • ~Ψx)

Quantification of the Square of Opposition[124]

Now that we have quantified each of the four propositional forms, let us apply these quantified versions to the Square of Opposition:

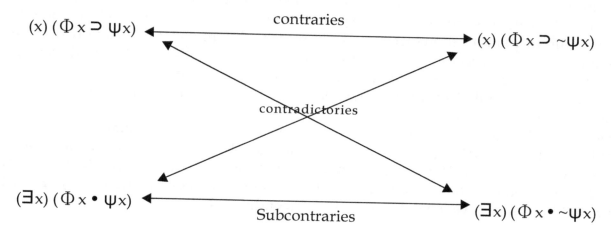

As you can see, the "A" and the "E" propositions are considered contraries, in that they both can be false but they both cannot be true. Likewise, the "I" and the "O" propositions are subcontraries in that they both can be true but they both cannot be false. We also see that the "A" and the "O" are contradictories, as are the "E" and the "I".

Why is there no relationship between the "A" and the "I" or the "E" and the "O"? Because, in the case of unicorns or things that do not exist, while the "A" proposition is true, the "I" would be false. Take the unicorn example, now that we see the internal structure of an "A" proposition, we see that it is a conditional, and if we write out, "IF it is a unicorn, then it is a horse with a horn in the middle of its forehead" we see that this conditional is true, because the antecedent, "unicorns" does not exist, and is therefore false, making the conditional true. But now look at the "I" proposition. Some unicorns are both horses and have a horn in the middle of their forehead. This is a conjunction, as we know for a conjunction to be true, both sides of the "•" must be true, but because there are NO unicorns, at least one side is false, thus rendering the "I" proposition false while the "A" proposition is true.

This helps to explain why Boole had concerns about Aristotle's Square of Opposition, and why there can be no relationship between the "A" and the "I" propositions. The same is true with the "E" and the "O" propositions. Again, with the "E" being a conditional, having a false antecedent makes it true, while the "O" proposition is a conjunction, and having even one side false makes the whole thing false. For example; If there are Unicorns then they are not black. Again, because the antecedent is false, the conditional is TRUE! Conversely, if you say "Some things are both unicorns and not black" we can see that being a conjunction, if one side of the conjunct is false, the whole thing is false. So again, while the "E" proposition is true the "O" proposition is false.

Quantification has allowed us to take Aristotle's Syllogistic Logic and clarify the internal structure of complex propositions by treating the "A, E, I and O" as compound propositions and not simple propositions. Now we can understand what is meant by "existential" import when it comes to the difference between universal and particular propositions.

Biconditionals[125]

Something else quantification allows us in logic, the development of bi-conditionals. A bi-conditional is another way of saying that if one thing is true, then the negation of its negation is also true. Take for example the proposition:"Nothing is perfect". How would we symbolize this in quantification theory? Let's look at the different ways we can say the same thing, for example, "Everything is imperfect", or "Given any individual thing whatever, it is not perfect", which can be rewritten:Given any "x", "x" is not perfect.

Ok, now say "P" symbolizes the attribute of being perfect, we can symbolize "Nothing is perfect" by writing:(x) ~Px.

Does this lead us to a connection between universal and existential quantification, yes. How? If we say "Everything is perfect" is this not negated by the existential statement, "Something is not perfect"? So, we would say that (x) Px is negated by ($\exists$x) ~Px, and if that is the case, is it not, therefore, also true that ~(x) Px is logically equivalent to ($\exists$x) ~Px? Of course, and in this way we have developed the biconditional:

$$(\exists x) \sim Px \leftrightarrows \sim(x) \, Px$$

Ok, let's go over that again. If I say "Everything is perfect", which is an "A" proposition, and we look at the quantification of the Square of Opposition, we know that the contradictory or negation of the "A" proposition is an "O" proposition, so the negation would be "Something is not perfect" which is an "O" proposition. So, if the "O" proposition is the negation of the "A" proposition, then we get:

$$(\exists x) \sim Px \leftrightarrows \sim(x) \, Px$$

Now, is it not the case that to say "Everything is perfect" means the same as saying "There is nothing that is not perfect"? So, we have another biconditional:

$$(x) \, Px \leftrightarrows \sim(\exists x) \sim Px$$

It is equally clear that the universal general proposition "Nothing is perfect" is denied by the existential general proposition "Something is perfect", again, the "E" proposition's contradiction, or negation, is the "I" proposition, and so if we negate the universal general proposition, would it not be logically equivalent to the existential general proposition. If we say, "it is not the case that nothing is perfect" would mean the same thing as saying "something is perfect". So, we get yet another biconditional:

$$\sim(x) \sim Px \leftrightarrows (\exists x) \, Px$$

Finally, there is a fourth biconditional. Is it not the case that to say "Everything is not perfect" is the same thing as saying "There is nothing that is perfect"? So, we have this biconditional:

$$(x) \sim Px \leftrightarrows \sim(\exists x) \, Px$$

This is simply another way of taking (x) ~Px, which is an "E" proposition and negating it's contradictory which is an "I" proposition. So, by negating the negation of the "E" proposition we get:~(∃x) Px.

Why are these biconditionals so important? When working on determining the validity of a complex argument, we must make certain that all negations refer directly to the variable and not the quantifier. What that means is, if you run into this in your argument:

~(x) ~Px

You want to get rid of the ~ on the quantifier (x) and have it directly related to the variable, in this case, ~Px. So, because we have a biconditional that shows you what is logically equivalent to ~(x) ~Px, we can convert it to its biconditional (∃x) Px, and therefore have gotten rid of the ~ on the quantifier. Or, if we have ~(∃x) Px, we need to get the ~ off of the existential quantifier, we can convert it to its biconditional, (x) ~Px.

Below are all of the biconditionals that are possible with the specific capital letters replaced with Φ :

$$(x) \, \Phi x \leftrightarrows \sim(\exists x) \sim \Phi x$$
$$(x) \sim \Phi x \leftrightarrows \sim(\exists x) \, \Phi x$$
$$(\exists x) \, \Phi x \leftrightarrows \sim(x) \sim \Phi x$$
$$(\exists x) \sim \Phi x \leftrightarrows \sim(x) \, \Phi x$$

This symbol "$\leftrightarrows$" simply means that you can go either way, you could have ~(∃x) ~Φx in you problem and to get rid of the ~ you simply use its biconditional (x) Φx .

Having now established these biconditionals, we need to put them into their respective forms, that is, the proper forms for an "A, E, I and O" form. So, by doing that, the biconditionals now look like this:

$$(x) \, (\Phi x \supset \psi x) \leftrightarrows \sim(\exists x) \, (\Phi x \cdot \sim \psi x)$$
$$(x) \, (\Phi x \supset \sim \psi x) \leftrightarrows \sim(\exists x) \, (\Phi x \cdot \psi x)$$
$$(\exists x) \, (\Phi x \cdot \psi x) \leftrightarrows \sim(x) \, (\Phi x \supset \sim \psi x)$$
$$(\exists x) \, (\Phi x \cdot \sim \psi x) \leftrightarrows \sim(x) \, (\Phi x \supset \psi x)$$

Why is it important for us to have these biconditionals? Simple, you will find after UI and EI are explained, that we cannot come up with formal proofs of validity if we have to deal with a "~" on the outside of the quantifier. So, if you have a "~" on the outside of the quantifier, as you do in the right column above, then you know you can convert it to its Quantified Equivalent (QE) to the left, thus eliminating the "~" on the outside of the quantifier.

Formal Proof of Validity

Having now established the quantified versions of the "A, E, I and O" propositions, and by putting them into the forms of symbolic logic, that is, the conditional and the conjunctive, we can now apply Elementary Valid Argument Forms and Rules of Replacement to the forms of Categorical Syllogisms and their respective propositions. In this case you will find that we have borrowed the "A, E, I and O" propositional forms from Categorical Syllogistic Logic, but have left behind the rules that claim a syllogism may only have three terms and two premises and a conclusion. Instead, we are going to continue to use the logic trees of symbolic logic, knowing now that the conjunctions and the conditionals represent the propositions of categorical logic.

The problem we run into now is how to apply EVAF and rules of replacement to:

(x) (Mx ⊃ Sx)?

We know how to apply EVAF and rules of replacement to Mx ⊃ Sx, but how do we get there from (x) (Mx ⊃ Sx)?

To do that we need to add four additional rules of replacement to our current list of rules of replacement in order to be able to derive Mx ⊃ Sx from (x) (Mx ⊃ Sx). Let's take the following for an example:

> (x) (Mx ⊃ Sx)
> Mb
> ∴ Sb

We know, looking at this argument that we are seeing Modus Ponens. The problem is, how do we apply Modus Ponens when there is a quantifier (x) outside the conditional (Mx ⊃ Sx)? In order for the universal quantification of a propositional function to be true, ALL substitution instances of that universally quantified proposition must be true. Therefore, we can assume that Mb ⊃ Sb is a substitution instance of (x) (Mx ⊃ Sx), where the lower case "b" represents a specific instance of the "x" that it replaced.

Therefore, we add the rule we call **Universal Instantiation(UI)**[126,] that is to say, any substitution instance of a propositional function can validly be inferred from its universal quantification, then we can give a formal proof of the validity of the given argument through the use of EVAF and rules of replacement.

So, by applying (UI) to the above problem, we get this:

> 1. (x) (Mx ⊃ Sx)
> 2. Mb
> ∴ Sb
> 3. Mb ⊃ Sb 1, UI
> 4. Sb   3, 2 M.P.

Ok, so we have gotten this far, but what happens if we have a complex, compound argument that does not have any specific substitution instances as we did above with Mb and Sb? What if we have this problem:

> 1. (x) (Hx ⊃ Sx)
> 2. (x)(Sx ⊃ Ix)
> ∴ (x)(Hx ⊃ Ix)

Again, you look at this and you certainly must see that this is a pure hypothetical syllogism. But, again, how do you get around the quantifiers in order to apply the rule of Hypothetical Syllogism? You can apply UI and get the following, and note, we are using "y" as the lower case substitution simply because the original argument does not demonstrate any particular substitution instance, so we are "fabricating" a substitution instance by using the "y" as simply a place holder as we apply UI. So, it would look like this:

1. (x) (Hx ⊃ Sx)
2. (x)(Sx ⊃ Ix)
   ∴ (x)(Hx ⊃ Ix)
3. Hy ⊃ Sy 1, UI
4. Sy ⊃Iy   2, UI
5. Hy ⊃ Iy 3,4 H.S.

Ok, so far so good, the problem is, Hy ⊃ Iy is not the actual conclusion, the actual conclusion is:(x)(Hx ⊃ Ix). So, how do we go back to the quantifier and the universal generalization? We add another rule to our rules of replacement; this new rule is call **"Universal Generalization"**[127] or UG. This rule simply states that from any substitution instance of a universal generalization, we can infer the universal quantification from which that substitution instance came. So, we can now apply UG to our problem from above and get this:

1. (x) (Hx ⊃ Sx)
2. (x)(Sx ⊃ Ix)
   ∴ (x)(Hx ⊃ Ix)
3. Hy ⊃ Sy 1, UI
4. Sy ⊃Iy   2, UI
5. Hy ⊃ Iy 3,4 H.S.
6. (x) (Hx ⊃ Ix) 5, UG

Now, we have the tools to provide a formal proof of validity for a problem with universal quantifiers. The problem with this is obvious, when was the last time we saw a complex compound argument with just universal quantifiers and no existential quantifiers, so we need to also know how to convert existentially quantified propositions into substitution instances so that the rules of replacement may be applied.

From the existentially quantified proposition, we can infer the truth of a substitution instance with respect to any individual constant that occurs nowhere else in the context of the argument.[128] In other words, we can get rid of the existential quantifier by providing a substitution instance, however, we cannot use any substitution instance that has been used before. What this means is that when we have an argument that has both a universal and an existential proposition, we must apply the existential instantiation first. Why? Take for example the argument, "Some monkeys are domesticated. Some cats are domesticated. Therefore, some monkeys are cats." If we did not pay attention to the existential instantiation rule governing the substitution instance, that is exactly what we would end up with. Let's write it out in symbolic form to see what we are talking about:

1. $(\exists x)(Mx \cdot Dx)$ (M for monkeys and D for domesticated)
2. $(\exists x)(Cx \cdot Dx)$ (C for cats and D for domesticated)
   ∴ $(\exists x)(Mx \cdot Cx)$
3. Ma • Da   1, EI
4. Ca • Da   2, EI (wrong!)
5. Ma   3, Simp
6. Ca   4, Simp
7. Ma • Ca   5, 6 Conj
8. $(\exists x)(Mx \cdot Cx)$ 7, EG

Notice that we used "a" as the single substitution instance with both complex compound existential propositions. That is wrong, because it now means we can relate the Ma to the Ca, thus ending up with the absurd conclusion that some monkeys are cats! So, what we have to do is never use a substitution instance that has been used before when applying EI. Now we have added two more rules of replacement, **Existential Instantiation (EI) and Existential Generalization (EG)** for the same rule holds true for getting the substitution instance back to the general existentially quantified proposition[129].

What happens if you have a problem that has both existential propositions and universal propositions? Remember, when you begin to convert each proposition you must start with the existential quantifier, because it cannot use any substitution instance that has already been used. So, if we have this problem:

1. $(x) (Hx \supset Lx)$
2. $(x) (Lx \supset Kx)$
3. $(\exists x) (Hx \cdot Zx)$
∴ $(\exists x) (Kx \cdot Zx)$

Notice that as was the case in Categorical Syllogisms, if you have a particular premise, your conclusion must be a particular proposition. The same is true here, if you have an Existential Proposition as a premise, then you must have an Existential Proposition for a conclusion. Conversely, if you have all universal propositions for premises, you must have a universal proposition for a conclusion.

Now, we will begin to convert this argument:

1. $(x) (Hx \supset Lx)$
2. $(x) (Lx \supset Kx)$
3. $(\exists x) (Hx \cdot Zx)$
∴ $(\exists x) (Kx \cdot Zx)$

We begin with the existential proposition $(\exists x) (Hx \cdot Zx)$ and apply EI and get:

4. Ha • Za   3, EI

Now when we go about translating the universal quantifiers, what sub letter do we use? We have to use the "a" as we did in the EI translation, why? Because, in order to apply rules consistently and to have these various propositions relate to each other, they have to share the same sub letter. (Right about now you might wonder what happens when you have more than one existential proposition among your premises. You are right to ask, because then you cannot reuse the same sub letter again, so you have to introduce as many new sub letters as you have existential propositions, which means those particular propositions will NOT be able to relate to each other, which will basically prevent any solution to the problem!)

So, we apply UI to the universal propositions and use the sub letter "a" established by the existential quantifier. Remember, in any problems that have both existential quantifiers and universal quantifiers, the existential quantifier establishes the sub letter. However, if you have more than one existential quantifier, you will probably have an invalid argument, unless the argument can be formally proved valid without applying EI to any other existential quantifiers in the argument stack..

5.	Ha ⊃ La	1, UI
6.	La ⊃ Ka	2, UI

Now our problem looks like this:

1.	(x) (Hx ⊃ Lx)	
2.	(x) (Lx ⊃ Kx)	
3.	(∃x) (Hx • Zx)	
∴	(∃x) (Kx • Zx)	
4.	Ha • Za 3, EI	
5.	Ha ⊃ La	1, UI
6.	La ⊃ Ka	2, UI

Now we can apply the EVAF and Rules of Replacement.

1.	(x) (Hx ⊃ Lx)	
2.	(x) (Lx ⊃ Kx)	
3.	(∃x) (Hx • Zx)	
∴	(∃x) (Kx • Zx)	
4.	Ha • Za3, EI	
5.	Ha ⊃ La	1, UI
6.	La ⊃ Ka	2, UI
7.	Ha ⊃ Ka	5,6 H.S.
8.	Ha	4, SIMP
9.	Ka	7,8 M.P.
10.	Za • Ha	4, COMM
11.	Za	10, SIMP
12.	Ka • Za	9,11 CONJ
13.	(∃x) (Kx • Zx) 12, EG	

Quantification Rules of Inference

Universal Instantiation   UI $(x)(\Phi x)$
$\therefore \Phi v$

Universal Generalization   UG Φy (where y denotes any selected individual)
$\therefore (x)(\Phi x)$

Existential Instantiation   EI $(\exists x)(\Phi x)$
$\therefore \Phi v$ (where **v** is any individual constant not appearing previously in the argument)

Existential Generalization   EG Φv
$\therefore (\exists x)(\Phi x)$

SUMMARY

To review what we have now presented, we have quantified the "A, E, I, and O" categorical propositions by applying the conditional to the universal propositions and the conjunctive to the particular propositions. By so doing we have clarified the inner structure of the propositions showing them to be compound rather than simple. We have also developed four biconditionals that allow us to remove the ~ from outside a quantifier so that we may then apply either UI or EI, depending upon the nature of the compound proposition, to provide a formal proof of validity. Now let's give it a try and see what happens.

EXERCISES (*See the back of the book for some answers*)

Sample:

    1.   (x) (Dx ⊃ Bx)
    2.   (∃x) (Cx • Dx)
    3.   (x) (Bx ⊃ Mx)
        ∴ (∃x)(Cx • Mx)
    4.   Ca • Da   2, EI
    5.   Da ⊃ Ba   1, UI
    6.   Ba ⊃ Ma   3, UI
    7.   Da ⊃ Ma   5, 6 H.S.
    8.   Da • Ca   4, Com
    9.   Da   8, Simp
    10.   Ma   7, 9 M.P.
    11.   Ca   4, Simp
    12.   Ca • Ma   11, 10, Conj
    13.   (∃x)(Cx • Mx)   12, EG

1.   1.   (x)(Bx ⊃ Dx)
       2.   (∃x)(Cx • Bx)
        ∴ (∃x)(Cx • Dx)

2.   1.   (x)(Fx ⊃ Yx)
       2.   (x)(Yx ⊃ Zx)
       3.   (∃x) (Dx • Fx)
        ∴ (∃x)(Dx • Zx)

3.　1.　$(\exists x)(Kx \cdot Cx)$
　　2.　$(x)(Kx \supset Dx)$
　　∴ $(\exists x)(Cx \cdot Dx)$

4.　1.　$(x)(Bx \supset Cx)$
　　2.　$(x)(Cx \supset Dx)$
　　3.　$(x)(Dx \supset Fx)$
　　4.　$(\exists x)(Bx \cdot Mx)$
　　∴ $(\exists x)(Mx \cdot Fx)$

5.　1.　$(\exists x)[Px \cdot (Sx \cdot \sim Ix)]$
　　2.　$(x)(Px \supset Ax)$
　　3.　$(\exists x)(Px \cdot \sim Sx)$
　　4.　$(x)(Jx \supset Sx)$
　　∴ $(\exists x)(Ax \cdot \sim Jx)$
　　5.　$Pa \cdot \sim Sa$　_____
　　6.　Pa　_____
　　7.　$Pa \supset Aa$　_____
　　8.　Aa　_____
　　9.　$\sim Sa \cdot Pa$　_____
　　10.　$\sim Sa$　_____
　　11.　$Ja \supset Sa$　_____
　　12.　$\sim Ja$　_____
　　13.　$Aa \cdot \sim Ja$　_____
　　14.　$(\exists x)(Ax \cdot \sim Jx)$ _____

(notice, there are two existential quantifiers in this argument, and so I ignored line 1, which is permissible. Line 1 was unnecessary to this argument)

6.　1.　$(x)\{[Ex \cdot (Sx \vee Dx)] \supset \sim Px\}$
　　∴ $(x)[(Dx \cdot Ex) \supset \sim Px]$

2. [Ey · (Sy ∨ Dy) ⊃ ~Py _____
3. ~[Ey ·(Sy ∨ Dy) ∨ ~Py _____
4. ~[Ey ·(Dy ∨ Sy) ∨ ~Py _____
5. ~[(Ey · Dy) ∨ (Ey · Dy)] ∨ ~Py _____
6. ~Py ∨ ~[(Ey · Dy) ∨ (Ey · Dy)] _____
7. ~Py ∨ [~(Ey · Dy) · ~(Ey · Dy)] _____
8. [~Py ∨ ~(Ey · Dy)] · [~Py ∨ ~(Ey · Dy)] _____
9. ~Py ∨ ~(Ey · Dy) _____
10. ~(Ey · Dy) ∨ ~Py _____
11. ~(Dy · Ey) ∨ ~Py _____
12. (Dy · Ey) ⊃ ~Py _____
13. (x) [(Dx · Ex) ⊃ ~Px] _____

7. 1. (x) {[Cx · (Lx ∨ Ox)] ⊃ ~Fx}
    2. (x) (~Fx ⊃ ~Ex)
        ∴ (x) [(Cx · Lx) ⊃ ~Ex]
    3. [Cy · (Ly ∨ Oy)] ⊃ ~Fy _____
    4. ~Fy ⊃ ~Ey _____
    5. [Cy · (Ly ∨ Oy)] ⊃ ~Ey _____
    6. [(Cy · Ly) ∨ (Cy · Oy)] ⊃ ~Ey _____
    7. ~[(Cy · Ly) ∨ (Cy · Oy)] ∨ ~Ey _____
    8. [~(Cy · Ly) · ~(Cy · Oy)] ∨ ~Ey _____
    9. ~Ey ∨ [~(Cy · Ly) · ~(Cy · Oy)] _____
    10. [~Ey ∨ ~(Cy · Ly)] · [~Ey ∨ ~(Cy · Oy)] _____
    11. ~Ey ∨ ~(Cy · Ly) _____
    12. ~(Cy · Ly) ∨ ~Ey _____
    13. (Cy · Ly) ⊃ ~Ey _____
    14. (x) [(Cx · Lx) ⊃ ~Ex] _____

8. 1. (x) [Cx ⊃ (Sx ∨ Ox)]
    2. (x) (Sx ⊃ ~Wx)
    3. (∃x) (Cx · Wx)
        ∴ (∃x) (Cx · Ox)

    4. _____
    5. _____
    6. _____
    7. _____
    8. _____
    9. _____
    10. _____
    11. _____
    12. _____
    13. _____
    14. _____
    15. _____

9. 1. ~(∃x)(Wx · Cx)
    2. (x)(~Cx ⊃ Hx)
    3. ~(∃x)(Hx ·~ Kx)
        ∴ (x)(~Kx ⊃ Cx)

10. 1. ~(x) (Jx ⊃ ~Bx)
     2. ~(∃x) (Jx · ~Mx)
     3. (x) (Mx ⊃ Kx)
     ∴   (∃x)(Kx · Bx)

11. 1. ~(☐x) (Hx · Kx)
     2. ~(☐x) (~Kx · ~Nx)
     3. (x) (Nx ⊃ Jx)
     ∴ (x) (Hx ⊃ Jx)

Chapter Fifteen

PRACTICAL APPLICATION OF LOGIC

We have come a long way in our study of logic. You have learned Aristotelian Categorical Syllogistic Logic, Modern Symbolic Logic, and finally, Quantification or Predicate Logic. This chapter will attempt to take all that has been covered in this book and apply it to a few arguments that appear a bit difficult but prove to be quite analyzable due to the powerful tools found in logic. I have selected Anselm's (1033-1109) logical proof of the existence of God as the source of the arguments we will review. Below are excerpts from Anselm's "Proslogion". First, read through the arguments and then you will see a need to translate the propositions from 12th century language to language we are more familiar with in the 21st century. Please find the translations below marked as translations.

CHAPTER III.

AND it assuredly exists so truly, that it cannot be conceived not to exist. For, it is possible to conceive of a being which cannot be conceived not to exist; and this is greater than one which can be conceived not to exist. Hence, if that, than which nothing greater can be conceived, can be conceived not to exist, it is not that, than which nothing greater can be conceived. But this is an irreconcilable contradiction. There is, then, so truly a being than which nothing greater can be conceived to exist, that it cannot even be conceived not to exist; and this being thou art, O Lord, our God.

So truly, therefore, dost thou exist, O Lord, my God, that thou canst not be conceived not to exist; and rightly. For, if a mind could conceive of a being better than thee, the creature would rise above the Creator; and this is most absurd. And, indeed, whatever else there is, except thee alone, can be conceived not to exist. To thee alone, therefore, it belongs to exist more truly than all other beings, and hence in a higher degree than all others. For, whatever else exists does not exist so truly, and hence in a less degree it belongs to it to exist. Why, then, has the fool said in his heart, there is no God (Psalms xiv. 1), since it is so evident, to a rational mind, that thou dost exist in the highest degree of all? Why, except that he is dull and a fool?

CHAPTER II.

AND so, Lord, do thou, who dost give understanding to faith, give me, so far as thou knowest it to be profitable, to understand that thou art as we believe; and that thou art that which we believe. And indeed, we believe that thou art a being than which nothing greater can be conceived. Or is there no such nature, since the fool hath said in his heart, there is no

God? (Psalms xiv. 1). But, at any rate, this very fool, when he hears of this being of which I speak -- a being than which nothing greater can be conceived -- understands what he hears, and what he understands is in his understanding; although he does not understand it to exist.

For, it is one thing for an object to be in the understanding, and another to understand that the object exists. When a painter first conceives of what he will afterwards perform, he has it in his understanding, but he does not yet understand it to be, because he has not yet performed it. But after he has made the painting, he both has it in his understanding, and he understands that it exists, because he has made it.

Hence, even the fool is convinced that something exists in the understanding, at least, than which nothing greater can be conceived. For, when he hears of this, he understands it. And whatever is understood, exists in the understanding. And assuredly that, than which nothing greater can be conceived, cannot exist in the understanding alone. For, suppose it exists in the understanding alone:then it can be conceived to exist in reality; which is greater.

Therefore, if that, than which nothing greater can be conceived, exists in the understanding alone, the very being, than which nothing greater can be conceived, is one, than which a greater can be conceived. But obviously this is impossible. Hence, there is no doubt that there exists a being, than which nothing greater can be conceived, and it exists both in the understanding and in reality.

CHAPTER IV.

BUT how has the fool said in his heart what he could not conceive; or how is it that he could not conceive what he said in his heart? since it is the same to say in the heart, and to conceive.

But, if really, nay, since really, he both conceived, because he said in his heart; and did not say in his heart, because he could not conceive; there is more than one way in which a thing is said in the heart or conceived. For, in one sense, an object is conceived, when the word signifying it is conceived; and in another, when the very entity, which the object is, is understood.

In the former sense, then, God can be conceived not to exist; but in the latter, not at all. For no one who understands what fire and water are can conceive fire to be water, in accordance with the nature of the facts themselves, although this is possible according to the words. So, then, no one who understands what God is can conceive that God does not exist; although he says these words in his heart, either without any or with some foreign, signification. For, God is that than which a greater cannot be conceived. And he who thoroughly understands this, assuredly understands that this being so truly exists, that not even in concept can it be non-existent. Therefore, he who understands that God so exists, cannot conceive that he does not exist.

I thank thee, gracious Lord, I thank thee; because what I formerly believed by thy bounty, I now so understand by thine illumination, that if I were unwilling to believe that thou dost exist, I should not be able not to understand this to be true.[130]

TRANSLATIONS

AND so, Lord, do thou, who dost give understanding to faith, give me, so far as thou knowest it to be profitable, to understand that thou art as we believe; and that thou art that which we believe. And indeed, we believe that thou art a being than which nothing greater can be conceived. Or is there no such nature, since the fool hath said in his heart, there is no God? (Psalms xiv. 1). But, at any rate, this very fool, when he hears of this being of which I speak -- a being than which nothing greater can be conceived -- understands what he hears, and what he understands is in his understanding; although he does not understand it to exist.

God has given us understanding through our faith which leads us to understand God is as we believe God to be. What we believe is that God is that than which nothing greater can be conceived. Or is there no such nature as a being that than which nothing greater can be conceive, for the fool has said in his heart "there is no God"? (Psalms 14:1). Yet, this very fool who claims there is no God does understand what I mean when I say "a being that than which nothing greater can be conceived". The fool understands what he hears, and if he understands it, then it must be in his mind (understanding) even though he does not understand it to exist.

For, it is one thing for an object to be in the understanding, and another to understand that the object exists. When a painter first conceives of what he will afterwards perform, he has it in his understanding, but he does not yet understand it to be, because he has not yet performed it. But after he has made the painting, he both has it in his understanding, and he understands that it exists, because he has made it.

It is one thing for something to be in our mind (understanding) and quite another for it to actually exist. When a painter thinks about the picture he wishes to paint, he has it in his mind (understanding), but he does not yet think of it as actually existing because he has not yet painted it. After he has actually painted the picture he then has it both in his mind (understanding) and he knows (understands) it to exist.

Hence, even the fool is convinced that something exists in the understanding, at least, than which nothing greater can be conceived. For, when he hears of this, he understands it. And whatever is understood, exists in the understanding. And assuredly that, than which nothing greater can be conceived, cannot exist in the understanding alone. For, suppose it exists in the understanding alone:then it can be conceived to exist in reality; which is greater.

Thus, even a fool is convinced that something exists in his mind (understanding) when he thinks of that than which nothing greater can be conceived, because hearing this he understands it. Whatever is understood exists in the mind (understanding). It must be that than which nothing greater can be conceived must exist in more than just our minds (understanding). Why? If it existed only in our minds (understanding) then could it not then be conceived as existing in reality outside our minds? If that is so, then would it not be the case that to exist both in the mind and in reality would be greater than just existing in the mind?

Therefore, if that, than which nothing greater can be conceived, exists in the understanding alone, the very being, than which nothing greater can be conceived, is one, than which a greater can be conceived. But obviously this is impossible. Hence, there is no doubt that there exists a being, than which nothing greater can be conceived, and it exists both in the understanding and in reality.

Therefore, if that than which nothing greater can be conceived exists only in the understanding, then it cannot be that than which NOTHING GREATER can be conceived if we can conceive of it existing both in the mind and in reality. Because, if we can conceive of it existing in both mind and reality, then surely that is greater than just existing in the mind, therefore, it MUST exist in both the mind and reality in order for it to be that than which NOTHING GREATER can be conceived.

AND it assuredly exists so truly, that it cannot be conceived not to exist. For, it is possible to conceive of a being which cannot be conceived not to exist; and this is greater than one which can be conceived not to exist. Hence, if that, than which nothing greater can be conceived, can be conceived not to exist, it is not that, than which nothing greater can be conceived. But this is an irreconcilable contradiction. There is, then, so truly a being than which nothing greater can be conceived to exist, that it cannot even be conceived not to exist; and this being thou art, O Lord, our God.

It therefore must be the case that this being cannot be conceived not to exist. It is possible to conceive of a being which must exist, and this is greater than one which can be conceived not to exist. Therefore, that than which NOTHING GREATER can be conceived must necessarily exist, for to claim that we can conceive in our minds of that than which nothing greater can be conceived and then claim it doesn't exist contradicts the very meaning of the phrase, "that than which nothing greater can be conceived" because we can conceive of it existing, and to actually exist outside the mind in reality is greater than just existing in the mind, so to claim that than which nothing greater can be conceived exists only in our minds is a contradiction. God is that than which nothing greater can be conceived.

So truly, therefore, dost thou exist, O Lord, my God, that thou canst not be conceived not to exist; and rightly. For, if a mind could conceive of a being better than thee, the creature would rise above the Creator; and this is most absurd. And, indeed, whatever else there is, except thee alone, can be conceived not to exist. To thee alone, therefore, it belongs to exist more truly than all other beings, and hence in a higher degree than all others. For, whatever else exists does not exist so truly, and hence in a less degree it belongs to it to exist. Why, then, has the fool said in his heart, there is no God (Psalms xiv. 1), since it is so evident, to a rational mind, that thou dost exist in the highest degree of all? Why, except that he is dull and a fool?

We understand God as the Creator, and to conceive of God not existing and everything created does exist is to place the created above the Creator, and this is absurd. So it must certainly be the case that "that than which nothing greater can be conceived" must be God. Furthermore, that which is created exists temporarily, and not by necessity, whereas that than which NOTHING GREATER can be conceived MUST exist necessarily, therefore God must exist necessarily, for that which exists necessarily is greater than that which does not.

BUT how has the fool said in his heart what he could not conceive; or how is it that he could not conceive what he said in his heart? since it is the same to say in the heart, and to conceive.

But, if really, nay, since really, he both conceived, because he said in his heart; and did not say in his heart, because he could not conceive; there is more than one way in which a thing is said in the heart or conceived. For, in one sense, an object is conceived, when the word signifying it is conceived; and in another, when the very entity, which the object is, is understood.

In the former sense, then, God can be conceived not to exist; but in the latter, not at all. For no one who understands what fire and water are can conceive fire to be water, in accordance with the nature of the facts themselves, although this is possible according to the words. So, then, no one who understands what God is can conceive that God does not exist; although he says these words in his heart, either without any or with some foreign, signification. For, God is that than which a greater cannot be conceived. And he who thoroughly understands this, assuredly understands that this being so truly exists, that not even in concept can it be non-existent. Therefore, he who understands that God so exists, cannot conceive that he does not exist.

If the fool can understand that than which nothing greater can be conceived, then how is it he cannot conceive of it? It is the same to understand and to conceive.

There are two ways a thing can be conceived or understood, one is by the meaning of the words used to describe such a thing, in another way of conceiving such a thing is to understand the very entity itself. In just the understanding of the meaning of words, God could be conceived as not existing. However, if one understands the entity itself, in this case God, than it is impossible for God not to exist, for knowing fire and water as entities themselves one does not mistake fire for water or water for fire. One understands their true nature, and thus the true nature of God is that he exists necessarily. If one claims then, that God does not exist, then truly they do not properly conceive of the entity itself, in this case God. Anyone who truly understands God cannot claim he does not exist.

ANALYSIS

Having translated Anselm's argument as I understand it, I have already begun the process of analysis. What needs to be done now is to summarize the entire argument so that we can more easily re-write the propositions into proper categorical propositions. Summarizing the argument requires that we pull together all of the translations and lay them one after another to better get a glimpse of the entire scope of the argument. Once we have done that we will determine the ultimate conclusion Anselm is attempting to establish. Once we have the final conclusion in hand, we can reconstruct the argument from the conclusion by first building categorical syllogisms and finally applying predicate logic to further determine validity. Remember, however, we are seeking to determine whether or not this is a sound argument, that is, an argument both valid in structure and made up of all true propositions.

The Translated Argument

God has given us understanding through our faith which leads us to understand God is as we believe God to be. What we believe is that God is that than which nothing greater can be conceived. Or is there no such nature as a being that than which nothing greater can be conceive, for the fool has said in his heart "there is no God"? (Psalms 14:1). Yet, this very fool who claims there is no God does understand what I mean when I say "a being than which nothing greater can be conceived". The fool understands what he hears, and if he understands it, then it must be in his mind (understanding) even though he does not understand it to exist.

It is one thing for something to be in our mind (understanding) and quite another for it to actually exist. When a painter thinks about the picture he wishes to paint, he has it in his mind (understanding), but he does not yet think of it as actually existing because he has not yet painted it. After he has actually painted the picture he then has it both in his mind (understanding) and he knows (understands) it to exist.

Thus, even a fool is convinced that something exists in his mind (understanding) when he thinks of that than which nothing greater can be conceived, because hearing this he understands it. Whatever is understood exists in the mind (understanding). It must be that than which nothing greater can be conceived must exist in more than just our minds (understanding). Why? If it existed only in our minds (understanding) then could it not then be conceived as existing in reality outside our minds? If that is so, then would it not be the case that to exist both in the mind and in reality would be greater than just existing in the mind?

Therefore, if that than which nothing greater can be conceived exists only in the understanding, then it cannot be that than which NOTHING GREATER can be conceived if we can conceive of it existing both in the mind and in reality. Because, if we can conceive of it existing in both mind and reality, then surely that is greater than just existing in the mind, therefore, it MUST exist in both the mind and reality in order for it to be that than which NOTHING GREATER can be conceived.

It therefore must be the case that this being cannot be conceived not to exist. It is possible to conceive of a being which must exist, and this is greater than one which can be conceived not to exist. Therefore, that than which NOTHING GREATER can be conceived must necessarily exist, for to claim that we can conceive in our minds of that than which nothing greater can be conceived and then claim it doesn't exist contradicts the very meaning of the phrase, "that than which nothing greater can be conceived" because we can conceive of it existing, and to actually exist outside the mind in reality is greater than just existing in the mind, so to claim that than which nothing greater can be conceived exists only in our minds is a contradiction. God is that than which nothing greater can be conceived.

We understand God as the Creator, and to conceive of God not existing and everything created does exist is to place the created above the Creator, and this is absurd. So it must certainly be the case that "that than which nothing greater can be conceived" must be God. Furthermore, that which is created exists temporarily, and not by necessity, whereas that than which NOTHING GREATER can be conceived MUST exist necessarily, therefore God must exist necessarily, for that which exists necessarily is greater than that which does not.

If the fool can understand that than which nothing greater can be conceived, then how is it he cannot conceive of it? It is the same to understand and to conceive.

There are two ways a thing can be conceived or understood, one is by the meaning of the words used to describe such a thing, in another way of conceiving such a thing is to understand the very entity itself. In just the understanding of the meaning of words, God could be conceived as not existing. However, if one understands the entity itself, in this case God, than it is impossible for God not to exist, for knowing fire and water as entities themselves one does not mistake fire for water or water for fire. One understands their true nature, and thus the true nature of God is that he exists necessarily. If one claims then, that God does not exist, then truly they do not properly conceive of the entity itself, in this case God. Anyone who truly understands God cannot claim he does not exist.

Now that we have the translated argument at our disposal, let us look at some of the main points of the argument. It appears that the final conclusion is:

Therefore, God necessarily exists.

The following are propositions appearing in the argument:

Proposition #1:   God has given us understanding, and revealed himself through that understanding. God exists.

Proposition #2:   God is that than which nothing greater can be conceived.

Proposition #3:   That which exists both in the mind and in reality is greater than that which exists only in the mind.

Proposition #4:   That which exists in reality is greater than that which does not.

Proposition #5:   That which exists necessarily is greater than that which does not.

Proposition #6:   There are two ways to understand something, one is simply by understanding the meaning of the words used to describe something and the second is knowing the nature of the entity itself.

Proposition #7:   The nature of God is to exist necessarily.

Proposition #8:   To claim to understand God and not believe him to exist is to not know God's nature and thus not know God.

Now we will begin to re-write the propositions in the form of an A, E, I or O proposition. First, the conclusion. We have to assign letters to stand for each of the elements of each proposition, and we have to apply these substituted letters consistently. So, here are the letter substitutions:

G = God exists
EN = Exists Necessarily
T = That than which nothing greater can be conceived
GR = Greater
M = Exists in the Mind
R = Exists in Reality

This will give us something to begin with. Let us begin with the conclusion:

All G is EN

With an A proposition as the conclusion, we have only one mood and figure that will provide a valid argument structure, AAA-1. So, let us reconstruct the first argument into a categorical syllogism:

All _____ is EN
All G is _____
Therefore, All G is EN

What is missing in this argument? Correct, the middle term. In Anselm's argument, what did he claim is something that would always exist necessarily? Right, That than which nothing greater can be conceived, or T. So, we rewrite the argument:

> All T is EN
> All G is T
> Therefore, All G is EN

You are probably concerned that we have done nothing to challenge Anselm's argument, but we are just getting started. Let us take the first premise, All T is EN and treat it as a conclusion:

> All _____ is EN
> All T is _____
> Therefore, All T is EN

So what would be the missing middle term?

We might try inserting "that which is greater" or GR as the middle term. So, it would look like this:

> All GR is EN
> All T is GR
> Therefore, All T is EN

But what do we mean by "Greater"? Anselm argued that which existed both in the mind and in reality was Greater, so that proposition would be a compound proposition and look like this:

> $(M \cdot R) \supset GR$

But greater than what? Something that only existed in the mind, according to Anselm.

So, we would have to create an E proposition that would look something like: $(M \bullet \sim R) \supset \sim GR$

Now, however, we have moved past Aristotelian logic into modern symbolic logic. That being the case, we will move to predicate logic simply because it brings together both Aristotelian logic and modern symbolic logic, thus giving us more power to address this argument.

Because we are speaking in universals, we will refer back to the universal quantification of the A and E propositions. $(M \cdot R) \supset GR$ would look like this: $(x)(Mx \cdot Rx) \supset GRx)$. And $(M \bullet \sim R) \supset \sim GR$ would look like this: $(x)((Mx \bullet \sim Rx) \supset \sim GRx)$ The final conclusion would look like: $(x)(Gx \supset ENx)$

If we begin to re-write all of the propositions in quantitative form we would get:

Proposition #1:   God has given us understanding, and revealed himself through that understanding. God exists. $(x)Gx$

Proposition #2:   Proposition #2: If God exists then God is that than which nothing greater can be conceived.

$$(x)(Gx \supset Tx)$$

Proposition #3:   That which exists both in the mind and in reality is greater than that which exists only in the mind.

$$(x)\{[(Mx \cdot Rx) \supset GRx] \bullet [(Mx \bullet \sim Rx) \supset \sim GRx]\}$$

Proposition #4:   That which exists in reality is greater than that which does not.

$$(x)[(Rx \supset GRx) \bullet (\sim Rx \supset \sim GRx)]$$

Proposition #5:   That which exists necessarily is greater than that which does not.

$$(x)[(ENx \supset GRx) \bullet (\sim ENx \supset \sim GRx)]$$

Proposition #6:   (My added proposition) That than which nothing greater can be conceived is greater than that which may not exist therefore it must exist necessarily.

$$(x)(Tx \supset GRx) \ (x)(Tx \supset ENx)$$

Proposition #7:   There are two ways to understand something, one is simply by understanding the meaning of the words used to describe something and the second is knowing the nature of the entity itself. (We will not pursue this and the following propositions in our analysis. The reason being, to claim that the nature of God is the exist necessarily is simply another way of saying God is that than which nothing greater can be conceived if we accept the premise that something is greater if it exists in reality and not just in the mind.)

Proposition #8:   The nature of God is to exist necessarily. $(x)(Gx \supset ENx)$

Proposition #9:   To claim to understand God and not believe him to exist is to not know God's nature and thus not know God.

Now, if we stack this propositions so re-written with the final conclusion, it should look like this:

1. $(x)(Gx \supset Tx)$
2. $(x)(Tx \supset ENx)$
    $\therefore (x)(Gx \supset ENx)$

Now, to generate a proof.

5.	$Gy \supset Ty$	1, UI
6.	$Ty \supset ENy$	2, UI
7.	$Gy \supset ENy$	5, 6 H.S.
8.	$(x)(Gx \supset ENx)$	7, U.G.

Ok, this is the simple argument that Anselm makes, if you accept that God is that than which nothing greater can be conceived, and if you can accept that that than which nothing greater can be conceived must exist necessarily, then you have a valid argument. But is it sound? Remember what $Gy \supset Ty$ actually means, IF God exists, THEN God would be that than which nothing greater can be conceived. The conclusion simply claims, IF God exists, THEN God exists necessarily.

How do we arrive at the conclusion that God necessarily exists? Do we simply stipulate that that than which nothing greater can be conceived must exist necessarily because not to would not make it the greatest thing to be conceived? Let's try another argument:

1. $(x)Gx$
2. $(x)(Gx \supset Tx)$
3. $(x)(Tx \supset GRx)$
4. $(x)[(Mx \cdot Rx) \supset GRx) \cdot (Mx \cdot {\sim}Rx) \supset {\sim}GRx)]$
5. $(x)[(Rx \supset GRx) \cdot ({\sim}Rx \supset {\sim}GRx)]$
6. $(x)[(ENx \supset GRx) \cdot ({\sim}ENx \supset {\sim}GRx)]$
    $\therefore (x)(Tx \supset ENx)$

7.	Gy	1, UI
8.	$Gy \supset Ty$	2, UI
9.	$Ty \supset GRy$	3, UI
10.	$Gy \supset GRy$	8, 9 H.S.
11.	GRy	10, 7, M.P.
12.	$({\sim}ENy \supset {\sim}GRy) \cdot (ENy \supset GRy)$	8, Comm
13.	$(My \cdot Ry) \supset GRy$	4, Simp
14.	$(My \cdot {\sim}Ry) \supset {\sim}GRy$	5, Simp
15.	$(Ry \supset GRy)$	6, Simp
16.	$({\sim}Ry \supset {\sim}GRy)$	7, Simp
17.	$(ENy \supset GRy)$	8, Simp
18.	$({\sim}ENy \supset {\sim}GRy)$	9, Simp
19.	ENy	18, 11 M.T.
20.	$ENy \vee {\sim}Ty$	18, Add
21.	${\sim}Ty \vee ENy$	19, Comm
22.	$Ty \supset ENy$	20, Impl
23.	$(x)(Tx \supset ENx)$	22, U.G.

Notice, this argument works so long as we assume God exists. We have shown it is a valid argument, but is it sound? Has it taken us any closer to deciding whether or not God actually exists. No, it hasn't. We are still stipulating that God exists.

Looking at the stack above, if you take line 8 and line 22:

24. $Gy \supset Ty$
25. $Ty \supset ENy$

You get the original conclusion:

$Gy \supset ENy$

What does this analysis show us? It clarifies for us the fact that to claim God exists necessarily requires one to stipulate that God exists in the first place. What Anselm's argument has failed to do is prove the existence of God from the outset. The best we can conclude is IF God exists then God exists necessarily.

This extensive analysis is simply one more example of how one can use the tools of logic to analyze what on the surface appears to be a very complex argument. To further understand what is being claimed in this argument we provide a translation of the symbols found in the extended argument above:

1.	(x)Gx	(God exists)
2.	(x)(Gx ⊃ Tx)	(If God exists then God is that than which nothing greater can be conceived)
3.	(x)(Tx ⊃ GRx)	(If it is that than which nothing greater can be conceived, then it is greater than…)
4.	(x)[(Mx · Rx) ⊃ GRx) • (Mx • ~Rx) ⊃ ~GRx)]	(If it exists in both the mind and in reality then it is greater, and if it exists ONLY in the mind and not reality then it is NOT greater.)
5.	(x)[(Rx ⊃ GRx) • (~Rx ⊃ ~GRx)]	(If it exists in Reality then it is greater and if it does not exist in reality then it is NOT greater.)
6.	(x)[(ENx ⊃ GRx) • (~ENx ⊃ ~GRx)]	(If it exists necessarily then it is greater and if it does not exist necessarily then it is NOT greater.)

∴ (x)(Tx ⊃ ENx) (If it is that than which nothing greater can be conceived then it exists necessarily.)

7.	Gy	1, UI (God exists)
8.	Gy ⊃ Ty	2, UI (If God exists then God is that than which nothing greater can be conceived)
9.	Ty ⊃ GRy	3, UI (If it is that than which nothing greater can be conceived, then it is greater than…)
10.	Gy ⊃ GRy	8, 9 H.S. (If God exists then it is a greater existence.)
11.	GRy	10, 7, M.P. (Greater than…)
12.	(~ENy ⊃ ~GRy) • (ENy ⊃ GRy)	8, Comm (If it does NOT exist necessarily then it is NOT Greater and if it does exist necessarily then it is Greater.)
13.	(My • Ry) ⊃ GRy	4, Simp (If it exists both in mind and reality then it is Greater.)

14.	$(My \cdot \sim Ry) \supset \sim GRy$	5, Simp (if it exists ONLY in mind and not reality then it is NOT Greater.)
15.	$(Ry \supset GRy)$	6, Simp (If it exists in reality then it is greater.)
16.	$(\sim Ry \supset \sim GRy)$	7, Simp (If it does NOT exist in reality then it is NOT greater.)
17.	$(ENy \supset GRy)$	8, Simp (If it exists necessarily then it is greater.)
18.	$(\sim ENy \supset \sim GRy)$	9, Simp (If it does NOT exist necessarily then it is NOT greater.)
19.	ENy	18, 11 M.T. (It exists necessarily.)
20.	$ENy \lor \sim Ty$	18, Add (It exists necessarily or it is NOT that than which nothing greater can be conceived.)
21.	$\sim Ty \lor ENy$	19, Comm (It is NOT that than which nothing greater can be conceived or it exists necessarily.)
22.	$Ty \supset ENy$	20, Impl (If it is that than which nothing greater can be conceived then it exists necessarily.)
23.	$(x)(Tx \supset ENx)$	22, U.G. (If it is that than which nothing greater can be conceived then it exists necessarily.)

Having established by way of a valid argument that that than which nothing greater can be conceived exists necessarily, we can further conclude that IF God exists then God exists necessarily. Again, this conclusion cannot be reached without stipulating in the first place that God exists, which begs the question, is Anselm's Ontological Argument an elaborate example of the fallacy of the circular argument?

ANSWER GUIDE TO CHAPTERS ONE THROUGH FOURTEEN
ANSWERS TO PROBLEMS BEGINNING ON PAGE 32

3.   Sam is lonesome, but of course anyone who is without a date for this dance would be lonesome, so it stands to reason to conclude that Sam is without a date.

S   =   Sam
L   =   is lonesome
D   =   Without a date

	All L is D
	All S is L
∴	All S is D

1. Therefore, Kentucky won the NCAA College Basketball Championship.

All College Basketball Teams that win the final game in the NCAA Tournament are College Basketball Teams that have won the NCAA College Basketball Championship. Kentucky is a College Basketball Team that won the final game in the NCAA Tournament.

Therefore, Kentucky won the NCAA College Basketball Championship.

2. Therefore, all people in the Navy are people who can swim.

All people who serve in the Navy are people who can swim.
All people in the Navy are people who serve in the Navy.

Therefore, all people in the Navy are people who can swim.

3. Therefore, all Red Tractors are better than Green Tractors.

All tractors that win tractor pull contests are better than Green Tractors.
All Red Tractors are tractors that win tractor pulling contests.
Therefore, all Red Tractors are better than Green Tractors.
(OK, this is valid, I didn't claim it was true!)

ANSWERS TO PROBLEMS BEGINNING ON PAGE 32

3.   It breaks rule #3, if a term is distributed in the conclusion it must be distributed in the premise. In this case, the minor term, or the subject term in the conclusion is distributed but it is NOT distributed in the Minor Premise.

6. All P is M
   Some S is M
∴ Some S is P

It breaks rule #2, the middle term must be distributed at least once. Look at the Major Premise "All P is M", which position does it distribute? Right, the subject position, and the Middle term "M" is in the predicate position, so it is not distributed. Of course the Minor Premise "Some S is P" does not distribute anything.

ANSWERS FOR PROBLEMS BEGINNING ON PAGE 42

2. No P is M
   No S is M
∴ No S is P

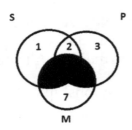

The conclusion is supposed to be No S is P, but look at this Venn Diagram, look at space #2, it is not filled in, which means that these two premises does NOT give you NO S is P, if the two premises did give you the conclusion, then space #2 would be filled in, but it is not, therefore we know that this argument is invalid and breaks rule #5, you cannot have two negative premises.

ANSWERS FOR PROBLEMS BEGINNING ON PAGE 44

OIE-3   Some M is not P
                Some M is S
      ∴   No S is P

(this is invalid, do you know why? It breaks Rule #2, the undistributed Middle, and Rule #3, an Illicit Minor)

ANSWERS FOR PROBLEMS BEGINNING ON PAGE 63

EXERCISES
Translate the following into proper form (A, E, I or O forms). *(check the back for answers)*

1.   Only the brave deserve the Medal of Honor.
        All who deserve the Medal of Honor are the brave.

3.   Nearly everyone who smokes will die of cancer.
        Some people who smoke are people who will die of cancer.

5.   It simply is not true that any Democrats would want to do anything to benefit small business!
        No Democrats are people who support benefitting small business.

7.   No one can participate except by invitation.
        All people who participate are people who were invited.

9.   Early detection of breast cancer saves lives.
        All cases of early detection of breast cancer are cases in which lives are saved.

ANSWERS TO PROBLEMS BEGINNING ON PAGE 79

Exercises using the Standard Square (Aristotelian) of Opposition. After completing using the Standard Square, answer using the Boolean Square and see what the differences are.
T___(true)   F___(false)   U___(undetermined)

Using the Standard Square of Opposition:

2.   If "All horses are brown" is false, what is the truth value of the following:

No horses are brown	T__	F__	U X		
Some horses are brown	T__	F__	U X		
Some horses are not brown	T X	F__	U__		

Using the Boolean Square of Opposition (notice, there is not difference in this case!):

2.   If "All horses are brown" is false, what is the truth value of the following:

No horses are brown	T__	F__	U X		
Some horses are brown	T__	F__	U X		
Some horses are not brown	T X	F__	U__		

Using the Standard Square of Opposition:

4.   If "No horses are thoroughbreds" is false, what is the truth value of the following:

All horses are thoroughbreds	T___ F___ U X___
Some horses are thoroughbreds	T X F___ U___
Some horses are not thoroughbreds	T___ F___ U X___

Using the Boolean Square would again give you the same answers as above.

Using the Standard Square of Opposition:

6.   If "Some men are immortal" is false, what is the truth value of the following:

All men are immortal	T___ F X U___
No men are immortal	T X F___ U___
Some men are not immortal	T X F___ U___

Using the Boolean Square of Opposition:

6.   If "Some men are immortal" is false, what is the truth value of the following:

All men are immortal	T___ F___ U X___
No men are immortal	T X F___ U___
Some men are not immortal	T___ F___ U X___

Using the Standard Square of Opposition (Aristotelian):

8.   If "Some dogs are not mammals" is false, what is the truth value of the following:

All dogs are mammals	T X F___ U___
No dogs are mammals	T___ F X U___
Some dogs are mammals	T X F___ U___

Using the Boolean Square of Oppostion:

8.   If "Some dogs are not mammals" is false, what is the truth value of the following:

All dogs are mammals	T X F___ U___
No dogs are mammals	T___ F___ U X___
Some dogs are mammals	T___ F___ U X___

Exercises using Conversion, Obversion and Contraposition

This exercise will be using both the standard square of opposition and the use of the Aristotelian version of Conversion, Obversion and Contraposition as well as the Boolean Square of Opposition and the Boolean version of Conversion, Obversion and Contraposition.

(After answering with the Standard Square, switch and answer with the Boolean Square and see the differences in your answers)

Using the Aristotelian or Standard Square of Opposition and the Aristotelian version of Conversion, Obversion and Contraposition:

9.   If "Some historians are philosophers" is true, what is the truth value of the following? (mark an "X" in what you believe to be the correct answer)

Some philosophers are not non-historians	T X F		U	
All philosophers are historians	T	F	U X	
No non-historians are philosophers	T	F	U X	
Some non-non-philosophers are not non-historians	T X F		U	

Using the Boolean Square of Opposition and the Boolean version of Conversion, Obversion and Contraposition (notice that in this case the answers are the same!):

9.   If "Some historians are philosophers" is true, what is the truth value of the following? (mark an "X" in what you believe to be the correct answer)

Some philosophers are not non-historians	T X F		U	
All philosophers are historians	T	F	U X	
No non-historians are philosophers	T	F	U X	
Some non-non-philosophers are not non-historians	T X F		U	

Using the four examples above, what if "Some historians are philosophers" is false, then what is the truth value of the above four (mark an "O" in what you believe to be the correct answer)

Using the Aristotelian or Standard Square of Opposition and the Aristotelian version of Conversion, Obversion and Contraposition:

9.   If "Some historians are philosophers" is FALSE, what is the truth value of the following? (mark an "X" in what you believe to be the correct answer)

Some philosophers are not non-historians	T	F X U		
All philosophers are historians	T	F X U		
No non-historians are philosophers	T	F X U		
Some non-non-philosophers are not non-historians	T	F X U		

Using the Boolean Square of Opposition and the Boolean version of Conversion, Obversion and Contraposition (this time, notice the difference in the answers to the second and third proposition):

9.   If "Some historians are philosophers" is FALSE, what is the truth value of the following? (mark an "X" in what you believe to be the correct answer)

Some philosophers are not non-historians	T ___	F X	U ___	
All philosophers are historians	T ___	F ___	U X	
No non-historians are philosophers	T ___	F ___	U X	
Some non-non-philosophers are not non-historians	T ___	F X	U ___	

Using the Aristotelian or Standard Square of Opposition and the Aristotelian version of Conversion, Obversion and Contraposition:

11.   If "Some farmers are nature lovers" is true, what is the truth value of the following: Enter an "X" in the correct answer:

Some nature lovers are farmers	T X	F ___	U ___
Some nature lovers are not non-farmers	T X	F ___	U ___
Some farmers are not non-nature lovers	T X	F ___	U ___
All farmers are nature lovers	T ___	F ___	U X
No farmers are nature lovers	T ___	F X	U ___
All nature lovers are non-farmers	T ___	F X	U ___

Using the Boolean Square of Opposition and the Boolean version of Conversion, Obversion and Contraposition:

11.   If "Some farmers are nature lovers" is true, what is the truth value of the following:

Enter an "X" in the correct answer (NOTE, THE ANSWERS DO NOT CHANGE IN THIS EXAMPLE):

Some nature lovers are farmers	T X	F ___	U ___
Some nature lovers are not non-farmers	T X	F ___	U ___
Some farmers are not non-nature lovers	T X	F ___	U ___
All farmers are nature lovers	T ___	F ___	U X
No farmers are nature lovers	T ___	F X	U ___
All nature lovers are non-farmers	T ___	F X	U ___

Using the Aristotelian or Standard Square of Opposition and the Aristotelian version of Conversion, Obversion and Contraposition:

11.   If "Some farmers are nature lovers" is FALSE, what is the truth value of the following: Enter an "X" in the correct answer:

Some nature lovers are farmers	T	F	X	U	
Some nature lovers are not non-farmers	T	F	X	U	
Some farmers are not non-nature lovers	T	F	X	U	
All farmers are nature lovers	T	F	X	U	
No farmers are nature lovers	T	X	F	U	
All nature lovers are non-farmers	T	X	F	U	

Using the Boolean Square of Opposition and the Boolean version of Conversion, Obversion and Contraposition:

11.   If "Some farmers are nature lovers" is FALSE, what is the truth value of the following: Enter an "X" in the correct answer (Note that the only different answer is the fourth proposition, it is undetermined because of the Boolean Square):

Some nature lovers are farmers	T	F	X	U	
Some nature lovers are not non-farmers	T	F	X	U	
Some farmers are not non-nature lovers	T	F	X	U	
All farmers are nature lovers	T	F	U	X	
No farmers are nature lovers	T	X	F	U	
All nature lovers are non-farmers	T	X	F	U	

ANSWERS TO PROBLEMS BEGINNING ON PAGES 88

4.
All Non-Divine Beings are Mortal
All Human Beings are Non-Divine Beings
∴ No Human Beings are Immortal

Obvert the Major Premise:

All Non-Divine Beings are Mortal obverts to No Non-Divine Beings are Immortal Now we have a valid argument:

No Non-Divine Beings are Immortal
All Human Beings are Non-Divine Beings
∴ No Human Beings are Immortal

We could have obverted the conclusion and gotten this instead:

All Non-Divine Beings are Mortal

All Human Beings are Non-Divine Beings
∴ All Human Beings are mortal

This is valid as well. At this point in Logic we begin to see that there is more than one way to eliminate complements.

5.
All who lay off their employees in order to give themselves a bonus are difficult to work for.
Some employers hate their employees
∴ Some Employers are Difficult to Work For

For this problem we see that there are actually four terms:
"People who lay off employees in order to get a big bonus"
"People who are difficult to work for"
"Employers"
"People who hate their employees"

We could convert this to a valid argument by starting with the conclusion:

Some Employers are Difficult to Work For

With this conclusion we see that "Employers" is the Minor Term, and so should appear in the Minor Premise (second premise) and "Difficult to Work For" is the Major Term, and so should appear in the Major Premise (first premise). So, we can recreate the argument to look like this:

All _____ are Difficult to Work For
Some Employers are _____
∴ Some Employers are Difficult to Work For.

Or, perhaps this approach:

Some People who are difficult to Work For are _____
All _____ are Employers
∴ Some Employers are Difficult to Work For.

We know we have an "I" proposition for a conclusion, and because the "I" does not distribute anything we do not need to worry about distributing either the Minor Term or the Major Term in the premises. However, we still have to distribute the Middle Term, and because we have an affirmative conclusion, we must have all affirmative premises, and because the conclusion is a particular proposition we must have one particular proposition and one universal proposition, therefore, we know we will need all affirmative propositions, one universal and one particular. So, we need one "A" proposition and one "I" proposition. Because we know that the "I" distributes nothing, we cannot try to distribute the Middle Term in the "I" proposition, but we do know that the "A" proposition distributes the term in the SUBJECT position, so we WILL distribute the Middle Term with the "A" proposition, thus the two possible approaches listed above. Truthfully, whichever premise is written as an "I" proposition, it does not matter what position the Minor or Major term is in or the Middle Term, simply because it distributes nothing. However, whichever premise we write as an "A" proposition, the Middle Term MUST be in the Subject position.

Let's go back to the original four terms:

"People who lay off employees in order to get a big bonus"
"People who are difficult to work for"
"Employers"
"People who hate their employees"

Because we have "Employers" as the Minor Term in the conclusion, and "People who are difficult to work for" as the Major Term in the conclusion, we are left with two other terms from which to choose our Middle Term:"People who hate their employees" and "People who lay off employees in order to get a big bonus". Let's try using "People who hate their employees" first as our Middle Term:

All People who hate their employees are Difficult to Work For
Some Employers are People who hate their employees
∴ Some Employers are Difficult to Work For.

That seems to work, how about this approach:

Some People who are difficult to Work For are People who hate their employees
All People who hate their employees are Employers
∴ Some Employers are Difficult to Work For.

That seems a bit more difficult to accept, I would hope that not ALL employers hate their employees.
Now let's try applying "People who lay off employees in order to get a big bonus" to the two argument forms and see if that works:

All People who lay off employees in order to get a big bonus are Difficult to Work For
Some Employers are People who lay off employees in order to get a big bonus
∴ Some Employers are Difficult to Work For.

That sort of makes sense…
Now, how about this approach:

Some People who are difficult to Work For are People who lay off employees in order to get a big bonus

All People who lay off employees in order to get a big bonus are Employers
∴ Some Employers are Difficult to Work For.

Ok, that makes sense as well. But can we create a totally different conclusion using the above mentioned terms?
Here is the original argument:

All who lay off their employees in order to give themselves a bonus are difficult to work for.
Some employers hate their employees
∴ Some Employers are Difficult to Work For

What if we did this:

All who lay off their employees in order to give themselves a bonus are difficult to work for.
Some employers are those who lay off their employees to give themselves a bonus.
∴ Some employers are difficult to work for

Or,
All people who lay off their employees in order to give themselves a bonus hate their employees
Some employers are people who lay off their employees in order to give themselves a bonus
∴ Some employers hate their employees

Or,
All people who are difficult to work for are people who lay off employees to give themselves a bonus.
Some people who are difficult to work for are employers who hate their employees.
∴ Some people who hate their employees are people who lay off employees to give themselves a bonus.

By creating these many different arguments from the four terms you can begin to get at what is implied in the original argument, but note, all of the arguments I have formed from the four terms are all valid, but are they sound?

ANSWERS TO PROBLEMS BEGINNING ON PAGE 95

1. Solve the following sorites:

All murderers deserve the death penalty
Alex is a murderer
Alex does not deserve leniency
Alex is a terrorist
∴ All terrorists deserve the death penalty

We will start with the conclusion:

"All terrorists deserve the death penalty."

We see that "terrorists" is the minor term and "deserve the death penalty" is the major term. Because the minor term must appear in the minor premise which is the second premise, and because the major term must appear in the major premise which is the first premise, we know what order they will appear in. We also know that we have an affirmative universal proposition for the conclusion, which means the only argument form valid for that kind of conclusion is an AAA-1 argument form. So, we can begin reconstructing one of the arguments imbedded in this sorites.

All _____ deserve the death penalty
All terrorists are _____
∴ All terrorists deserve the death penalty.

What is missing is the middle term. Do we see a proposition in the above sorites that might work? Yes, we see "All murderers deserve the death penalty." So, murderers must be the middle term. Now we can complete one of the imbedded arguments in the original sorites:

All murderers deserve the death penalty.
All terrorists are murderers.
∴ All terrorists deserve the death penalty.

Ok, do you agree that ALL terrorists are murderers?

Now to get another argument out of this, use the conclusion as a premise. Again, remember we are using all "A" type arguments, and so we have to stick with AAA-1 format. If we take the conclusion "All terrorists deserve the death penalty," as a premise, then we have to decide whether "terrorists" will be the middle term, or "deserve the death penalty" will be the middle term. We do have to distribute the middle term at least once. We also know that with an AAA-1 format we must also distribute the minor term.

Let's try treating "terrorists" as the middle term. It would then need to be the major premise, or the first premise:

All terrorists deserve the death penalty.

Is there another premise in the sorites that would work as the minor premise? Remember, in the minor premise the middle term should be in the predicate position. As a matter of fact there is such a proposition:

Alex is a terrorist.

Now, if we stack these two in proper order we should end up with yet another conclusion:

All terrorists deserve the death penalty.
Alex is a terrorist.
∴ Alex deserves the death penalty.

Now take that conclusion and use it as another premise and see what you can come up with. Determine whether the following are valid and whether they are pure hypothetical arguments, mixed hypothetical arguments or disjunctive arguments.

2. If I would have asked for your opinion then I wanted it, I did not ask for your opinion therefore I did not want it!
   Mixed-hypothetical syllogism form, invalid, commits the fallacy of denying the antecedent in order to deny the consequent.

4. If Joe did not do it, then Sam must have done it. If Sam did it, then Joe could not have been there. So, if Joe did not do it, then Joe could not have been there.
   Pure hypothetical syllogism form, valid.

6. If the death penalty does not curb violent crimes, then the death penalty is ineffective. If the death penalty is ineffective, then the only reason to have the death penalty is about vengeance. Therefore, if the death penalty does not curb violent crimes, then the only reason for having the death penalty is to get even.
   Pure hypothetical syllogism, valid.

8. If the cow jumps over the moon then I am a monkey's uncle.
   I am NOT a monkey's uncle.
   Therefore, the cow did NOT jump over the moon.
   Modus Tollens, valid.

10. If the price of gas goes up much more then electric cars will become more popular.
    Electric cars are becoming more popular.
    Therefore, the price of gas is going up much more.
    Invalid, commits the fallacy of affirming the consequent in order to affirm the antecedent.

ANSWERS TO PROBLEMS BEGINNING ON PAGE 112

1. Every time I walked a certain way, a rooster would crow, so it must be that if I walk that certain way, a rooster will crow, I think I will call it the Rooster walk!

   False Cause

3. Has anyone ever proved that there is no God? Then how can you deny that He exists?

   Ad Ignorantiam

5. How could you have nothing to do with the robbery, witnesses have seen you hanging around the boys who were caught in the robbery.

Ad Hominem Circumstantial

7. Everyone on that football team can bench press over 400 pounds, so they are the strongest team out there, so why aren't they number one in the polls?

Composition

9. Please, do as I say, because you really would not want to upset me!

Ad Baculum

19. Water is liquid, therefore the molecules that make it up are liquid.

Division

23. Trinitarianism holds that three equals one. Three does not equal one. Therefore: Trinitarianism is false.

Ignoratio Elenchi

ANSWERS TO PROBLEMS BEGINNING ON PAGE 119

1. 1504 West Indies DR, San Diego, CA
2. Joe.

ANSWERS TO PROBLEMS BEGINNING ON PAGE 133

Using the truth tables of "·"; "v"; "⊃", determine the truth values of the following compound propositions (circle the correct answer):

1. Columbus is the capitol of Ohio or Pierre is the capitol of South Dakota.   **T**
3. Juneau is the capitol of Alaska and Lawrence is the capitol of Kansas.   **F**
5. Austin is the capitol of Texas and Jackson is the capitol of Mississippi.   **T**
7. If Helena is the capitol of Montana, then Honolulu is the capitol of Hawaii   **T**

EXERCISE II
If P and Q is true and R and X is false, what is the truth value of the following complex propositions? (Circle the correct answer)

2. $P \cdot Q$ **T**
4. $(P \cdot R) \supset (R \lor X)$ **T**

6. {[(Q ⊃ R) ⊃ (P · X)] v [~(P · R) ⊃ ~(P v Q)]} v (P ⊃ X) **T**

8. ~{~[~(~P · ~X) ⊃ ~(~X ⊃ ~R)] · ~[~(P · X) · ~(Q ⊃ X)]} **T**

9. {~[(Q v R) v (X · R)] v ~[(P v X) · (X v R)]} ⊃ ~{~[~(P · R) ⊃ ~(Q ⊃ P)] · ~[~(P · X) v ~(Q ⊃ R)]} **T**

EXERCISE III

Translate the following into symbols and the correct compound proposition using proper punctuation:

1. Either Santa Fe is the capitol of New Mexico or Austin is the capitol of Texas.

    SF = Santa Fe is the capitol of New Mexico

    A = Austin is the capitol of Texas.

    SF V A

3. If the US government does not bail out the three big auto makers then the recession will get worse and if the recession gets worse, then more people will lose their jobs and if more people lose their jobs, then the recession could decline into a depression and the number of homeless would begin to escalate.

    US = US government does not bail out the three big auto makers

    R = the recession will get worse

    P = more people will lose their jobs

    D = the recession could decline into a depression

    H = the number of homeless would begin to escalate

    [(US ⊃ R) • (R ⊃ P)] • [(P ⊃ D) • H]

Determine the truth value of the following complex compound propositions if you know that the P is true and the Q is false but you do not know the truth value of X, Y or Z:

T

3.   **T**

1. {[~(Q ⊃ X) ⊃ (~Y v Y)] ⊃ ~[~(~Z ⊃ P) ≡ (X · ~X)]} **T**
   ≡ ~{~[~(X ≡ ~X) ⊃ ~(P ⊃ Q)] ⊃ [(X ⊃ Y) v (Z v X)]}

3. $\{\sim[\sim(X \cdot Z) \supset (Y \vee X)] \supset \sim[(Q \supset P) \supset (X \cdot Q)]\} \vee$ **T**
   $\{\sim[(X \cdot \sim X) \supset (Z \supset Y)] \supset [\sim(Z \vee Y) \vee (X \supset Y)]\}$

ANSWERS TO PROBLEMS BEGINNING ON PAGE 139

Determine what substitution instances on the left side match the argument form on the right side:

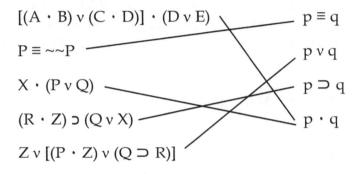

EXERCISES

Using truth tables, construct and determine the validity of each of the following arguments:

1.   P $\supset$ Q
          ~P
   $\therefore$ ~Q

There are two variables with two negations, so we construct a truth table using the formula 2^2 We do not count negations as a separate variable. This is what the truth table would look like:

~P~QP $\supset$ Q

There are two variables with two negations, so we construct a truth table using the formula 2^2 We do not count negations as a separate variable. This is what the truth table would look like:

P	Q	~P	~Q	P ⊃ Q
T	T	F	F	T
T	F	F	T	F
F	T	T	F	T
F	F	T	T	T

Now, do we see anywhere that the ~Q is false (F) and the two premises are both true. Yes, we can, see line three there we see the conclusion is False and the premises are both True, which means this argument form is invalid. We knew that to be the case because we had already discussed the fact that you cannot negate the antecedent in order to negate the consequent, that is referred to as the fallacy of negating the antecedent.

ANSWERS TO PROBLEMS BEGINNING ON PAGE 148

EXERCISES

Now try these out and see which are valid and which invalid:

1. (P·Q) v (R ⊃ X)   *T*
    X v Y   *T*
    ~(X · R) v (P v Q)   *T*
    ~[~(P ⊃ Q) · (R v Y)]   *T*
    ∴   P ⊃ Q   *F*

    Here are the variables in this argument:
    P__T__
    Q__F__
    R__F__
    X__T__
    Y__F__

    This argument is invalid.

2. {[(P · Q) v (Z ⊃ Y)] ⊃ [(R ⊃ X) · (Z ⊃ P)]} v {[(Q ⊃ X) · (R ⊃ Z)] v [(P · R) · (Q · Z)]}
    P ⊃ Q
    Z ⊃ Y
    (R ⊃ X) v (P · Q)
    ∴ X v Y

X__F__
Y__F__
Z__F__
P__T__
Q__T__
R__F__

This argument is invalid.

ANSWERS TO PROBLEMS BEGINNING ON PAGE 164

2. 1.   P ⊃ Q
    2.   Q ⊃ R
    3.   R ⊃ X
    4.   P
    ∴   X   (How many steps do you suppose this could take?)
    5.   P ⊃ R   *1,2 H.S.*
    6.   R   *5,4 M.P.*
    7.   X   *3,6 M.P.*

Fill in the blanks provided how I arrived at each step using the EVAF:

4. 1.   P ⊃ Q
    2.   ~Q
    3.   R ⊃ S · Q ⊃ S
    4.   P v R
    ∴   **S**
    5.   R ⊃ S ____3, SIMP_____
    6.   (P ⊃ Q) · (R ⊃ S)_____1,5 CONJ_____
    7.   Q v S _____6,4 C.D._____
    8.   S_____7,2 D.S._____

6. 1.   (P ⊃ Q) • (S v T)
    2.   (Q ⊃ R) • (Z ⊃ Y)
    3.   P
    ∴.. P • R
    4.   (P ⊃ Q)   _____1, SIMP_____

5.   (Q ⊃ R)_____2, SIMP_____

6.   (P ⊃ R)_____4,5 H.S._____

7.   *P ⊃ (P • R)____6, Abs_____*

8.   *P • R _____7,3 M.P._____*

8. 1.   (F ⊃ G) · (H ⊃ I)

     2.   J ⊃ K

     3.   (F v J) · (H v L)

    ∴. G v K

     4.   *F ⊃ G   1, SIMP*

     5.   *(F ⊃ G) • (J ⊃ K) 4, 2 CONJ*

     6.   *F v J   3, SIMP*

     7.   *G v K   5,6 C.D.*

ANSWERS TO THE PROBLEMS BEGINNING ON PAGE 172

1. 1.   Q

     2.   S

   ∴. [P ⊃ (Q ⊃ S)]

     3.   *S v ~Q   2, ADD*

     4.   *~Q v S   3,COMM*

     5.   *Q ⊃ S   4, IMPL*

     6.   *(Q ⊃ S) v ~P   5, ADD*

     7.   *~P v (Q ⊃ S)   6, COMM*

     8.   *[P ⊃ (Q ⊃ S)]7, IMPL (is there another way to solve this one?)*

EXERCISE II

3. 1.   P ⊃ Q

     2.   P

   ∴. ~(~P v ~Q)

     3.   *Q   1,2 M.P.*

     4.   *P • Q 2,4 CONJ*

     5.   *~(~P v ~Q) 4, DEM*

     5. 1.   (P · Q) ⊃ R

          2.   ~(Q ⊃ R)

          3.   X ⊃ P

4.   Z ⊃ R

    ∴X ⊃ (X · R)

5.   *P ⊃ (Q⊃ R)   1, EXP*

6.   *X ⊃(Q⊃ R)   5,3 H.S.*

7.   *~X   6,2 M.T.*

8.   *~X ∨ R   7, ADD*

9.   *X ⊃ R   8, DEM*

10. *X ⊃ (X · R) 9, ABS*

8. 1.   P⊃(Q⊃R)

   2.   ~R

   3.   P

∴ ~Q

   4.   *(P • Q) ⊃ R   1, EXP*

   5.   *~(P • Q)   4,2 M.T.*

   6.   *~P ∨ ~Q   5, DEM*

   7.   *~Q   6,3 D.S.*

12. 1.   (D ⊃ F) • (P ⊃ N)

   2.   D ∨ P

   3.   (D ⊃ ~N) • (P ⊃ ~F)

∴ F ≡ ~N

   4.   *F ∨ N*   1, 2, C.D.

   5.   *~N ∨ ~F.*   3, 2, C.D

   6.   *N ∨ F*   4, COMM.

   7.   *~~N ∨ F*   6, D.N

   8.   *~N ⊃ F*   7, IMPL

   9   *~F ∨ ~N*   5, COMM

   10. *F ⊃ ~N*   9, IMPL

   11. *(F ⊃ ~N) • (~N ⊃ F)*   10, 8, CONJ

   12. *F ≡ ~N*   11, EQUIV

13. 1.   M ⊃ ~C

   2.   ~C ⊃ ~A

3.　　　　D ∨ A

　　　　　∴ ~M ∨ D

4.　　　　M ⊃ ~A　　　　1, 2, H.S.

5.　　　　A ∨ D　　　　　3, Comm.

6.　　　　~~A ∨ D.　　　 5, D.N

7.　　　　~A ⊃ D.　　　　6, Impl

8.　　　　M ⊃ D4　　　　 7, H.S.

9.　　　　~M ∨ D.　　　　8, Impl

ANSWERS TO PROBLEMS BEGINNING ON PAGE 189

2.　1.　　(x)(Fx ⊃ Yx)

　　2.　　(x)(Yx ⊃ Zx)

　　3.　　(∃x) (Dx • Fx)

　　　　　∴ (∃x)(Dx • Zx)

　　4.　　Da • Fa　　　　3, EI

　　5.　　Fa ⊃ Ya　　　　1, UI

　　6.　　Ya ⊃ Za　　　　2, UI

　　7.　　Fa • Da　　　　4, COMM

　　8.　　Fa　　　　　　　7, SIMP

　　9.　　Ya　　　　　　　5,8 M.P.

　　10.　Za　　　　　　　6,9 M.P.

　　11.　Da　　　　　　　4, SIMP

　　12.　Da • Za　　　　11,10 CONJ

　　13.　(∃x)(Dx • Zx)　12, EG

10　1.　　~(x) (Jx ⊃ ~Bx)

　　2.　　~(∃x) (Jx • ~Mx)

　　3.　　(x) (Mx ⊃ Kx)

　　∴　　(∃x)(Kx • Bx)

　　4.　　(∃x)(Jx • Bx)　　1, QE

　　5.　　(x) (Jx ⊃ Mx)　　2, QE

　　6.　　Ja • Ba　　　　　4, EI

　　7.　　Ja ⊃ Ma　　　　 5, UI

　　8.　　Ma ⊃ Ka　　　　3, UI

　　9.　　Ja　　　　　　　6, SIMP

10.	Ma	7,9 M.P.
11.	Ka	8,10 M.P.
12.	Ba • Ja	6, COMM
13.	Ba	12, SIMP
14.	Ka • Ba	11,13 CONJ
15.	$(\exists x)(Kx • Bx)$	14, EG

11	1.	~$(\exists x)$ (Hx • Kx)	
	2.	~$(\exists x)$ (~Kx · ~Nx)	
	3.	(x) (Nx $\supset$ Jx)	
	∴	(x) (Hx $\supset$ Jx)	
	4.	(x) (Hx $\supset$ ~Kx)	1, QE
	5.	(x) (~Kx $\supset$ Nx)	2, QE
	6.	Hy $\supset$ ~Ky	4, UI
	7.	~Ky $\supset$ Ny	5, UI
	8.	Ny $\supset$ Jy	3, UI
	9.	Hy $\supset$ Ny	6,7 H.S.
	10.	10.Hy $\supset$ Jy	9, 8 H.S.
	11.	(x) (Hx $\supset$ Jx)	10, UG

Introduction to Logic: Entering the Realm of Reasonableness
End Notes

1. See Irving Copi and Keith Burgess-Jackson's book, "Informal Logic", 3rd Edition, Prentice Hall, 1996, Page 1-3.
2. Ibid.
3. For further discussion of "Formal" or "Modern" Logic, see Irving Copi and Carl Cohen's book, "Introduction to Logic", 12th Edition, Prentice Hall, 2005, pages 307-308.
4. For a cogent discussion of "Categorical Syllogisms", go to Stephen Layman's book, "The Power of Logic", 3rd Edition, McGraw Hill, 2005, pages 167-168.
5. See Aristotle's "Organon", translated by E. M. Edghill, Philosopher's Stone, 2009, ISBN:978-1-928565-10-9, section entitled "Prior Analytics" beginning on page 51.
6. For additional information on the distinction between "Inductive" and "Deductive" arguments, go to Stan Baronett's book, "Logic", Prentice Hall, 2008, page 28.
7. Ibid.
8. See Irving Copi and Carl Cohen's book, "Introduction to Logic", 12th Edition, Prentice Hall, 2005, page 7.
9. Ibid.
10. See Irving Copi and Carl Cohen's book, "Introduction to Logic", 12th Edition, Prentice Hall, 2005, page 6.
11. See Irving Copi and Carl Cohen's book, "Introduction to Logic", 12th Edition, Prentice Hall, 2005, page 13.
12. Go to Stephen Layman's book, "The Power of Logic", 3rd Edition, McGraw Hill, 2005, page 191. See also Aristotle's "Organon" Part 4, page 57, where Aristotle discusses the nature of a perfect syllogism.
13. See Aristotle's discussion of the categorical syllogism and its structure in the "Organon", Part 25 of the Prior Analytics, beginning on page 94.
14. Go to Stephen Layman's book, "The Power of Logic", 3rd Edition, McGraw Hill, 2005, page 169.
15. Go to Stephen Layman's book, "The Power of Logic", 3rd Edition, McGraw Hill, 2005, page 192.
16. Ibid. See also Aristotle's discussion of the middle term in the "Organon", page 57.
17. Go to Stephen Layman's book, "The Power of Logic", 3rd Edition, McGraw Hill, 2005, page 239.
18. Go to Stephen Layman's book, "The Power of Logic", 3rd Edition, McGraw Hill, 2005, page 169.
19. Go to Stephen Layman's book, "The Power of Logic", 3rd Edition, McGraw Hill, 2005, page 169.

John H Bolen

20. See Irving Copi and Carl Cohen's book, "Introduction to Logic", 12th Edition, Prentice Hall, 2005,pages 185-185.

21. See Irving Copi and Carl Cohen's book, "Introduction to Logic", 12th Edition, Prentice Hall, 2005,page 226-227.

22. See Irving Copi and Carl Cohen's book, "Introduction to Logic", 12th Edition, Prentice Hall, 2005,page 214.

23. See Irving Copi and Carl Cohen's book, "Introduction to Logic", 12th Edition, Prentice Hall, 2005,pages 214 and 184-185.

24. Ibid.

25. See Irving Copi and Carl Cohen's book, "Introduction to Logic", 12th Edition, Prentice Hall, 2005,pages 184-185

26. For additional information on how to reconstruct regular propositions into standard form categorical syllogisms, go to Stan Baronett's book, "Logic", Prentice Hall, 2008, pages 70-73.

27. See George Boole's discussion in his paper published in 1848 in the *Cambridge and Dublin Mathematical Journal, Vol. III, pp. 183-98.* Another excellent discussion of "Existential Import" is that by Keith Burgess-Jackson, to be found at:http://www.toodoc.com/pdf2text.php?u=aHR0cDovL3d3dy51dGEueZWR1L3BoaWxvc29waHkvZmFjdWx0eS9idXJnZXNzLWphY2tzb24vRXhpc3RlbnRpYWwlMjBJbXBvcnQucGGm&title=%20Existential%20%20%20Import%20%20Keith%20Burgess-Jackson

28. Go to Stephen Layman's book, "The Power of Logic", 3rd Edition, McGraw Hill, 2005, pages 208-214.

29. For other versions of these rules, go to:Go to Stephen Layman's book, "The Power of Logic", 3rd Edition, McGraw Hill, 2005, page 242. Or go to:Irving Copi and Carl Cohen's book, "Introduction to Logic", 12th Edition, Prentice Hall, 2005,page 241.

30. Ibid.

31. Irving Copi and Carl Cohen's book, "Introduction to Logic", 12th Edition, Prentice Hall, 2005,page 179.

32. For an excellent explanation for using Venn diagrams in the analysis of Categorical Syllogisms, go to Stephen Layman's book, "The Power of Logic", 3rd Edition, McGraw Hill, 2005, pages 208-214.

33. Ibid.

34. Irving Copi and Carl Cohen's book, "Introduction to Logic", 12th Edition, Prentice Hall, 2005, page 229.

35. Irving Copi and Carl Cohen's book, "Introduction to Logic", 12th Edition, Prentice Hall, 2005, page 231.

36. Go to Stephen Layman's book, "The Power of Logic", 3rd Edition, McGraw Hill, 2005, pages 192-193.

37. Go to Stephen Layman's book, "The Power of Logic", 3rd Edition, McGraw Hill, 2005, page 193.

38. Go to Stephen Layman's book, "The Power of Logic", 3rd Edition, McGraw Hill, 2005, pages 192-193. See also Aristotle's discussion of "figure" in Parts 6 and 7 of the Prior Analytics in the "Organon".

39. The Des Moines Register, Editorial Page, September 30, 2008.

40. Irving Copi and Carl Cohen's book, "Introduction to Logic", 12th Edition, Prentice Hall, 2005, page 19.

41. For another approach to this problem, go to Stephen Layman's book, "The Power of Logic", 3rd Edition, McGraw Hill, 2005, page 170. See also Irving Copi and Carl Cohen's book, "Introduction to Logic", 12th Edition, Prentice Hall, 2005, pages 263-270

42. See Irving Copi and Carl Cohen's book, "Introduction to Logic", 12th Edition, Prentice Hall, 2005, page 263.

43. See Irving Copi and Carl Cohen's book, "Introduction to Logic", 12th Edition, Prentice Hall, 2005, page 267.

44. See discussion in Irving Copi and Carl Cohen's book, "Introduction to Logic", 12th Edition, Prentice Hall, 2005, pages 263-270.

45. Go to Stephen Layman's book, "The Power of Logic", 3rd Edition, McGraw Hill, 2005, page 177.

46. See Irving Copi and Carl Cohen's book, "Introduction to Logic", 12th Edition, Prentice Hall, 2005, page 190. Aristotle discusses these concepts in his Prior Analytics found in the Organon.

47. Go to Stan Baronett's book, "Logic", Prentice Hall, 2008, pages 394-398. See also Stephen Layman's book, "The Power of Logic", 3rd Edition, McGraw Hill, 2005, pages 181-186. Note the additional memorization technique Layman provides for the student on page 185.

48. Stephen Layman's book, "The Power of Logic", 3rd Edition, McGraw Hill, 2005, page 175.

49. Go to Stan Baronett's book, "Logic", Prentice Hall, 2008, pages 394-398. See also Stephen Layman's book, "The Power of Logic", 3rd Edition, McGraw Hill, 2005, pages 181-186. Note the additional memorization technique Layman provides for the student on page 185.

50. Ibid. See Aristotle's excellent explanation about the limitations of conversion found on page 56 of the Prior Analytics, "The Organon", Philosopher's Stone, 2009.

51. Ibid.

52. Ibid.

53. For an excellent discussion and further explanation of Boolean theory and the problem with existential import, go to Stan Baronett's book, "Logic", Prentice Hall, 2008, pages 402-408.

54. Go to Stephen Layman's book, "The Power of Logic", 3rd Edition, McGraw Hill, 2005, pages 230-232.

55. Go to Stan Baronett's book, "Logic", Prentice Hall, 2008, pages 78-80 for an excellent discussion of how to handle "missing information". For the language of First Order, Second Order and Third Order Enthymemes, I used Irving Copi and Carl Cohen's book, "Introduction to Logic", 12th Edition, Prentice Hall, 2005, page 280.

56. For a good alternative approach to the Disjunctive Syllogism, Go to Stan Baronett's book, "Logic", Prentice Hall, 2008, page 206.

57. For a good description of a Hypothetical Syllogism, Go to Stan Baronett's book, "Logic", Prentice Hall, 2008, pages 206-207.

58. For an excellent review of modus ponens and modus tollens, go to Stephen Layman's book, "The Power of Logic", 3rd Edition, McGraw Hill, 2005, pages 22-26.

59. Go to Stephen Layman's book, "The Power of Logic", 3rd Edition, McGraw Hill, 2005, page 24.

60. Go to Stephen Layman's book, "The Power of Logic", 3rd Edition, McGraw Hill, 2005, page 25.

61. See an excellent discussion of the nature of fallacies in Stephen Layman's book, "The Power of Logic", 3rd Edition, McGraw Hill, 2005, pages 123 – 124. See also Irving Copi and Carl Cohen's book, "Introduction to Logic", 12th Edition, Prentice Hall, 2005, page 125.

62. Irving Copi and Carl Cohen's book, "Introduction to Logic", 12th Edition, Prentice Hall, 2005, pages 135. See also Aristotle's discussion of what he referred to as "sophistic refutations" or fallacies. The discussion can be found in "On Sophistical Refutations" beginning on page 285 of "The Organon", Philosopher's Stone, 2009.

63. See Irving Copi and Carl Cohen's book, "Introduction to Logic", 12th Edition, Prentice Hall, 2005, page 140. I disagree with Copi and Cohen's classifications, and so you will see a distinction in how I classify the various fallacies. I collapse Fallacies of Defective Induction in with the Fallacies of Relevance.

64. See Irving Copi and Carl Cohen's book, "Introduction to Logic", 12th Edition, Prentice Hall, 2005, page 142.

65. See Irving Copi and Carl Cohen's book, "Introduction to Logic", 12th Edition, Prentice Hall, 2005, page 131.

66. See Irving Copi and Carl Cohen's book, "Introduction to Logic", 12th Edition, Prentice Hall, 2005, page 132.

67. See Irving Copi and Carl Cohen's book, "Introduction to Logic", 12th Edition, Prentice Hall, 2005, page 127.

68. See Irving Copi and Carl Cohen's book, "Introduction to Logic", 12th Edition, Prentice Hall, 2005, page 129.

69. Ibid.

70. See Irving Copi and Carl Cohen's book, "Introduction to Logic", 12th Edition, Prentice Hall, 2005, page 133.

71. See Irving Copi and Carl Cohen's book, "Introduction to Logic", 12th Edition, Prentice Hall, 2005, page 148.

72. Ibid.

73. See Irving Copi and Carl Cohen's book, "Introduction to Logic", 12th Edition, Prentice Hall, 2005, page 144.

74. See Irving Copi and Carl Cohen's book, "Introduction to Logic", 12th Edition, Prentice Hall, 2005, page 151.

75. See Irving Copi and Carl Cohen's book, "Introduction to Logic", 12th Edition, Prentice Hall, 2005, page 148.
76. See Irving Copi and Carl Cohen's book, "Introduction to Logic", 12th Edition, Prentice Hall, 2005, page 146.
77. For further discussion on informal fallacies, go to Stephen Layman's book, "The Power of Logic", 3rd Edition, McGraw Hill, 2005, pages 124 – 159.
78. Go to Stephen Layman's book, "The Power of Logic", 3rd Edition, McGraw Hill, 2005, page 140.
79. Go to Stephen Layman's book, "The Power of Logic", 3rd Edition, McGraw Hill, 2005, page 141.
80. Ibid.
81. Go to Stephen Layman's book, "The Power of Logic", 3rd Edition, McGraw Hill, 2005, page 143.
82. Go to Stephen Layman's book, "The Power of Logic", 3rd Edition, McGraw Hill, 2005, page 144.
83. Ibid.
84. For a discussion of how to solve riddles, see Irving Copi and Carl Cohen's book, "Introduction to Logic", 12th Edition, Prentice Hall, 2005, pages 59 – 64. Also see the Penny Press published "Original Logic Problems" magazine available at all major bookstores. Many students of Logic are preparing for the LSAT test, and there are many excellent resources online, free. This is one of them, just copy and paste this url into your browser:http://www.purelocal.com/landing.aspx?slk=lsat+practice+test+ free+online&nid=2&cid=7507596537&kwid=20888820319&akwd=lsat%20practice%20 test%20free%20online&dmt=b&bmt=bb&dist=s&uq=lsat%20practice%20test&device =c&ismobile=false&msclkid=a3ae023433124268b26a1cb825eda8bd&vx=0
85. You will find that there is some latitude in what symbols are used in symbolic logic. For example, go to Stephen Layman's book, "The Power of Logic", 3rd Edition, McGraw Hill, 2005, page 249. I will use the same symbols Layman uses, except for the "if-then" conditional. For that I will use the also familiar "horseshoe" as found in Irving Copi and Carl Cohen's book, "Introduction to Logic", 12th Edition, Prentice Hall, 2005, pages 322 – 325.
86. Irving Copi and Carl Cohen's book, "Introduction to Logic", 12th Edition, Prentice Hall, 2005, page 309.
87. Ibid.
88. Stephen Layman's book, "The Power of Logic", 3rd Edition, McGraw Hill, 2005, page 250 – 251.
89. Irving Copi and Carl Cohen's book, "Introduction to Logic", 12th Edition, Prentice Hall, 2005, page 311.
90. Stephen Layman's book, "The Power of Logic", 3rd Edition, McGraw Hill, 2005, page 249.
91. Irving Copi and Carl Cohen's book, "Introduction to Logic", 12th Edition, Prentice Hall, 2005, page 313.
92. Stephen Layman's book, "The Power of Logic", 3rd Edition, McGraw Hill, 2005, pages 252 - 254.

93. Irving Copi and Carl Cohen's book, "Introduction to Logic", 12ᵗʰ Edition, Prentice Hall, 2005, page 314.

94. Stephen Layman's book, "The Power of Logic", 3ʳᵈ Edition, McGraw Hill, 2005, page 252.

95. Irving Copi and Carl Cohen's book, "Introduction to Logic", 12ᵗʰ Edition, Prentice Hall, 2005, page 322.

96. Irving Copi and Carl Cohen's book, "Introduction to Logic", 12ᵗʰ Edition, Prentice Hall, 2005, page 325.

97. Irving Copi and Carl Cohen's book, "Introduction to Logic", 12ᵗʰ Edition, Prentice Hall, 2005, page 324.

98. Ibid.

99. Irving Copi and Carl Cohen's book, "Introduction to Logic", 12ᵗʰ Edition, Prentice Hall, 2005, page 346 - 350.

100. Irving Copi and Carl Cohen's book, "Introduction to Logic", 12ᵗʰ Edition, Prentice Hall, 2005, page 315.

101. Stephen Layman's book, "The Power of Logic", 3ʳᵈ Edition, McGraw Hill, 2005, pages 263 – 277.

102. Irving Copi and Carl Cohen's book, "Introduction to Logic", 12ᵗʰ Edition, Prentice Hall, 2005, page 342.

103. Irving Copi and Carl Cohen's book, "Introduction to Logic", 12ᵗʰ Edition, Prentice Hall, 2005, page 343.

104. Ibid.

105. Go to Stan Baronett's book, "Logic", Prentice Hall, 2008, pages 168 – 177 for an excellent explanation from a different angle the one I developed.

106. Go to Stan Baronett's book, "Logic", Prentice Hall, 2008, pages 197 – 209 for another approach to these rules of inference. I have chosen the abbreviation EVAF in an effort to simplify what is a complex system.

107. I refer the reader to Stephen Layman's book, "The Power of Logic", 3ʳᵈ Edition, McGraw Hill, 2005, page 342, where a sketchy definition is presented in symbols.

108. Go to Stan Baronett's book, "Logic", Prentice Hall, 2008, pages 197 – 209 for another approach to these rules of inference.

109. See Irving Copi and Carl Cohen's book, "Introduction to Logic", 12ᵗʰ Edition, Prentice Hall, 2005, page 362.

110. Ibid.

111. Ibid.

112. Ibid. See also Stephen Layman's book, "The Power of Logic", 3ʳᵈ Edition, McGraw Hill, 2005, page 307.

113. See Irving Copi and Carl Cohen's book, "Introduction to Logic", 12ᵗʰ Edition, Prentice Hall, 2005, pages 370 – 374.

114. See the discussion in Irving Copi and Carl Cohen's book, "Introduction to Logic", 12ᵗʰ Edition, Prentice Hall, 2005, pages 360, 361 and at the top of the Overview on page 371.

115. See Irving Copi and Carl Cohen's book, "Introduction to Logic", 13ᵗʰ Edition, Prentice Hall, 2009, page 437.

116. Ibid., page 441

117. See Howard-Snyder, Frances and Daniel Howard-Snyder, "The Power of Logic", 4th Edition, McGraw Hill, 2009. Page 420-429.
118. See Irving Copi and Carl Cohen's book, "Introduction to Logic", 13th Edition, Prentice Hall, 2009, page 447
119. Ibid. page 448.
120. See Baronett, Stan "Logic", Prentice Hall, 2008, page 251.
121. See Irving Copi and Carl Cohen's book, "Introduction to Logic", 13th Edition, Prentice Hall, 2009, page 447
122. Ibid.
123. Ibid.
124. Ibid. Page 449.
125. See Cohen, Carl and Irving Copi, "Introduction to Logic", 12th Edition, Prentice Hall, 2005, Page 406.
126. Ibid. Page 416.
127. Ibid. Page 418.
128. Ibid. Page 420.
129. Ibid. See also Baronett, Stan "Logic", Prentice Hall, 2008, page 265 and following.
130. Excerpt from Anselm's "Proslogion", www.thriceholy.net.

BIBLIOGRAPHY

Anselm, "Proslogion", www.thriceholy.net

Aristotle, "Organon", translated by E. M. Edghill, Philosopher's Stone, 2009.

Baronett, Stan "Logic", Prentice Hall, 2008.

Boole, George, "The Calculus of Logic", *Cambridge and Dublin Mathematical Journal, Vol. III, 1848, pp. 183-98.*

Boss, Judith, "Think", McGraw Hill, 2010.

Burgess-Jackson, Keith, "Existential Import" to be found at:http://www.toodoc.com/pdf2text.php?u=aHR0cDovL3d3dy51dGEuZWR1L3BoaWxvc29waHkvZmFjdWx0eS9idXJnZXNzLWphY2tzb24vRXhpc3RlbnRpYWwlMjBJbXBvcnQucGRm&title=%20Existential%20%20%20Import%20%20Keith%20Burgess-Jackson

Burgess-Jackson, Keith, Copi, Irving "Informal Logic", 3rd Edition, Prentice Hall, 1996.

Cohen, Carl and Irving Copi, "Essentials of Logic", 2nd Edition, Prentice Hall, 2007.

Cohen, Carl and Irving Copi, "Introduction to Logic", 12th Edition, Prentice Hall, 2005.

Cohen, Carl and Irving Copi, "Introduction to Logic", 13th Edition, Prentice Hall, 2009.

Howard-Snyder, Frances and Daniel Howard-Snyder, "The Power of Logic", 4th Edition, McGraw Hill, 2009.

Layman, C. Stephen"The Power of Logic", 3rd Edition, McGraw Hill, 2005.

May, Matthew E. "The Elegant Solution:Toyota's Formula for Mastering Innovation",

Free Press, 2007

Vaughn, Lewis, "The Power of Critical Thinking", 2nd Edition, Oxford University Press, 2008.